Drew,
Happy
Merry Xmas, happy new year..
LOL!
I hope you enjoy this book,
is always good to know how
people got rich, and someday,
you will be there as well,
I have faith on you. ☺

Best,
Annie Gutierrez
(formerly known as "Chikis")

December 2013

CARLOS SLIM

THE RICHEST
MAN IN THE WORLD

CARLOS SLIM
RICHEST
MAN IN THE WORLD

TitleTown Publishing, LLC
P.O. Box 12093 Green Bay, WI 54307-12093
920.737.8051 | titletownpublishing.com

Translator and Editor: Alecs Kakon
Original Designer: Natasha Dierwechter
Copy Editor: Amanda Bindel
Cover Design: Howard Grossman
Interior Layout and Design: Erika L. Block

PUBLISHER'S CATALOGING-IN-PUBLICATION DATA:

Martínez, José (Martínez M.)
Carlos Slim : the richest man in the world / an authorized biography by José Martínez. -- Bob Oré ed. -- Green Bay, WI : TitleTown Pub., c2012.

p. ; cm.
ISBN: 978-0-9852478-1-2

Summary: Carlos Slim has become synonymous with business success and economic power. Starting to build his fortune at the age of 14, this authorized biography reveals the boy and the man behind the name, complete with advice from the richest man on Earth on how to maintain a balanced life, inspiring readers to achieve their own destiny. He is a blueprint for how to turn adversity into success.

1. Slim Helú, Carlos, 1940- 2. Businessmen--Mexico--Biography. 3. Entrepreneurship--Mexico. 4. Philanthropists--Mexico--Biography. 5. Mexico--Economic conditions--20th century. 6. Mexico--Economic conditions--21st century. 7. Success in business. 8. Work-life balance. I. Title.

HC132.5.S55 M37 2012
338/.04092--dc23 1211

Printed in the USA

CARLOS SLIM

THE RICHEST
MAN IN THE WORLD

AN AUTHORIZED BIOGRAPHY
BY JOSÉ MARTINEZ

BOB ORÉ EDITION

Title Town
PUBLISHING

CONTENTS

To my mother, Elvia Mendoza Jaramillo, a life example and to the memory of my father Ismael Martinez Leon, teacher and guide.

"Money is the most important thing in the world. It represents health, strength, honor, generosity and beauty as conspicuously as the want of it represents illness, weakness, disgrace, meanness and ugliness."

George Bernard Shaw

INTRODUCTION

In 2010, *Forbes* magazine placed Carlos Slim at the top of the list of the world's richest men. Slim, whose fortune was estimated at that time at US $53.5 billion[1], has captured the spotlight for quite some time. Consequently, public interest in Slim's story grows more and more each day.

The Slim family arrived in Mexico more than one hundred years ago. During that time, four generations have been born and raised. His immense wealth has made the name "Slim" one of the most popular in Mexico. Unlike other rich Mexicans who have often been caught between glamour and scandal, the Slim dynasty has maintained an unusual respectability. Although not directly involved in politics, the charismatic tycoon has become an influential personality in Mexico's economic, political, social, and cultural life.

In other times, the economic empire of the Slim family might have made them the undisputed ruling family of Mexico. Though rich and powerful, the Slim family is simple, well mannered, and seemingly informal, far from the expected posh attitude of the financial elite. Fifth in the line of six brothers, Slim began to build the foundations of his vast empire at the age of twenty-five.

At his bedside, he keeps Bertrand Russell's *The Conquest of Happiness*. Slim believes Russell to be one of the last great humanitarians of the West. Russell held that the secret to happiness consists of not being a complete imbecile. He said in order to be reasonably happy, one needs only to think and behave properly. He further asserted that one must never stop being inventive or stop doing and if at all possible, doing whatever it is he is doing selflessly. Undoubtedly with this in mind, Slim has said many times that his main job is to "think."

Thus, this journalistic investigation aims to portray, without distortion, the richest and most powerful man in the history of Mexico who has emerged as the largest investor in the twenty-first century.

His name is associated with the world of money, but serving others has been one of the keys to his success. A vital character of globalization, he built his empire in a country that opened its doors to his parents. The vast majority of entrepreneurs began to jump ship by safeguarding their capital in banks abroad while the nation's coffers emptied, Slim put his trust in his country.

Far from the stories of avarice and greed of the past, when the meaning of life was equated with amassing wealth, the rise of neo-liberal economics has created a new class of wealthy Mexicans with a fresh, energetic and ambitious mentality. This modern mindset has secured their association with international business. Slim, the creator of Mexico's largest business, is one of the main representatives of this elite class that symbolizes the growth and power of new financial capital.

His story is one that is typical of a self-made man: Slim lost his father when he was barely thirteen years old, but it was from him that he inherited his entrepreneurial spirit.

Because of his prominent position in the economic world, he is seen from abroad as one of the "builders of the country." He has been considered by the specialized media in the United States, Japan and Europe as among the most important leaders of globalization

THE EASTERN EXILE
The Promised Land

In the late nineteenth century, during the reign of Porfirio Díaz when the spotlight shone on the ambition of the bourgeoisie to accumulate money, the first group of Lebanese immigrants arrived in Mexico in pursuit of a better life. The country's top three fortunes back then belonged to two Spaniards, Avelino Montes Molina and Iñigo Noriega Laso, and the American, Thomas Braniff. At that time, there were forty-four fortunes exceeding one million pesos in Mexico. Of the total assets, 26.4 percent belonged to nine Spanish immigrants, 8.2 percent to two Americans, 1.4 percent to a German, and 0.7 percent to a Frenchman.

In Lebanon, the Ottoman Empire was shuddering. It is estimated that the total number of emigrants who left Lebanon between 1860 and 1914 was a bit more than one million people. The majority, around 40 percent, went to the United States while most of the remainder settled in Brazil and Argentina. In that time, a mere two percent immigrated to Mexico, or about 20,000 Lebanese people.

Most of them fled the excesses of the Ottoman Empire. The government's immigration records state that the first Lebanese people arrived in Mexico at the port of Veracruz in early 1878, right after General Porfirio Díaz finished his first term as President of the Republic. According to the census of 1900, there were 391 Lebanese people in Mexico. Ten years later, that number increased to over two million, representing 2.5 percent of the foreign population under the rule of Porfirio Díaz.

The Lebanese population continued to grow until Díaz was overthrown by Francisco I. Madero and the dictator was forced to leave Mexico. As his hour came and went, Porfirio Díaz, the man who saw to it that immigrants from the Middle East were welcomed, was exiled and fled to Spain. He left Veracruz aboard the ship steamer *Ypiranga* after spending five days waiting in port. He proceeded to Coatzacoalcos and embarked on a painful journey across the Atlantic to Europe. From the bay, Teodoro Dehesa, Governor of the state, gave the last farewell to the dictator who ended his life in Paris in 1915. In the first months of exile, Díaz withdrew his savings that amounted to 1.5 million francs, the equivalent to approximately a half million pesos at that time, earned from seventy years of pension funds for having been a General in the Mexican army.

In 1936, he saw the first rays of light in the city of Bloiz, France. Bernardo Díaz Casasús, the last great-grandson of General Díaz, was born in exile. Meanwhile, in Mexico, the first generation of native Slims was born. Originally attracted to a mirage of social peace and money in the twilight of the Díaz era, the Slim family gradually established themselves as the richest family of Lebanese origin in the country.

Born Khalil Slim Haddad in 1887, Slim Helú's father arrived in Mexico after leaving his hometown of Jezzine at the age of fourteen. He arrived through the port of Veracruz and traveled to the port of Tampico, following the footsteps of his four older brothers, Elías, José and Pedro. During a time when all Middle Eastern people were subjects of the Ottoman Empire, many Lebanese people fled due to the imposition of Turkish rule. Slim too left in search of better horizons.

"My paternal and maternal ancestors arrived in Mexico a hundred years ago, in order to escape the yoke of the Ottoman Empire," said Slim Helú. "At that time, the boys were forced by conscription to join the army. It was because of this that mothers would force their children into exile before they turned fifteen years old."

This is how Khalil Slim Haddad was brought to Mexican territory in the year 1902. He later changed his name to Julián (Khalil is a common Arab name meaning faithful friend or loyal friend). He was just one of thousands of Lebanese immigrants who arrived in the country by way of Mexico's three main ports: Veracruz, Tampico in Tamaulipas, and Progreso in Yucatan.

One of the earliest Lebanese immigrants was José María Abad, who became the first Lebanese street vendor in Mexico in 1878. Abad's sales as a peddler were about fifty percent higher than the average vendor.

Lebanon is in the Middle East and is one of the smallest nations in the world with just under 27,000 square miles. Of its 3.6 million inhabitants, 3.5 million were born in the country, but the Lebanese diaspora in the world is approximately 16 million people. Lebanon is populated by twenty-four villages, twenty-three of which are Arabic and one Jewish. Since the prophets of the three great monotheistic religions come from this region, many of its people bear deep scars from the wars fought in the Holy Lands throughout history.

The Lebanese writer Amin Maalouf tries to find an explanation for this warring spirit in his book *The Crusades Through Arab Eyes*. Maalouf maintains that for the West, the threat of Islam has been permanent. Nearly a century after the prophet's death in AD 632, the Moors conquered Spain. Finding themselves on the threshold of France, they continued to expand, but their progress was hindered by Charles Martel in the year 732. In 1453, the Turks and the Ottomans captured Constantinople and were at the gates of Vienna in 1529 until they were defeated definitively in 1683.

In the eyes of Islam, conflict with the West has taken different forms: Byzantium versus the Islamic empire, the Christian Kingdoms versus Al-Andalus, Europe versus the Ottoman Empire, colonialism versus Arab nationalism, and so on. For the Muslim world, the West has for a long time attempted to define itself in contrast to Islamic culture and religion.

Always a fragmented territory throughout its five-thousand-year history, Lebanon has survived its tragedy and despair. Though the Lebanese in exile say that the cedar tree—a symbol of their country—is disappearing, they insist that the spirit of the cedar as well as the thistle, the rose, and the Lebanese poet Khalil Gibran, will live forever.

Lebanon, the country for which King Solomon sang, "He who adorned the temple and palace with its cedars," stood for more than 400 years under Turkish rule, the rule of the Sublime Porte[2]. When the First World War ended, the Lebanese coast was occupied by the French, the interior by the English and the mountainous region by the nationalists, who had banded together to resist the great Turks.

As a result of ancestral war, the first Middle Eastern immigrants to Mexico were Lebanese, arriving between the late nineteenth and early twentieth century when the inhabitants of this small nation were subjects of the Ottoman Empire.

Mexican sociologist and historian Martínez Assad recounts in detail the vicissitudes suffered by Lebanon throughout its long history and explores why they have left it in such a fragmented state.

Slim describes that it was between 1918 and 1920, when Lebanon was under an occupation regime, that a new phase in political history began in the small country. Fierce diplomatic negotiations between France and England led to the Treaty of Sevres, which forced the Turks to give up their claims to Syria and Lebanon and left them under French mandate. Palestine remained under the supervision of the British. In 1920, when Greater Lebanon was created, they also added four Muslim-Arab territories. And so a bi-national state was built where a State, in the modern sense of the word, had never previously existed. It was not until Lebanon gained its independence on November 22, 1943, that it became a truly modern state and asserted its place in the world.

Lebanon continued to be weighed down by old problems of secular government. Why? Because the right to command, to do justice, to protect and exploit the people in the Ottoman Empire was distributed across a multitude of local cells. The chiefs, men of the sword, considered themselves God's representatives and felt responsible for maintaining order; the order that God himself wanted to be represented on Earth. Amin Maalouf, in *Rock of Tanios*, explained what life was like in Lebanon in the second-half of the nineteenth century. He said:

The whole village then belonged to the same feudal lord. He was the heir of an ancient system of sheikhs ... He was one of the most powerful characters in the world. Among the eastern plains and the sea, there were dozens of properties larger than theirs ... Above them, and for those who were of the same circumstance, there was Emir of the mountain. And above the Emir, the Pasha of the provinces: those of Tripoli, Damascus, Sidon and Acre. And above him was the Sultan of Istanbul ...

So when independence came to Lebanon, they didn't have to resign themselves as the people of a State nor did they have to settle to the core idea of modernization. This was due to the departure of thousands of immigrants who sought other lands as a reaction to the impossibility of achieving better living conditions in their homeland. But among these immigrants were many intellectuals. It became very common in the early twentieth century to find important Lebanese intellectuals outside of their home state, particularly throughout Europe. The nationalists met in Paris, most notably in 1913 when the Arab Congress met to announce their support for the independence of Lebanon and urge the international community to recognize their distinct national character. In 1914, Turkey was allied with the Germans and thrust their regime on tiny Lebanon. The following year, the military invaded and announced the end of *Mutasarrifiyya* autonomy. The repression that followed was brutal. Many decided to emigrate, never to return.

As a result, most of the immigrants who came to Mexico from the Middle East at the turn of the nineteenth century were Lebanese. On a much smaller scale, Iraqis, Palestinians and Syrians also entered the country. It was usual to call these immigrants Turks because of their passports, though they were not Turkish. Until 1918, they were subjects of the Ottoman Empire and were then mistakenly called Arabs because of the language they spoke and wrote. The language, food, traditions and social customs of Lebanese affairs are reflected in a book by Patricia Jacobs Barquet, author of a dictionary[3] about Mexicans of Lebanese origin. Jacobs recounts in detail how the Lebanese who drifted to Mexico from the East were initiated into Mexican social customs.

The Middle Eastern immigrants who arrived in Mexico left their small territories and came to a developing host country with sparsely populated peripheral territories. They were grateful that they were able to contribute to a developing country, contributions from which they directly benefitted.

They became more and more integrated into Mexican culture. As part of the trend of assimilation, many were marrying outside of their own Lebanese community. Today, a number of descendants of first, second, third, fourth and fifth generation immigrant families from various countries are prominent Mexicans whose work and participation in the cultural activities of Mexico hold major significance.

Their ancestors came from lands that had been passed from civilization to civilization, like the Egyptians, Greeks, Romans and Persians, as well as various conquerors such as the Byzantines, Crusaders, Arabs, Ottomans and Alexander the Great. They went in search of a better life, some through a desire to expand their horizons and others because they were forced to run from Turkish rule. The majority were Christians, Maronites and Orthodox; some were Sunni and Shi'a Muslims, and a few Druze and Jews. In Mexico, they found a territory rich in history and ethnicities. Despite their lack of knowledge of the language and customs of their new home, and despite their lack of experience and financial resources, in most cases, they found ways to adapt and grow. They left their families and were attracted by the enchanting land of Central America and the opening of its immigration laws. Young and fearless, they began as merchants in their new adventure and were favored by conditions such as the instability of the Mexican currency. This allowed their goods and services to be converted into capital that would increase in value. They were able to save and invest their earnings. In their struggle to survive, they explored untapped markets in villages that were cut off from all communication, and in these places, they introduced the concept of a market. Since this was both necessary and attractive for the locals, the Lebanese immigrants were welcomed. Earning money became second nature.

This is how they gained their reputation and became the precursors to credit sales; they facilitated the integration of marginalized areas and they favored internal markets. Their austerity and constant struggle made it so that, to become a *barillero* (a peddler), they had to establish small outposts in markets. They began in the ports and then traveled by foot, mule or rail into villages, cities and towns across the country. They learned to live in back rooms before they had the capital to pay rent or become homeowners. The first to immigrate helped others who sought to do the same. There was always a peasant who was willing to carry a *Kashshi* (the traditional box filled with knickknacks identified with peddlers). They opened credit accounts so that they could act as creditors. Those who prospered in trade ventured into industry; those who were professionals served the new communities. They did their best to integrate so that their future generations would be better prepared and able to penetrate the world in other professions.

Not forgetting their values, love and connection to a country that had always been coveted and envied by its neighbors as the gateway to the East for Europeans, the Lebanese people and their descendants came to form one of the largest and most prosperous communities in Mexico. Although they never stopped showing their solidarity, they were a community made up of individuals who chose their own paths – individuals who, business aside, were diversified in their activities.

In terms of quantity and ability to integrate, the Lebanese community formed one of the largest and most significant groups of immigrants in Mexico. It has been said that by 1905 they numbered five thousand and were established in several provincial cities as well as the Federal District. This number increased considerably after the First World War, a fact that, along with other factors, stimulated a desire for more Lebanese people to emigrate. The only specific census that has ever been conducted about this population was that of Salim Abud and Julian Nasr in 1948. It recorded about twenty thousand immigrants and their descendants, in a total Mexican population of twenty million, which were then established in more than three hundred cities and towns in all states of the republic. This census assumed all immigrants from the East as a single community.

However, in 1927, Julián Slim Haddad had already conducted an initial survey of Lebanese businessmen and traders.

Among Mexicans of Lebanese descent who arrived in Mexico since about 1878, more than a thousand have excelled at some point in Mexican history.

The Lebanese have been mainly businessmen and traders. The majority is Catholic (Maronite), although there have been Lebanese Muslims, of whom built their first mosque in Torreón, Coahuila. It is not uncommon to see the image of Saint Charbel in Catholic churches in Mexico.

In Mexico, there are around half-a-million Lebanese descendants mainly concentrated in the states of Puebla, Guanajuato, Hidalgo, Oaxaca, San Luis Potosí, Coahuila, Jalisco, the State of Mexico, Yucatan and the capital.

Furthermore, the scholar Martínez Assad highlights in the book *Veracruz: Port of Arrival* the involvement of some Lebanese and their identification with the political life of Mexico. "When the Americans invaded Veracruz, a Lebanese with the last name Nicholas offered the President Victoriano Huerta and his sons MX$200,000 to defend the country."

The name Slim, rooted in Arabic, means peace, tranquility, and repose. However, the semantics of the language create many versions of peace. In the name Slim, the character for peace represents the peace that comes from having one's own affairs in order.

THE EASTERN STAR
Pioneers

The Slim family, like thousands of their countrymen, arrived on Mexican soil following the footsteps of the first Lebanese who left their homeland to "live the American dream."

The first Lebanese people settled in New York in 1870; their businesses multiplied. New Yorkers were struck by the attire of this group of immigrants. Thus, it was these immigrants who formed the first "Oriental" or "Middle Eastern" neighborhood called Little Syria.

Although official documents of the Ministry of Foreign Affairs did not record the names of the first Lebanese immigrants who arrived in Mexico, it is an accepted fact that the precursor was the priest Boutros Raffoul, who arrived in 1878 through the port of Veracruz. However, other sources cite a merchant named Santiago Sauma as one of the initiators of the first Lebanese colony established in 1880 in Yucatan.

Julián Slim Haddad, born July 17, 1887, in Jezzine, Lebanon, arrived in Mexico in 1902 through the Tampico port where he began working alongside his brother José, thirteen years his senior. José Slim Haddad had arrived in 1893, and was followed by his three older brothers, Elías, Carlos, and Pedro, in 1898. This family was part of an era that saw thousands of people leaving their homeland for different parts of the world. In fact, one-fourth of the population had left Lebanon before the outbreak of the First World War, leading to their empire's dismemberment.

Within years, there were approximately ten thousand Lebanese people in Mexico. The Mexican government began to impose regulations that would act as obstacles for Middle Eastern immigrants.

It was at the time of these regulations that José and Pedro moved from Tampico and made their way to the capital. Once there, they founded their own shops in the city center and José Slim Haddad became the first Lebanese merchant in Mexico City.

The Slim brothers moved to the capital in search of new horizons. They arrived as the Díaz dictatorship was coming to an end. Social unrest was growing and the number of armed peasants was increasing. Despite the imminent war, the Slim family hoped to keep working in order to forge their future.

Those were the times when businessmen, rather than those of rich ancestry, received support from the dictatorship, which had a taste for unimaginative and lucrative activities. The business class of that era was made up of foreign bourgeoisie, primarily French, British and newly rich Mexicans. Apart from delighting in the *joie de vivre*, they did in fact continue to encourage progress.

Gold production between the years of 1902 and 1903 reached fifteen tons and silver rose to two thousand tons in the same period. Before concluding the first decade of the century, gold production reached more than thirty tons.

But all that glitters is not gold. The fire of the revolution set the social and political environment ablaze. The Slim brothers remained undaunted and continued to work. They had made the decision to settle in Mexican territory, their new homeland, so they had to make it work.

THE DYNASTY
Family Portrait

Slim Helú, unlike his parents, did not have a traumatic childhood. His parents had to survive the devastation of their nation, as did hundreds of thousands of other Lebanese. But, Slim is the symbol of the new generation of Mexicans of Lebanese descent who gave an economic boost to their adopted country.

He inherited from his father the art of doing business. He learned the gift of sniffing out the money, making him somewhat of a modern King Midas.

He forged his destiny from childhood, and by the age of fifty, Slim began to top the charts as one of the richest men in the world.

Slim Helú was born to Julián and a Chihuahuense[4] of Lebanese descent named Linda Helú on January 28, 1940. At the time, his parents lived on Mexico Avenue, Number 51, in the Hippodrome Condesa colony, one of the areas of Lebanese ancestry in the Mexican capital.

When his parents were married in 1926, his maternal grandfather, José Helú, one of the most distinguished intellects in the Mexican-Lebanese community, who brought the first Arabic newspaper to Mexico and was the founder of the *Al-Jawater* (The Ideas), read to those present, the following letter of blessing by Muhamad Abu-Shajín, entitled "Fatherly Love":

How should I behave on the wedding day of my dear child? How can I be eloquent and meet the needs of my sweet daughter? Oh! How I wish I could do it! I would weave the shining stars together to create the image of two crowns, and perhaps that would be enough.

Linda! To describe you, I will not mimic the mannerisms of a poet. To avoid the swords of the critics, better to speak the language I can best employ in order to give you advice.

Linda: Because you followed the law of the Creator, which is the law of the centuries and of the hidden secret, since you left my arms for another man's arms, similar to mine, and you left my lap for your groom's chest, and came out of the soft shadow of your father to find the sweet shade of your love, emulate your mother's virtues and her intelligence; imitate her character and her purity.

Be a princess in prosperity and be compassionate, without malice, toward the poor. Docility in a woman is a jewel that distances her from insignificant and meaningless fortune. And ostentation! How many were humiliated and how many tyrants fell from their thrones!

If poverty afflicts you, do not lament, nor should you let yourself be defeated: quite the contrary, accept with certainty the troubles of life and drain the bitter cup until the dregs, and if the envious slander you, rise with nobility over whomever afflicts you, because forgiveness destroys the evil with more precision than the blade of any weapon.

Be faithful to your husband and meet his needs without a murmur; if he smiles with joy, do not furrow your brow; if he gets angry, take it into account, and be strong for him, be bound by loyalty to him, his family and his friends, never do them wrong.

And if your brother hurts your husband, be angry with him, and if your husband is fond of your enemy, welcome them, for happiness in a marriage is a mutual exchange; therefore, learn the intentions of your husband and try to fulfill them.

And if you follow the advice I give you, because I know you so well, you will reap the rewards of virtue and you will be given much more.

Oh! Khalil! Welcome: she is "a portion of my liver," to the point that I would not hesitate to keep from feeding her with my own blood and give my soul for her happiness; she is a beautiful and chaste virgin; virtuous, noble and educated. And if she offends you, without reason, be understanding and loving and forgive her. And if any unhappiness is ever thrust upon her, protect her with serenity from the evildoer who offended her, because you are the only one who is the master of this house and you will be her refuge on the day she shall be tested.

For you, little children, I bless you with my best wishes: that prosperity and the pleasures of life are with you always.

To all of you, thank you for taking my words of advice, because with these wise words, I have done you a priceless favor.

Khalil, diners, the honorable Slim family and Yúsuf-El-Helú, I thank you.

Slim was the fifth of six children, three girls and three boys: Nour, Alma, Linda, Julián, and José. Josefina the nanny, a Oaxacan who was with the family for more than half a century, played a vital role in Carlos' childhood and was second only to his mother.

Out of all the siblings, Carlos was the one who inherited his father's knack for doing business. Slim remembers his father fondly as the patriarch of the Slim family.

"My father gave us an education based on well-defined values," he said. "He was a loving person with very solid values who always gave thanks to the strong family bond he built. Family was a priority for him. He was able to establish a pleasant life built upon harmony, honor, sincerity and the most profound concern for Mexico."

Slim's father did not attach much importance to material things, but rather on the things that truly had significance. According to Slim, his father and mother were very close to him. His mother Linda was a woman with a lot of personality who was quite tidy. The tycoon reminisces about his parents being open-minded people with great human values.

Little Carlos often accompanied Julián to work. Though they talked about many subjects, they most often spoke of business, despite Slim's young age. He remembers listening to conversations his father had with friends: "They were people from whom I learned a great deal." From these gatherings, he spawned his own business sense and by ten years old, he was initiated into the business world. He ran a little shop at the foot of the stairs in his house where he would sell sweets and sodas to his relatives on the weekends.

He went to the Augustine College, Alonso Institute of Veracruz, for elementary and secondary school. During those years, Slim learned what "savings" meant. He opened his first checking account with $500 and later invested in National Savings Bonds. With this capital, he later bought his first shares of the National Bank of Mexico while studying for his bachelor's degree in the National Preparatory School in San Ildefonso.

However, not everything in Slim's life was pleasant. Although he left his family in a good financial situation, Slim's father died when he was just thirteen years old

Slim inherited the entrepreneurial spirit from his father. "My father was enormously dedicated to his work and his great entrepreneurial talent was quickly noticed," Carlos remembers. "The reasons for my father's commercial success were simple: vocation, talent and hard work. His advice on professional issues and moral and social responsibility was very clear. I quote, in his words: 'Business must implement a useful system; its activities and purpose lie in a small gain in sales. Fine and cheap articles should be provided to consumers and you should deal directly with them; give credit facilities to adjust their actions to the strictest morality and honesty.' "

According to Slim, his father was ahead of his time "because he had a deep knowledge of business. Already in the twenties, he talked about how efficient trade meant selling large volumes with low margins and with additional services, the latter of which stores today still do not incorporate."

Slim credits his father's training in making him a saavy investor.

"I must say that from the beginning, I could count on family support, which was not limited to material things, but mainly in being a good example and imparting proper training. In late 1952, when I was twelve, with the idea of administering our income and expenses, my father established that we had to carry a savings passbook, which he would review with us every week," Slim said. "Following this rule, I took care of my own personal passbook balances for several years. Thus, in January 1955, my personal capital was MX$5,523.32, and by August of 1957, it rose to MX$31,969.26. It continued to grow and I invested primarily in shares of the National Bank of Mexico, sometimes by using credit, and by early 1966 my personal capital was over MX$5 million, not including my inheritance."

Later, both the valuable and less valuable family investments were divided into six parts among the Slim siblings. In that way, Slim said, he was in contact with the properties on the streets of Corregidora, Alhóndiga, and Juan de la Granja corner Corregidora. After some time, they sold several properties such as Rubén Dario (now the Canadian Embassy), Martí (Hospital of Mexico), Venustiano Carranza 124, Corregidora, and three on Correo Mayor, with an amount of approximately US$20 million, standing today as only four condominiums.

Not everything in the Slim dynasty is money. Julián was something of a bohemian and his interests revolved around somewhat intellectual pursuits; a trait his son also inherited.

In the 1930s, José Helú, the maternal grandfather to Slim, and his cousin Alfredo Harp Helú met with journalists, writers and Lebanese intellects from the vicinity of Mexico City and formed the Literary League. Their gatherings, which Julián frequented, were held in members' homes or cafés. One favored meeting spot, the home of Antonio Letayf, had a vast library that boasted books on many themes in a multitude of languages that scholars and friends alike could consult.

The Literary League was formed by José Helú, Antonio Letayf, Nasre Ganem, Leonardo Shafick Kaim, Nacif Fadl, Salim Bacha, Anuar Merhy and William Jammal. The members would often invite other poets and writers as guests.

Those were the bohemian days in Mexico City when intellectual groups of all literary and political streams made up of Mexicans and immigrants from several countries, made it fashionable to frequent places like the opera, the Paris Café, the Regis, the Tupinamba and the Campoamor. In these places, cultural figures like José Gaos, León Felipe, Antonio Helú, Mauricio Magdaleno, Jaime Torres Bodet, Salvador Novo, Hugo Thilgman, Tufic Sayeg Frederico Heuer, the poet Antonio González Mora, brothers Gabriel and Armando Villagrán, among many others, would come together and talk about a plethora of things from boxing to philosopher and politician José Vasconcelos.

Antonio Helú, son of José Helú and uncle to Carlos Slim, was an accomplished writer, film director and a pioneer in the *policiaca* narrative, detective stories. He gained notoriety with one of his novels, *The Necessity to Murder*. He came to be a figure in the *Queen's Quorum* by Ellery Queen, one of the most important detective series ever.

A tireless promoter of culture, Antonio Helú founded the journal *Policromías*, a student publication in which the first verses of Jaime Torres Bodet, Salvador Novo, Xavier Villaurrutia and Pellicer were released. Antonio Helú launched three editions: a literary monthly, one weekly edition on combat, and a bi-weekly cartoon, which started the careers of Hugo Thilgman and Miguel Covarrubias.

Years later, one of Antonio Helú's works, *The Crime of Insurgencies* was brought to the public by a group called The Mysterious Company, which boasted such names as Andrea Palma, Villarías, José Luis Jiménez and Juan José Martínez Casado.

These were the times when the Lebanese in Mexico had a significant presence in the life of the country. The cultural, political and intellectual atmosphere enveloped society. They were complemented by a world of entertainment: actors such as Joaquín Pardavé and Sara García starred in stories about how Lebanese families settled in the country. Pardavé played Khalil the *harbano*, and lit up the stage with performances that were presented in the Principal Theater or the Lírico, where the Mexican comedian Leopoldo the Cautezón Beristáin brought in the laughs alongside Lupe Rivas Cacho, the Pingüica, Roberto the Panzón Soto, Celia Montalván, María Concesa and Herminia Quiles.

In 1940, the year Carlos Slim Helú was born, the Russian revolutionary Leon Trotsky was assassinated in Mexico City. Mexico was experiencing incipient political stability: two years earlier, President Lázaro Cárdenas had decreed the expropriation of oil and the country propped up its economy on petroleum. Its exports, however, were boycotted by companies that demanded that their interests be restored. Meanwhile, the rural sector was just emerging from its slumber after a bloody revolution that led to a reform whose motto was, "The land belongs to he who works it." Between 1934 and 1940, Cárdenas created about 180, 000 suburbs, covering more than twenty million hectares (approximately fifty million acres), benefiting 750 families. Sponsored by the government, the Confederación Nacional Campesina[5] (CNC) was formed to give a voice to farmers within the ruling party (Party of the Mexican Revolution), and so began a campaign to integrate the indigenous population from the country.

But Catholic groups and the middle class were disillusioned by President Cárdenas's radicalism; from this non-conformity was spawned the Partido Revolucionario de Unificación Nacional[6] (PRUN) and General Juan Andrew Almazán was nominated as a presidential candidate. As a man of great influence in such an enlightened revolution, the government once again turned conservative. He was stripped of his electoral victory by alleged fraud, which caused a political storm that could have led to a civil war. Finally, in December of 1940, the army, which was loyal to the system and backed Cárdenas, had the power handed to Manuel Ávila Camacho.

A mass exodus of farmers began during the rule of Ávila Camacho as they marched their way into the major cities where better jobs were being offered. Others opted for the United States in order to take advantage of an unspoken, strong-arm program between the US and the Mexican government.

Lebanon achieved independence from the Ottoman Empire

on November 22, 1943 when Carlos Slim was three years old. Meanwhile, the Lebanese community was being consolidated in his new homeland. As President Ávila Camacho's term was coming to an end in 1946, the Mexican and Lebanese government established diplomatic relations.

From his birth in January 1940 until 1953 when his father died, Carlos Slim, along with his siblings, enjoyed a golden childhood.

Slim recalls countless anecdotes that his father left behind and great memories of his everyday life. He remembers daily discussions and lessons his father shared with him and his siblings, hoping their destiny would grant them the same love with which he was blessed.

He explained that from a young age, they had to mature quickly. Even from his student days at prep school, he was very friendly and proved to have a contemplative nature. He liked going out with friends and going to parties, but his life did not revolve around that social environment. He sometimes preferred to stay home on the weekends with his introspective thoughts. He enjoyed analyzing everything that was problematic about his country and all that plagued society.

At seventeen years old, he enrolled at the National Autonomous University (UNAM) of Mexico to pursue a career in engineering. Before concluding his own studies, he taught algebra at UNAM.

In 1963, at the age of twenty-three, he graduated with his thesis: *Applications of Linear Programming in Civil Engineering* (his chosen area of study earned him the life-long nickname of "the engineer"). In 1962, he took a course in Economic Development and Evaluation of Projects. Later, he traveled abroad to further his studies and specialize in industrial programming at the Latin American Institute for Economic and Social Planning in Santiago, Chile.

In the sixties, for the vast majority of young entrepreneurs and intellectuals, Paris was seen as the place to be. But for Slim, Mexico was the land of opportunity. The time was called "stabilizing development," an epoch that some political economists qualified as the "Mexican Miracle." The economy was governed by a stabilizing of prices and the GDP grew at an annual rate of six percent. The model was not magic; it was a tight economic strategy with the central goal of maintaining exchange-rate stability above all, thereby preventing the devaluation pressures from openly manifesting. Thus, curbing inflationary pressures and seeking stability in the balance of payments were converted into central policies. This led to a sacrifice of wages and higher goals for social development. In fact, it was a time of growing poverty.

In short, the transition from an agricultural and rural country to one that was urban and industrial lapsed over fifty years. From 1933 to 1982, the economy grew to 6.8 percent, on average.

However, Slim found success in the business world, working in the housing industry with a company that specialized in real estate. Even then, he caused a stir with his administrative capacity and strategic genius.

During his first steps as a businessman, he married the love of his life Soumaya Domit Gemayel. The priest who officiated at the marriage ceremony was Marcial Maciel, founder of the Legionaries of Christ.

Soumaya, daughter of Antonio Domit Dib and Lili Gemayel, was born in Mexico in 1948. From a young age, she dedicated herself to charitable causes. She supported her husband in good times and bad.

Of Lebanese descent, Domit Dib was a Bechele native. He was adorned with the title Orden del Cedro[7] by the government of Lebanon. He promoted the footwear industry in Mexico and for years was president of the National Chamber of the Footwear Industry.

Soumaya's mother, Lili Gemayel, belonged to a prominent family of politicians in her country. Soumaya's uncle Amin Gemayel was president of Lebanon.

When they married in 1966, Carlos Slim was given a gift by Soumaya's mother of one million dollars, with which he bought land in Polanco. The custom in the Lebanese community was to build a house for the new family, but the new couple decided to construct a building in its place. They lived in an apartment and rented the empty rooms. Among the tenants was Slim's lifelong friend, Ignacio Cobo.

In their home on Bernard Shaw Road, the newlyweds Slim-Domit divided the work according to conventional roles. Soumaya was devoted to raising their six children, Carlos, Marco Antonio, Patricio and Soumaya, Vanessa and Johanna. Meanwhile, Slim went to work on the trading floor of the Bolsa Mexicana de Valores[8] (BMV), in an old building on Uruguay Street.

At that time, Slim spent his days with a group of *casabolsero,* or friends. Since his youth, Slim associated with the group referred to as the Generation 29 that included Luis Rosenfeld and Doro Pérez. After a hectic day, they would gather to play dominoes, and the evenings resembled that of the bohemian brotherhood. Slim listened attentively to the teachings of a sophisticated Rosenfeld and the great conversationalist Doro Perez. Those who caught his interest were Jorge de León Portilla, brother of the historian Miguel León Portilla, Xavier de la Barra, Aldo Olivieri, Rafael Morales Blumenkron, Silvino Aranda, Antonio López Velasco, Edward Watson, and Jorge Caso Brecht; all men who were clever and bright.

As adults, they spent all morning on the trading floor, at lunch they played dominoes in one of the bars downtown, and in the evening, they did clerical work involving financial and security investments. Carlos and Soumaya would occasionally host his friends with whom they would spend pleasant evenings playing guitar, after having sent the children to bed. Back then, others who came to join in the domino games with Slim included Ernesto Riveroll, Luis Madrigal, Enrique Trigueros, Ignacio Haro and Silviano Valdés.

In those years, Slim founded Inversora Bursátil. In 1967, he employed his cousin Alfredo Harp Helú, who was an accountant at Price Waterhouse. Three years later, in 1970, Slim employed Roberto Olivieri and Roberto Hernández Ramírez.

When Slim would finish his work at around ten o'clock at night, he went home to be with his family. Everyone would gather in the kitchen as they all got back from their various activities. Together with their children, they prepared dinner and talked about what happened during the day. Sometimes, the couple went out for dinner to celebrate their anniversary or other such events. This was the routine until Soumaya Domit's death on March 7, 1999.

During Soumaya's battle with chronic kidney failure, Slim studied the disease until he had amassed knowledge that rivaled her doctors'. When the doctors came to see her, he was well versed in Therapeutic methods they should employ to ease her suffering.

In 1992, when Slim was not yet known as King Midas, but was already established as one of the richest and most powerful men in Mexico, he faced severe health problems. In December of that year, Slim underwent emergency cardiovascular surgery in Mexico City and went to recuperate in Acapulco. When he was admitted to the hospital, he registered under the name Delgado[9] to avoid any harassment from the media. He was still not feeling very well after being released. As he came to learn, he was given excessive amounts of anticoagulants that would not allow the surgery wounds to heal. After spending Christmas with family in Mexico City, he spent New Year's Eve in Acapulco. While there, his health faltered once more. Acting swiftly, his daughter Johanna rented a plane to take him to an emergency room in Mexico and then on to Houston the next day where he was hospitalized. There, a team of specialists used a syringe to draw blood that had forcefully invaded his heart. Within hours, he was at ease.

The two eminent physicians who cared for Slim's health were Dr. Michael Duncan and Dr. Victor Letayf. Latayf is a disciple of the celebrated surgeon Rafael Muñoz Kapellmann, one of the glories of Mexican medicine who pioneered the National Institute of Medical Sciences and Nutrition.

Though Slim soon recovered enough to begin directing his empire once again, five years later he checked himself into the hospital for an aortic aneurysm.

was already too late. The Grupo Carso stock had fallen 6.5 percent and Telmex fell 3.35 percent.

The false news spread to New York, but the executives of Grupo Carso stopped speculation effectively when they announced that Slim had undergone cardiovascular surgery.

Although there had been a risk of pneumonia during his convalescence, the danger had passed and within a couple of weeks, he returned to work. He lost twenty-three kilos (fifty pounds), but fought very hard to get back to good physical health. Notwithstanding his health conditions, Slim was aware of everything that was going on in his business and communicated with his inner circle.

Being on the brink of death made him reconsider his own personal and discreet style of doing business. Health restored, Carlos Slim reconvened with his staff to announce changes in the direction of his companies. He put his sons and sons-in-law in charge, but stayed on as honorary president for life. He would continue to make strategic decisions for Carso and would maintain his presidency as chairman of the board of directors for Telmex, Carso Global Telcom and Grupo Financiero Inbursa.

While the decision to change directions was made even before his surgery, it wasn't implemented until November 1998. His eldest son, Carlos Slim Domit, came to occupy the position of general director of Grupo Carso and Grupo Sanborns. Patricio Slim Domit was assigned to be general director of Condumex-Nacobre and all manufacturing and industrial activities derived from these companies. Marco Antonio Slim Domit was placed at the head of Grupo Financiero Inbursa and its subsidiaries. Jaime Chico Pardo was placed at the head of Telmex with Slim's son-in-law, Arturo

In October of 1997, he underwent an operation to change his aorta where the hemorrhaging had occurred by removing the stitching that had originally been placed to patch it up. Many pints of blood were transfused and one doctor even left the operating room to announce Slim's death. Slim was in fact alive and after a miraculous three-and-a-half-month recovery, he was released, but not before replacing the doctors who had treated him. However, a series of rumors had already been set in motion: "Carlos Slim is dead."

Thus, the issue caused a stir in financial circles. Before eight a.m. on Wednesday, November 12, 1997, brokerage firm executives met to discuss the information they had read in the newspapers. Nervousness was felt all around, but they tried to ward off consultations and various phone calls, which only further fed the rumors. There was a great deal of confusion. Was Slim really dead?

That was the news reported in *Fin Fax*, an exclusive service that provided news summaries by fax from the newspaper *El Financiero*. The service began distribution to subscribers at six o'clock in the morning.

Senior officials of Grupo Carso and Teléfonos de México were unprepared and therefore, reacted with delay. They did not know how to stop the rumors. They began making phone calls to hundreds of brokerage firms and the media to clarify that the tycoon was recovering from his surgery and would be back at work in no time.

By noon, the directors of *El Financiero* were forced to send a "clarification" to their subscribers, admitting their mistake. But it

Elias Ayub, as advisor to the general director of Mexico. Ayub had previously been the chairman of the board of directors of T1msn. In 1995, Daniel Hajj, another of Slim's sons-in-law, was named CEO of the powerful cell phone company Telcel.

Daniel Hajj is exceptional because not only was he one of the craftsmen of the telecommunication giant América Móvil, but he is also the most important one. A golf aficionado, Hajj ran the company much like he played the game: with extreme attention and accuracy placed in the details. Under Hajj's guidance, América Móvil went from a mere one million subscribers to approximately ten million customers in just three years. Thanks to his vision, today eight out of ten new customers in most Latin American countries are with América Móvil.

Due to his excellent results, Slim's son-in-law was designated "El Hombre Expansión[10]" in 2007 by the magazine *Expansión*, which specializes in business and investments.

The last Slim son-in-law, the internationally renowned architect Fernando Romero Havaux, son of Raúl Romero Zenizo and María Cristina Havaux, married Soumaya Slim Domit on July 7, 2000. By the time of their marriage, Slim's daughter had become an art historian while Romero Havaux's professional experience included projects in the office of Rem Koolhaas in Rotterdam, Netherlands. It was he who was responsible for drafting the new Museo Soumaya in northern Mexico City, where the dominating Group Carso cooperative would eventually exist.

Having already determined the allocation of his empire by way of inheritance, the best advice tycoon Slim has given his children was "not to mix business with politics." This was confided to journalist Rossana Fuentes Berain in an interview he had given on the same day that Raúl Salinas de Gortari was arrested for allegedly masterminding the murder of his brother-in-law José Francisco Ruiz Massieu.

Fuentes Berain relates this anecdote:

In the Grupo Carso boardroom (a name resulting from the combination of and Soumaya), Slim Helú, the richest man in Latin America, talked with me while smoking, on February 25, 1995. We were talking about the devaluation of the Mexican peso, which occurred a few weeks earlier, when we were interrupted by Arnulfo, one of his personal assistants, who gave Slim a note: they had arrested Raúl Salinas de Gortari.

We sat in front of the TV and, remote control in hand, Slim tried unsuccessfully to find the signal. He turned up the volume instead of changing the channel, turned it off, and then turned it on again.

Finally, Arnulfo took control. He changed the satellite station and found what he was looking for: a special channel, unlike commercial television or cable. The black-and-white image was shocking: in a suit, without handcuffs, but with hands tucked behind his back, Raúl was being led into a car by men carrying guns.

That was the beginning of the end for the awkward brother, "Mister Ten Percent" as he was known in both Mexican and international business circles for the amount charged to conduct business during the term of his brother Carlos Salinas.

"That is why I always tell my kids not to mix business with politics," Slim mumbled through his teeth, wonder and surprise visibly marked his face.

Slim has said that his children have been "vaccinated" against the temptations of political power. None of his three male heirs has expressed a political inclination, although they have argued over the change of regime. Carlos Slim Domit, the eldest of the brothers, considered that the change in power of the PRI (Institutional Revolutionary Party) for the PAN (National Action Party) has shown no major differences in the proposals for the economic state. The second of the heirs, Marco Antonio, feels the change will interrupt the inertia already at work. He further believes that this is part of a global trend. Patricio, the youngest of the boys, argues that change in regime is most feasible.

As part of the empire forged by their father, the Slim-Domit brothers have several things in common: they are charismatic and sociable and there is no rivalry between them. The three say they are complementary and that is what makes them successful.

"If my children wanted to be boxers or athletes, they would've competed against each other," Slim said. "But in my opinion, in order to pursue and achieve happiness, one should not have to compete against anyone in your own company."

Carlos, the eldest of the brothers, is a loving and respectful son, loyal to those closest to him. When Patricio needed a kidney, he did not hesitate to donate his.

Indeed, if anything can be said without a doubt, it is that Slim is a man of principle. In his heirs, he has instilled honesty, patience, discipline, flexibility, courage, confidence and strength of character.

According to Slim, his legacy is genetic. "I think we all have vocations. There are some who are meant to be bullfighters, others are meant to be priests, doctors, and journalists. For me, since childhood, I liked investments."

After the transition of handing over the entrepreneurial conglomerate to the second generation, the structure of the empire still seems to be intact.

His children are pragmatic and astute in business and although they now exercise control over select companies in the group, there are still plenty of opportunities for everyone. There are executives not related to the family who have climbed to the top as well as family members who do not participate in the business simply because they are not interested. The Slim-Domit brothers work harder than anyone. Perhaps Daniel Hajj, senior executive of América Móvil, most personifies the tirelessly industrious spirit of the company, as he is one of the first to arrive and one of the last to leave.

Unlike other rich and powerful families who were forced into a generational takeover or who hired professional executives rather than divide the company amongst children and relatives, Carlos, Marco and Patricio have held key positions in the corporate structure for many years. Since an early age, they had been gradually preparing to take hold of the reins of the business.

When his children were teenagers, Carlos Slim would gather everyone in the library to teach them lessons in economics. He would present them with handwritten lists of examples such as how a Mexican insurance company sells policies at lower rates than an American company, or he would compare the drastic devaluation of Mexican manufacturers of sweets and cigarettes compared to European manufacturers.

In the early eighties, Slim used to take his firstborn to the Stock Exchange. "My father always included us in his business ventures," recalled Carlos Slim Domit. "He talked to us about the problems within his companies and he told us about the solutions. It is a process we have been involved in for many years."

Communication amongst the Slim family is common. For example, a few weeks before closing the tender offer for Telmex, Slim made a commitment to his six children (Carlos, Marco Antonio, Patricio, Soumaya, Vanessa and Johanna) that if the deal he was about to make succeeded, the phone company would remain in family hands for at least the next two generations.

Carlos Slim Domit spoke about the fifteen years following the privatization of Telmex in a magazine interview for *Líderes* in which he confirmed his commitment.

"Telmex is an extremely valuable company for the country," he said. "It is a company of top priority for the nation; a strategic support for the nation. It is important that it remain Mexican. These are not guidelines, but rather convictions, because commitment comes from outside and conviction comes from within. It is more a conviction than a commitment."

Carlos runs the Grupo Carso. He began working with his father at a young age and like the other two heirs, he studied business administration at the Universidad Anáhuac. All three are aware that an enormous responsibility falls on their shoulders. Marco Antonio has a passion for mathematics and is regarded as the financier of the family. He runs Grupo Financiero Inbursa, one of the top-tier companies in the country for management with assets over US$18 billion. Patricio, the youngest of the house, works with his brother-in-law Daniel Hajj at América Móvil. Since he became president of the company, its value has more than tripled. It is one of the main sources of the family's wealth.

Slim's decision to entrust the success of his businesses to his children must have been a weighty decision for the young trio. At first, they were subject to much criticism, but what can now be said with certainty is that the heirs have continued to expand the business. Since the late nineties, the heads of the companies had been preparing for the oncoming shift in power that would lie with the men of the family.

Since then, the heirs have not been without criticism. "I think sometimes, when you succeed in business, you have others trying to turn public opinion against you, because they're trying to compete with you," Carlos Slim Domit said.

However, one of Slim's most valuable insights was to share the company with business advisors and board members, including family members, who are integrated in different sectors of the company. It is with this insight that he has achieved flexibility, delegation, continuity and expansion.

To explain why the company was being transitioned from his hands to those of his sons, the tycoon once told a reporter, "These are not positions that my sons simply earned by being my children. In baseball, what do you do when you are throwing the ball to your son? Do you strike him out? And if you are pitching and your father or brother is at bat, what do you do? It is a matter of responsibility. In each instance, if you have the responsibility of being at bat, you always try to hit a homerun, no matter who is pitching. I think there are major problems that arise when you hand over high positions, or companies even, to your children simply because they are your children. A son should not feel obliged to enter into a business that he has no interest in; one he hasn't a taste for, a talent for, or strength in."

Carlos Slim Domit was trained in all areas of his father's business. He was groomed and raised in the area of financial operations of Inbursa and became involved in the hotel business, paper mills, the Sanborns chain stores, and Telmex.

"I don't think people noticed the transition much," Carlos explained. "My father's style of leadership is very similar to my own. My priority has always been to preserve Grupo Carso's values. The transition was very normal. For example, my biggest concern is that people feel good about what they do and that there is proper communication between all areas. This helps us to constantly evaluate the process and to know, with exact science, all of the potential successes and failures of each investment."

The Slim-Domit family has managed to win the respect of critics who are skeptical about their ability. The three brothers have given ample proof of their leadership and they know that they have the responsibility to set in motion a new phase of their father's dynasty.

Carlos Slim Domit remembers his father's teachings.

"Our philosophy is based on a few basic principles: to have an efficient and productive operation in addition to financial soundness," he said. "We do a lot on the financial side, especially when we are doing very well, which is normally when companies go soft and make bad investments or when bad decisions tend to be made."

When families work together daily, they deal with one another in an informal manner. In the Slim family, they all know that they can count on each person to meet their responsibilities. It is understood that they have the fate of hundreds of thousands of families in their hands. They respect their positions and accept the weight on their shoulders.

Carlos Slim Domit has stated that his father has never once pressured them to work for him, nor has he ever told them what they should do.

"We have always had the liberty to study whatever we wanted, to study or even not to study, to work or not to work with the group, and to do other things," he said. "Moreover, what my parents taught us is to do the things we like and to do them responsibly; not just for ambition, but for inspiration. My dad said that the worst thing to do is something you don't love. It hurts you and it ends up hurting the company. If you don't feel like you are doing something you love or working in a place that stimulates and challenges you, then you are better off dedicating yourself to something else."

The Slim heirs obtained a formal education in business administration in Mexico. There has never been an effort to reassure stock analysts by recruiting managers trained in the United States.

Patricio, a fighting-bull breeder and the youngest of the clan, remembers his mother's strong relationships and respect for others. She had a deep concern for people. From his father, he inherited a strong sense of honesty and a desire to work hard. "A friend once asked me, 'what did your father demand most from you?' It was honesty," Patricio said.

Slim's daughters, Soumaya, Vanesa and Johanna, have followed in their mother's footsteps in taking care of their own families and immersing themselves into cultural arenas, both altruistic and philanthropic. Two of the sisters are part of the board on the foundation; one runs Museo Soumaya while the other runs a foundation called Asociación de Superación por México[11] (ASUME), which specializes in personal development and self-improvement. Another sister heads up a program called Programa de Educación (Educational Program) in which kids learn to swim from a young age as part of a program to develop and stimulate physical activity.

In total so far, the tycoon has nearly two-dozen grandchildren. Slim gets together with all of his children and grandchildren on weekends.

During one of his regular lectures, a university student asked him, "What legacy will you leave your children?" The tycoon answered: "Someone asked me one day if I was going to leave money to my sons. I believe that when you leave them a company, you leave them work, responsibility and commitment. But when you leave them money—a hundred, fifty, thirty or twenty million—you leave that for them to be bums, right? It is different because when you have a company that you have to manage, even if there is a CEO, it is a job, a responsibility, an effort and a commitment to the company, to yourself and to the country, to generate wealth. The issue is not to have cash to spend and just idle for the rest of your life, the importance lies in continuity which requires commitment."

Slim has taught his children to be responsible. "We have to do things throughout our lifetime that make us efficient, careful and responsible. We must be smart about the way we manage our wealth," he said. "Many people want to leave a better country for their children; I try to leave better children for my country."

When asked how he would like to be remembered, Slim said that he tries not to think about that.

"What worries me is the future of my family, my children and my grandchildren. I hope they stay close, they continue to love each other, and they stay positive and optimistic for themselves and for their country," he said. "That is my primary concern. I don't concern myself with how I will be remembered, or *if* I will be remembered. My family and friends will remember me fondly."

Carlos, Marco Antonio and Patricio are the modern heirs of King Midas. Slim bet on his future and has put his children in contact with such men as the futurist Alvin Toffler and media technology professor Nicholas Negroponte. In 1985, Negroponte founded Media Lab at Massachusetts Institute of Technology, which is a center for unique research in the world. The laboratory coordinates and manages millions of dollars that companies invest in each year in order to create better communication for the future. Both of these men have been specifically invited to Slim's house to discuss future business and to prepare his heirs for long-term projects, several of which they have already begun to develop in Latin America.

SLIM'S PHILOSOPHY
Money Attracts Money

When Carlos Slim earned his undergraduate degree in civil engineering, he was already a millionaire. Fifteen years earlier, he had managed his investments in such a way that that allowed him to take a year-long sabbatical. He dedicated that year to doing anything he wanted: thinking, traveling and reading. He went to New York and observed how the global market worked over the course of a few months. He followed the advice of an old Arabic proverb that said: "One's best companions in times of leisure are good books." Alone in a city of skyscrapers, Slim secluded himself in the New York Stock Exchange Library where he consulted books and archives on the subject. He then traveled all over Europe where he once again visited numerous libraries. By the time he returned to Mexico, he was ready to sow the seeds of his knowledge and skill.

Slim was a young man of twenty-five when he started creating his own myth, much like many others who came before him in history. Slim is part of a generation that lived through great social and cultural transformations. As budding business emerged, the world was changing: the US intervened in Vietnam, Fidel Castro was growing stronger in Cuba, Che Guevara was becoming an icon, and rock bands like the Beatles were revolutionizing music. Meanwhile, in Mexico, the end of the idyllic Mexican Miracle was under way. Mexico was entering a period defined by economists as the "stabilizing development" model. This was a period of unstable progress in which a small segment of the population, those who were highly protected by political governments, were getting richer.

As much as the country's economic growth allowed the expansion of the middle class, not enough was being done to deal with the marginalized population. With such an inequality of income and the excessive protection of only a few economic agents, the system's weakness was growing; the same system that would fall into crisis only years later.

The tycoon who successfully positioned himself, in less than three decades, as one of the most powerful men in the world is good-natured man; he projects the image of a quiet and reserved person. He shies away from public life and media. But that just adds to Slim's charm. With the mentality of a chess master, he strategically places himself where he needs to be. In business, he is always three steps ahead. He's a moneymaker through and through. As Michel Tournier said, "Suffice it to say, he thought of money and money only since childhood."

Building his empire went beyond all previously set limits. To his admirers, he is a true genius; everything he touches turns to gold. The secret to becoming a multimillionaire for this King Midas stems from his admiration for philosophers and great financiers such as Jean Paul Getty, Benjamin Graham and Warren Buffet, all of whom are considered to be the masters of investment and speculation.

As a young man, Slim read Getty's articles in *Playboy* magazine and learned the formula to financial success: "Rise early, work hard and extract oil." Inspired by his principles and ideologies about money, Slim followed Getty's teachings to the letter.

Other tenets, such as Warren Buffet's ideas on work and money, also influenced Slim: "If something is not worth doing at all, it's not worth doing well."

Benjamin Graham, another one of his models, said, "An entrepreneur looks for professional advice in various facets of their business, but never expects to be told how to turn a profit."

So, surrounded by this small group of gurus, Slim built his empire. With his desire to expand his domain, he aligned himself with Bill Gates, who for years was ranked by *Forbes* magazine as the richest man in the world. The combined wealth of Gates, Warren Buffett and Slim, the three richest men on the planet, exceeds the GDP of one-quarter of the least developed countries in the world, a collection of about seventy nations.

In Mexico, Slim's companies report over US$5 billion annually to the treasury, only one position after PEMEX, the country's largest public sector, and bring in the largest amount of taxes.

Slim's empire extends to all corners. He has investments everywhere because he buys when stocks are low. He became a celebrity when *Forbes* magazine first included him on the 1992 list of the world's richest men when his capital was US$2.1 billion. Back in the eighties, Slim and his business group consisted of companies in several important industrial, commercial and financial sectors. This was the world from which he began to build his fortune as a professional in both financial and industrial sectors.

Fear and discouragement ran the globe when the 1982 crisis hit. No one wanted to invest in Mexico—nationals or foreigners. By investing in and acquiring numerous businesses that operated successfully for many years but were now going into bankruptcy, Slim increased Grupo Carso's standing as a very important company.

Jean Paul Getty, an oil tycoon so wealthy he didn't bother

keeping track of his fortune, learned that a true businessman is never satisfied with his achievements.

Getty used to say, "When you have no money, you are *always* thinking about it, and when you do have money you *only* think about it." Like Getty, who died thinking of the future as an aesthetic representation, Slim learned about art through his wife Soumaya's passion. One of Getty's legacies is his museum in Los Angeles, California, where diverse forms of art are mixed together, from architecture and sculpture to fine and mixed-media art.

Most of all, he assimilated the teachings of Benjamin Graham who maintained the following principles:

1. The investor must impose some sort of limit on the price he pays.
2. More important than knowing how much to buy and how much to sell is
    knowing when not to buy and when to sell.
3. No one tells the expert how to conduct his business or his life ... except the
    market.

There are three areas where an educated person should act mindlessly or as a child: religion, the market and mathematics. In all three cases not only is it "all right" to be considered perfectly ignorant, but it is impolite to even debate it, according to Graham.

Graham defended one principle of similarity between investment and speculation. For him, it was impossible to distinguish between one and the other because at the moment that it needs to be defined with precision, we fall into a paradox. If the discussion revolves around these terms, then at the end of the day, the cynic is right: "An investment is a speculation that went well, and speculation is an investment that went wrong."

To clarify the problem, Graham considered and rejected five claims:

1. Investing is buying bonds; speculating is buying shares. False.

2. Investing is buying for cash; speculating is buying credit. False.

3. Investing is buying with the intention of maintaining a long-term relationship; speculating is turning a quick profit. False.

4. Investing is waiting for the dividend; speculating is waiting for capital to appreciate. False.

5. Investing is buying safe securities; speculating is buying risky ones. False.

According to Graham's business philosophy, one could consider an investment: "buying stock on credit with the intention of a quick profit." Though this may seem like an accurate definition for speculation at first glance, in reality, the starting point in this tangled affair has to be put into context. People spend more time buying a refrigerator than they do buying stocks. Graham calls the process analysis. Investor and Wall Street consultant Peter Lynch calls it doing your homework.

Armed with this philosophy, Slim became the number one investor in Latin America at fifty years old, all the while creating his own legend. He accumulated his fortune during the eighties under the accusations of having been favored by those in power. "Slim was simply in the right place at the right time," according to banker

Manuel Espinosa Iglesias, who put an end to the discussion about the origin of Slim's fortune and how he became the richest man in Latin America. "Opportunities like this do not repeat themselves."

Slim's secret is simple: he is allergic to publicity and he leads a frugal life, which borders more on modesty than it does on solemnity. His existence revolves around business. He appears on the board of directors of the most important businesses in Mexico and he has a modest way of being seen as a great guru. When asked for his business secret, Slim said, "I can't be everywhere. My job is to think." However, he has a unique style to his work. In the morning, far from calls, meetings and distractions, he dedicates himself to the analysis of documents. He uses this solitary time to get to the bottom of the issues instead of becoming lost in the details.

Business, according to Slim, is comprised of three types of businessmen: the entrepreneur, the executive and the investor. The three should complement one another, to the point where they sometimes meld together. The entrepreneur is the one who conceives and undertakes, the executive is the one who operates the ventures, and the investor is the man who provides the means. Slim defines himself as the entrepreneur, but he said, "It can be said that there is a fourth type of businessman, the one who is the political entrepreneur," or the one who is entrenched in public relations.

"I differ from those who think that Mexican entrepreneurs cannot manage their own businesses. Many authorities believe it is better to favor foreign investment over domestic," he said.

Since opening the country to foreign capital, Slim has prompted a nationalist discourse. Perhaps it is not coincidental that on his main work desk, he keeps a framed letter from Benito Juárez to Matías Romero, dated, January 26, 1865. The letter reads:

Mr. Matías Romero

    Washington

    My dear friend: about your letter from November 14, and from official communication, which refers to the ministry stay tax that states that things have changed in that arena in our favor, which I am very grateful for, I am still concerned about certain news that the government was willing to recognize the empire of Maximilian. So, at the very least we will have the negative cooperation of the republic, and in terms of positive aid which can be given to you, I deem it to be quite remote and extremely difficult, because it is unlikely that the South will yield even an inch of their claims and if so, the government must conclude the matter by force of arms, and this demands much time and many sacrifices.

    The idea held by some, from what you've told me, that we offer part of our national territory in order to obtain the indicated aid, is not only unpatriotic, but also harmful to our cause. The nation, by legitimate authority of its representatives, has manifested in a strict and explicit manner, which is not its will to mortgage, or alienate its territory, which as you can see from the decree from which my extraordinary powers have been granted in order to defend the independence and if this regulation is opposed, we will fly over the country and we will give powerful arms to the enemy so that a conquest may be carried out. If it is our destiny, so be it that our enemy shall beat us and rob us, but we should not legalize this attack, or give into it voluntarily because of he who forces us by the hand. If France, the United States or whatever other nation supports any one of our regions, and due to our weakness we cannot defend ourselves against them, then we shall stop living out our rights so that the generations that succeed ours shall have a chance to recover them. How bad it would be to allow ourselves to be disarmed by a higher power but it would be even worse to disarm our children by depriving them of their rights. Braver and more patriotic than us, they have suffered, but they will know how to assert themselves and reclaim their independence one day.

It is all the more damaging the idea of alienating our territory in these circumstances, in terms of the states of Sonora and Sinaloa, which are the most coveted today, they make heroic efforts in national defenses, which are the most jealous of the integrity of their territory and they provide the government with firm and resolute support. Then, for such consideration, it is for prohibition which the law imposes on the government to mortgage or alienate the country and finally, because this prohibition conforms entirely with the view that I have always held on these matters, I repeat that which I have already stated in my letters from December 22 and earlier, namely that you should only follow the patriotic behavior I have observed of not supporting any similar idea, instead you should oppose it and work to dissuade it by ensuring that fatal consequences are brought to fruition.

I am grateful that you are satisfied with my opinion about General Grant's army, with respect to our cause. This opinion, and that which Mr. Seward formed, are guarantees that we will not recognize Maximilian's empire. This is the only positive that we can expect right now from such a republic.

I will not extend myself anymore, because I am under the impression of such profound regret that is eating at my heart like a deceased son whom I loved, I was barely able to draw the line between them. I say dead son that I loved because according to the letter that you received last night, I understood that such dismal the news (you didn't give it to me all in one shot); but in reality, my loving son will never exist, no longer exists. Is this not true? With all my heart, I hope I am wrong, and I would be happy to learn in your next letter, which I anxiously await, that you will tell me my son has been relieved.

Much hope that a gloomy presentiment will fade, saying that there is no remedy!

Goodbye my friend. You know that I am here for you with overwhelming affection,

Benito Juárez

From a young age, Slim was an ambitious entrepreneur, but his philosophy has always been very simple. His companies work on basic principles and a simple structure. "We are constantly looking into the fact that our team always has vocation, preparation and stimulating work that fuels self-confidence. This incites a sense of satisfaction in their responsibility more than a sense of obligation, and contributes to their own personal development," he said. "The team operates without a corporate staff and the company manager is always located in the production plant, in operations and in sales, with minimum operating costs, searching for the best personnel, the most trained and therefore best paid. Investments are made in the production plant and in the distribution and administrative teams, and not in buildings/real estate or other operations.

"We seek to minimize the hierarchy, keeping the directors as close to operations as much as possible. We want to strive for that and not for corporate structures. We try to combine executive work with the interest of shareholders through a representative council, who work together with managers looking to optimize investments, strategies and expenditures. We work systematically to improve the production process, optimizing investment and facilities, increasing productivity, improving quality, reducing wastage and trying to mass produce the best quality at the lowest cost; its reduction means sustaining or improving margins, expanding our markets, reducing prices and competing internationally.

"We guide our growth and our investments toward the most dynamic sectors in the medium- and long-term; we try to maintain flexibility and rapid decision-making and, finally, the advantages of a small business, which are those that make big businesses great.

"The enabling environment in a society gives it political and economic stability, sound public finances, with an open budget applied to economic and social programs in priority, with investments in infrastructure and social expenditures, with redistributive effects that promote consistent and gradual well being. Moreover, such a favorable environment motivates and stimulates confidence in the country, and also in the government. Furthermore, the government has to participate by organizing society and managing common effort. These are, without a doubt, the necessary conditions for national development.

"Hence, a domestic and foreign private investment is required. A market that produces wealth is also necessary. A government that orients and fosters growth and that spends and invests with redistributive purposes in education, health and lifestyle will benefit from a good percentage of gross domestic profit.

"In this new world of economic liberalization and globalization, initiated by multinationals and by technology—which at times seems to recede with economic blocks and the protection by force of the historic subsidies—even the most developed countries like the United States, the European Union and Japan have become entrenched.

"Especially in the agricultural sector, security, efficiency, productivity, quality, design, technology, high added value, large industrial and commercial expertise and competitive advantages, strong investments in research and development, higher education for the masses in science and technology, in times of rapid growth and good results, in the era of the fat cows, management often relaxes and organizations exceed their means instead of taking the opportunity to capitalize and fortify the company, which is deteriorating and aging. On the other hand, maintaining fixed costs and austerity in the growth of the company constitutes its rapid development.

"One must be constantly attentive when it comes to the company; to its modernization and growth capital, quality and simplification, incrementing productivity and reducing costs and expenditures.

"We must distinguish three vocations in the company: the entrepreneur, the executive and the investor. In the first-generation of the family business, one person usually performs all three functions. In large public companies, there are large investors, both individual and institutional, and frequently in developed countries the entrepreneurial function is diluted and shifted by the non-executive parties who pay quarterly sums to institutional investors.

"In the competition, companies no longer operate simply to the specification of the proprietor who must be socially and emotionally satisfied. His responsibility should seemingly be fulfilled. But, in contrast, societal resources must be optimized in order to reduce waste, and the first thing to do is to have references. As in sports, we know what the world record is, who the best athletes are and how long they've been competing. We must have the best international references for the field in which we play.

"In a company, profit should be present in purchasing, trade and cost. In the industry, now immersed in a highly competitive environment, lowering costs is like reducing time for an athlete. In both cases, perseverance is required, training, organization and above all, vocation and the desire to win, constantly pushing brands, improving at all times, keeping a demand for operations workers, managers and entrepreneurs to optimize investments, production, quality and costs. Like a sports team, managers are not the only requirement, but rather well trained middle management, with leadership qualities and a good sense of organization, is also a necessity.

"When forming a new company or a new plant, one should consider the location, size, the engineering of the project, marketing, and the corporate structure.

"Moreover, greater market efficiency should correspond to economic policy of tax revenue that has fundamentally redistributive ends. This would establish minimum social welfare standards, raised in favor of the less fortunate, to be gradually integrated into modern society by having better nutrition, health, education and more opportunities in general.

Just being a competitive country in international trade may help retain better-paid employees, create wealth within the market rules and redistribute it through tax among the most disadvantaged with a clear sense of justice and economic and human development.

"Not improving quality and productivity, not optimizing our investment and mediocre resources, not capitalizing on Mexico's advantageous openness to international capital markets, not obtaining the maximum production out of our machinery and equipment, not having competitive levels of quality and prices of our non-tradable goods would be unforgivable. This implies that we would have to import more, export less and reduce the production apparatus. In sum, not consolidating the virtuous process that we have already initiated and not taking advantage of the significant capital inflow (which will only continue to thrive if we succeed) would be a serious mistake with a high price to pay.

"Only quality, productivity, efficiency and optimization of our resources can enable us to compete successfully in this opening.

"With success, a structured market will generate more well-paid jobs, better and cheaper products and greater wealth in society. Only government action through tax initiatives can benefit all members of society through public investment with essentially redistributive ends. So, the economic market in and of itself is not sufficient to put an end to ancestral surplus.

"The entrepreneur has the social responsibility to optimize the company's resources by making it more and more efficient, competitive, and by re-investing the profit and preparing his well-paid staff through motivation. He should be satisfied in knowing that his responsibility lies in ensuring his staff always does to the best of their ability.

"In short, after all is said and done, businessmen are creators of the wealth they temporarily manage."

Slim's philosophy channels some basics of the biblical passages from Genesis. One story tells of a dream the Pharaoh had, which foresaw seven years of abundance followed by seven years of misery. John Maynard Keynes, English economist, refers to these theories as the cycle of seven fat cows and seven thin cows.

Slim found Keynes's exposition of *Theory of Regulated Capitalism* in *The General Theory of Employment, Interest and Money* unoriginal. His theory can be found in the Bible. When Joseph interpreted the Pharaoh's dream, he said, "You will have seven years of fat cows and seven years of thin cows. This means that in the years of the fat cows, you must collect and store food so the following years the thin cows will not die of famine." This means that in the new economy, the fat cows are the surplus (excess) and the thin cows are the deficit. In the fat-cow years, businesses should capitalize and accelerate their development, that way during the thin-cow years they won't have to fire anybody.

In other words, Slim follows the Chinese proverb: "He who saves in times of plenty does not lament in times of need."

Unlike other business, those belonging to Slim do not require headhunters for recruiting. All employees grow within their companies. In fact, many of its executives have walked the halls of the companies' own training center, the Instituto Tecnológico[12] (Inttelmex). Thanks to this center, the level of schooling has improved from six to fifteen years. Teléfonos de México, Telmex International and América Móvil boast employees with the highest level of education in all of Latin America; the great majority of the sons of the telecommunications employees are academians.

Many of the ideas contained in the ten basic principles that guide Slim's business decisions were taken from his father, Julián Slim Haddad, who brought young Carlos to work because he noticed his son's particular affinity for business. These principles have been transmitted to the families, colleagues, staff and team.

1. Prefer simple structures and organizations with flexibility, a minimum of hierarchical levels, and quickness in decision-making. The advantages of the small company are what make large companies big.

2. Maintaining austerity in time of fat cows strengthens, capitalizes and accelerates development of the company. This avoids drastic changes in times of crisis.

3. Always remain active and tireless in relation to modernization, simplification and improvement of the production processes. Seek improvement in productivity and competitiveness, as well as reduction of costs and expenses through the guidance of major world references.

4. The company must never be limited to the parameters of the owner or manager. We get big within our own small barnyard.

5. There is no goal we cannot reach if we work united, with clarity of objectives, and knowledge of the available tools.

6. Money leaving the company evaporates. Therefore, we re-invest profits.

7. Creativity applies not only to business, but also to the solution of many of the problems in our countries.

8. Firm and patient optimism always bears fruit.

9. All times are good for those who know how to work and have the means to do so.

10. Our premise is that nothing is taken from here. The businessman is a creator of wealth that he manages temporarily.

In the practice, day in and day out, Slim's style and philosophy is the exact opposite of the pompous, corporate brands in Santa Fe, or of the glamorous and luxurious offices in Monterrey and Guadalajara, which resemble museums laden with large marble furnishings and art. In all offices, austerity prevails. High- and mid-level executives share the same secretary; advisers do not exist. Ability and talent is what counts. All achieve their raise or promotion by their own merit. There are no privileges given to family members. In order to climb the ladder, one must demonstrate that he is extremely efficient. Promotions are not granted through flattery, glamour, charisma or ability in public relations. What counts are talent, discipline, and productivity.

Arturo Elías Ayub, Slim's son-in-law, works out of a modest office where some of the furniture looks older than the privatization of telecommunications companies in the 1990s. This reminds the boss not to waste money during his workday at Teléfonos de México. Taking care of resources extends all the way to payroll.

Telmex spends on average MX$20,000 a month on ten employees.

What matters are the values that underlie operational efficiency: always getting the most at a minimal cost. Based on the principles of the business group, each peso is valued; the organization defines itself as austere. There is no allowance for big restaurants, first-class trips, nor luxury cars or gym memberships. The working philosophy is not to squander and waste on luxuries and unnecessary expenses. Everything is focused on maximizing resources. Salaries are competitive and at market level, but big salaries are not granted. Instead there are incentives and rewards. Training is another plus for employees. The business spends on average, sixty hours per year per employee on training. One may start as a humble analyst, but hard work can lead to a position of leadership in businesses in Mexico or abroad.

In a way, students receiving university scholarships from Telmex are a future payroll investment. Grants are equivalent to minimum wage for the best students from poor families, who also get free computers and Internet through Telmex and Prodigy. These programs eventually benefit the company, as it is in line with their Corporate Social Responsibility programs. In the case of many, these students will become employees at Telmex, Condumex or Sanborns. Thus, Slim has first pick of the best talent available and in turn, he ensures their loyalty.

Although Slim is one of the hundred most influential men in the world, he has defined himself as a man of solemn mind.

"I would say that I'm solemn, as are my children, for taste and conviction, but not when it comes to discipline," Slim told Chilean reporter Margarita Serrano during a visit to Santiago. He was in the country at the time to give a talk at the Entrepreneurs Club along with friend and former Spanish Prime Minister Felipe González.

Slim spoke of his philosophy of life and business when he spoke to a group of university students in Mexico City on June 25, 1994.

Dear young students,

I write you this letter in order to share some of my life experiences, hoping it will contribute to your education, your way of thinking and living, your emotional well-being, your sense of responsibility to yourselves and to others, your maturity, and above all, to your happiness, which should be the result of your daily existence.

You are privileged within society due to your talents and efforts, and for the best reason, your own worth.

Success is not about doing things well or even very well, or being acknowledged by others. It is not an external opinion, but rather an internal status. It is the harmony between the soul and your emotions, which requires love, family, friendship, authenticity and integrity.

To be as exceptional as you are, is a privilege, but it also entails many risks that can have an impact on values that are much more important than professional, economic, social or political "success." Emotional strength and stability are in the interior life, and in avoiding emotions that erode the soul such as envy, jealousy, arrogance, lust, selfishness, vengeance, greed and laziness, which are a poison that is ingested little by little.

When you give, do not expect to receive. "Fragrance clings to the hand that gives the rose," said a Chinese proverb. Do not allow negative feelings and emotions to control your mind. Emotional harm does not come from others; it is conceived and developed within ourselves.

Do not mix up your values or betray your principles. Life's road is very long, but it is traveled fast. Live the present intensely and fully, do not let the past be a burden, and let the future be an incentive. Each person forges his or her own destiny and it may influence reality. Do not ignore it.

Live with positive feelings and emotions such as love, friendship, loyalty, courage, joy, good humor, enthusiasm, peace, serenity, patience, trust, tolerance, prudence and responsibility. Do not allow their opposites to invade your soul, may they pass quickly from your mind, do not allow them to stay there, banish them. You will make mistakes many times, it is normal and human; but try to make them small, then accept, correct and forget them. Do not be obsessed by them; heaven and hell are within us. What is most valuable in life does not cost anything but is very precious: love, friendship, nature and what man has been able to achieve with it; the forms, colors, sounds, smells that we perceive with our senses can only be appreciated when we are emotionally awake.

Live without fear and guilt; fear is the worst feeling men can have, it weakens them, inhibits action and depresses them. Guilt is a tremendous burden in our lives, the way we think and act. Guilt and fear make the present difficult and obstruct the future.

To fight them, let us have good sense and accept ourselves as we are, with our realities, our merits and our sorrows.

Staying occupied displaces preoccupation and problems, and when we face our problems, they disappear. Thus, they make us stronger every day. We should learn from failure and successes should be silent incentives. Act always as your conscience dictates, because it never lies. Fear and guilt will then be minimal. Do not block yourself in, do not ruin your life, live it with intelligence, with soul and senses aware and on the alert; get to know their manifestations and train yourselves to appreciate and enjoy life.

Work well done is not only a responsibility to yourselves and society; it is also an emotional need.

At the end we depart with nothing. We leave behind only our work, family and friends, and perhaps a positive influence, which we have planted.

My very best wishes,
Carlos Slim Helú

In 1991 Slim's name first appeared on the list of the richest men in the world. Slim had no vested interest in the people at *Forbes*. For several years, when his first business ventures were starting out, he was driving an old red Mustang. By 1993, upon appearing on the list among great businessmen worth more than a billion dollars, he was driving a 1989 black Mustang. Up until recently, when he was recognized as the richest man in Latin America, he continued to maintain such humility. On rare occasions, he does give into his whims. Cars have always tempted him and he regularly pulls up to meetings in a Suburban or a Mercedes.

He rarely wears anything as elegant as a Brioni suit. He is informal: he works in shirts and rarely wears cufflinks. He doesn't own ostentatious jewels and he wears clothes from his own companies, like Saks[13]. He is the antithesis of tycoons who pose for magazines like *Jet Set*. He usually flies on the Telmex plane or helicopter and sticks to an agenda because "time is money."

One of Slim's greatest pleasures is to converse with intelligent people. While other millionaires like to play golf or tennis, cruise through the Caribbean, ride along in yachts, take exotic trips to the Orient, go on African safaris, mountaineer, or drive luxurious cars, Slim prefers to visit national parks or stroll along the Sea of Cortez. He leans more toward natural sites and cities that have historical value and pre-Hispanic ruins, but he is also passionate about new technology, culture, art and sports. Until three years ago, he smoked Cohiba cigars, but never indulged in extravagant foods; his favorite cuisine is Mexican. He enjoys *cochinita* tacos (a slow roasted pork taco), refried beans, handmade tortillas, *pambazos* (Mexican white bread), tamales, mole, enchiladas, salsa, and some traditional Lebanese dishes such as bulgur and chickpeas. Even in recent years, when he leaves for a road trip to Acapulco, he always makes a stop at the Cuernavaca's booth to eat the giant *tortas* (traditional Mexican sandwich) sold there.

One of his hobbies is film. His favorite movies that have most influenced him are *El Cid* and *Modern Times*. His favorite actors are María Félix, Sophia Loren, Charlie Chaplin, Joaquín Pardavé, Pedro Infante and Marcello Mastroianni. In music, his favorites are Elvis Presley and Little Richard. He had a very warm and affectionate relationship with la Doña, *née* María Félix[14], in her later years. She had a special soft spot for Slim's eldest son Slim Domit.

One time, Slim told la Doña that he would have loved to be a journalist so that he could have interviewed her and asked about her life, about love, about friendship. The diva, he remembers, had a wonderful concept of happiness.

Although he belongs to the Rock 'n' Roll generation, Slim is passionate about classical music as well as the *bolero*, the *mambo* and *danzón*.

One of his tiny indulgences is his personal security, which he reinforced after his financial information appeared on a Nicaraguan list of prominent businessmen to kidnap. This document, attributed to *Patria Vasca y Libertad*[15], targeted one hundred fifty Latin American businesses, seventy-seven of which were Mexican, and some of whom were defrauded, including Fernando Senderos, Juan Bosco Gutiérrez Cortina, Juan Robinson Bours, Alfredo Harp Helú and Ángel Losada Moreno.

Like Gates, who became a billionaire by revolutionizing the computer industry with Microsoft colleague Paul Allen, Slim began to climb the rungs of wealth in the eighties with his gift for business.

From then on, Slim, with his extensive business experience, became an authority in the world of money. From his position as a money guru, he wrote a few articles in the newspaper *Novedades* on October 3 and 4, 1988. This was one year after the stock market crash of October 5, 1987, when the Price and Quotation Index (IPC) of the Mexican Stock Exchange had risen to more than 26,000 points. The IPC didn't move more than that because the computer operators and staff, who manually work the stock market board, could not face the relentless pace of transactions. The National Banking and Securities Commission (NBSC) was forced to intervene, under the argument that the law allows the termination of the auction when there are fluctuations that are too abrupt, be it upward or downward.

Stock analysts argued that the market responded the way it had because of an information leak amongst investors about the nomination of Salinas de Gortari for President of the Republic, which was a sign that he was guaranteed to continue the economic policy.

In this context, Slim wrote two installments of his personal understanding of what had happened, entitled "Four Epochs of Mexican Economy: What Started in 1952 Ends Today" and "Excessive Debt and Deficit; Rising to the Oil Nightmare."

The first article published by *Novedades* read:

In the economic development of Mexico, since the post-war period and its immediate effects, three periods can be distinguished with similar economic characteristics across six different governments.

The first period lasted twenty years, beginning in 1952 and ending in 1972. The second period, which lasted little less than ten years, ended in 1981, having exhausted the sources that life provided: external credit, high oil prices and public deficit spending. The third period, the crisis, lapsed over seven years from 1982 to date. Currently, a new period is being envisioned beginning early 1989.

First period—1952-1972: During these years, substantial development was achieved by maintaining the proposed balance, stable prices and moderate external debt. Domestic debt was reduced to equate that of deficit, despite significant population growth and a major effort to provide public services. Domestic products almost quadrupled; income per capita doubled. Income was distributed through increasingly better-paid jobs—still far from the desired level—and by way of public spending, which covered the needs of more and more Mexicans.

The rapid substitution of imports and income from services, chiefly from tourism, attenuated the needs of foreign savings despite the rising importation of capital goods and more elaborate consumables. The State increasingly participated in economic activity.

Second period—1973-1981: Lasting nine years, it was expected to jeopardize the development process because of unhealthy strategies, like excessive external and internal debt, an exaggerated public deficit with a consequential imbalance of public finances and the excessive growth of bureaucracy. This reduced the possibilities of substituting imports, which affected the previous development model. There is a fundamental difference in the international financial, monetary system, technological changes and consumption patterns that affected the traditional primary materials and their terms of trade.

In the early years of this stage, participation in the private sector of productive economic activity was reduced, the deterioration of the economic situation of the country was accelerated by the handling of incompatible financial and economic policies (inflation, parity, interest rates), causing not only domestic savings to move abroad, but also the greater part of foreign loans was used to pay interest and consumption, and the waste caused by unproductive investments.

Extraordinary income derived from oil was wasted, as was US$76 billion of net external credit. Coincidentally, this stage began with the discovery of rich oil fields of Chiapas and Tabasco, which entered in production years later causing the "oil boom," and concluded with the drop in price along with foreign credit.

In the last five years, there was also a stretched out private investment, substantially financed by foreign savings, which threatened the production plant and employment; public finances and external accounts were upset, public and private external debt were in excess. Inflation was rampant and the country's reserves exhausted.

However, at the end of this period, the country produced large, modern facilities in all fields of economic activity, mostly operated by Mexicans, at all levels.

Third period—1982-1988: The Challenge of Crisis. Having lost the historical opportunity that gave us "oil *wealth" by trying to force growth, the current government, since its inception, faced every serious potential economic problem. I believe there is nothing missing: triple-digit inflation, fiscal deficit of 17.6 percent, external debt of US$88 billion, current account deficit: the productive apparatus of debt without liquidation fearing massive closures, without international reserve and an excessive dependence on oil revenues.*

Moreover, we still did not know what would come of the earth tremor of 1985, the collapse of oil prices in 1986 and Hurricane Gilberto shortly thereafter.

To address many problems, it was necessary to act in several directions at once, some of which had undesirable and unpopular consequences. So, to clean up the public accounts, it was necessary to increase the revenue by raising prices and public services and taxes, and reducing or eliminating subsidies; public investment and current expenditure were reduced as well.

In 1987, a primary surplus close to 4.5 percent was obtained that would consider us more than healthy. In 1988, it was necessary to bring this effort to a point of pursuing achievement of a primary surplus of approximately eight percent of GDP, despite having lost strong revenue from the decrease in oil. This surplus is a useful target for curbing inflation, along with other measures that periodically come along with the Economic Solidarity Pact, and which allowed inflation to dominate.

JOSÉ MARTINEZ

The success of the Pact was faster than anticipated and its success was recognized by pessimists. Inflation in the second half of 1988 should be less than fifteen percent annually and it is possible that in 1989 it will reach single digits annually, especially since we have learned to deduct: to stop one has to not only decelerate, but one must slow down (negative acceleration). Economists should study physics.

To disallow inflation quickly, not only does one have to maintain without changing certain variables, but one has to allow certain negatives; that way, stopping the flow of inflation becomes possible.

Inflation is reduced by setting it at zero, but it vanishes when lowering certain variables. It was impossible to bring inflation down gradually from three digits to one. Public accounts could not be attacked at the source without sufficient reserves to face it dead on.

The problems with the external accounts and its solutions have been: heavy reliance on oil revenues that have been replaced by several manufactures making it possible to absorb the debt service to maintain a slight current account surplus and the huge external debt of private and public sectors. The private sector has been practically solved through FICORCA[16], from financial restructuring with capitalization of liabilities of several large companies and the negotiation of foreign debt that many companies have been acquired at market value, close to fifty percent of their nominal value through debt swaps with Mexican external debt.

77

Private enterprise in the crisis has excelled in making itself efficient and incrementing productivity and quality, being competitive in other markets, and reducing internal prices facing economic openness.

In the case of public external debt, there have also been important advances: for the most part, short-term restructures every twenty years and the reduction of interest rates.

This new term, the lowest rate and the implicit recognition of creditors of which payment growth is a priority, has meant that the debt is listed at fifty percent of its nominal value, which is the most diverse option to stop trading, reduce principal debt and interest, such as swaps, buying debt in the market, the exchange of debt for investment (venture capital) and recognition of the value of the creditor that really gives its role to the market, all to benefit debt and move it into new restructuring.

Moreover, according to the president, in December 1982 to date [October 1988], *the effective use of external credit resources has been negative by US$7,113,000. To this, one must add that the dollars that are now worth more than that of 1982, and that debt will be reduced by more than US$20 billion, despite the loss of more than US$30 billion of revenue in the last three years due to the decrease in oil (an amount through which actual market prices could have practically bought the debt).*

The United States has become the world's largest debtor. Its debt is more than US$500 billion and is increasing by more than US$150 billion annually. Soon (and I use the term *loosely), they will have similar problems that we had if they do not change their fiscal deficit and current accounts.*

In our country, all this effort has only been achieved with high costs: deterioration of real wages, underemployment, informal economic growth, and deferred public investment. However, if we avoid falling into an increasingly serious chronic underdevelopment and structural change, we have the foundations for a new national project of a larger and fairer country.

Oil wealth was a chance opportunity that ended in nightmare, an ephemeral wealth that put us right back where we were. The current basis and immediate prospects represent a new historic opportunity, the only firm path to development: efficient and constant hard work, with steady steps. We cannot take this second chance for granted, or in less than ten years our children and our grandchildren may not forgive us.

In the second part of his analysis, published in *Novedades*, Slim wrote an article entitled, "A New Path to the Future Has Begun."

Fourth period—1989 – ?: A new historic opportunity, the economic picture is opposite that of 1982: annual inflation is one digit; public finances are sound; we have eight percent primary surplus; the production plant is healthy and highly efficient, exporting in a great way, with high liquidity; and we have an expected annual inflation of a single digit. The best alternative to production is productivity; the private sector has the capacity to invest and is ready to take responsibility.

We have a surplus in current accounts and high international reserves.

The external debt problem has not been resolved, but as I said before, progress is substantial: the solution is long term, its market value is half, and bankers are willing to do much more than they were six years ago, including changing their debt for venture capital. Worst-case scenario, we could "aficorcar" the debt, that is to say, pay only the real interest and capitalize on the inflationary component, keeping the debt at the same level of constant dollars. In the best-case scenario, that banks would recognize as debt that which the market recognizes: fifty percent, and that will change into long-term investments, leaving a minor foreign debt to two years of exportation, or three years of reserves, or twenty percent of the GDP, reducing it to a third and reopening it to new financial markets.

Some call for not paying the debt on the grounds that we have already paid more in interest, but I ask them if they would accept that argument as investors if a bank gave them that as a reason to not repay the principal.

Many complain that they are lowering the nominal interest rate, though Mexico is paying a higher interest rate than I've ever seen before (more than three percent per month for September). On the other hand, there is a rapid change in global finance, by giving the largest transfer of wealth in history to Southeast Asian countries, mainly Japan.

They are concentrating wealth, savings, financial strength and trading in Japan and the NICs (Newly Industrialized Countries), countries that despite not having the resources became very strong after the oil shock: a basis for work, imagination and efficiency.

Mexico can count on foreign savings for development, but must extend and intensify their economic transactions with more countries and in new ways.

It should be a super-macro plan, with a wide horizon of space and time in which large national projects, economic and social projects with long-term goals, defined priorities, and the origin of resources to achieve all of this can be determined. This should complement the public sector with national savings so it can coordinate with national interests when they come along, with more foreign investments or foreign debt conversion in productive investment.

Economic recovery will require more work and more efficiency, especially at the management level, and higher incomes to reactivate the economy. The public sector will increase its revenue and in order to resume economic growth, may invest more by reducing the primary surplus at levels of three percent of GDP and the nominal interest rate will be fiscal.

Export does not need dramatic increases like in recent years. It would suffice for it to consolidate and continue to grow, along with tourism and other services, to maintain our ability to import the capital goods and inputs that growth requires. With a consistent recovery of real wages and employment, the process of investment, productivity, income distribution, economic recovery, and tax revenue would be simultaneous and provide feedback.

The recovery of real wages is not just for social justice or political reasons, it is an economic necessity: the force of our recovery and development, the reason for our growth and ultimate goal is the emotional and material welfare of the population. Work is not only a social responsibility, but also an emotional necessity.

In late 2005, in a lecture to students at the Universidad Anáhuac, Slim explained his insight on the challenges Mexico faces in a global context:

I am both pleased and honored to be with you here today. If it is all right with you, I would like to start off with a bit of history of the evolution of Mexico's economy and then go on to current events, so as to give you a broader perspective.

Evolution of Mexico's economy

Owing to the difficult situation the country was undergoing as a result of recession, in 1931 Mexico arrived at an unprecedented agreement, which was called Congress's Revolutionary Movement, made up of congressmen, as well as representatives of the Chamber of Commerce and the Chamber of Industry. This decision led to a campaign, which was called the Nationalist Campaign, the slogan of which was "Buy what the country produces." Whether this is a coincidence or not, I do not know. Nevertheless, this campaign marked the beginning of fifty years of growth in

*Mexico at a rate of 6.2 percent: **fifty continuous years**. This growth was also spurred by Mexico having gone from an agricultural and rural era into a much-delayed urban and industrial stage.*

The golden era of those fifty years was from 1958 to 1970, when Mr. Antonio Ortiz Mena worked for both the Ministry of Finance & Public Credit and Mexico's Central Bank, growth was accelerated, inflation was low, interest rates and financing were long term, etc.

This sustained growth not only allowed for Mexico to grow substantially, it become industrialized and was no longer a predominantly rural and agricultural country that mostly lived off of self-consumption (in other words, people lived practically with what they produced and used and did not buy any other goods besides the necessary tools to work). It also gave rise to an enormous population growth, which as we all know was more than three percent as the economy grew at a rate of 6.2 percent.

Mexico went from an agricultural and rural country to an industrial and urban country

During the 1930s, the country's population was about seventeen million, perhaps sixteen or fifteen million, and by the 1940s, there were already twenty million. During those days, there was a beer commercial, Corona, I believe, that went like this: "Twenty million people cannot be wrong"; anyway, I had not yet been born when that commercial was popular. The Chamber of Commerce, Mr. Cayetano Blanco Vigil—the father of Nieves Noriega—and my own father as a chamber member, participated in that campaign; that was back in 1931.

Mexico was greatly strengthened by this transition from an agricultural and rural country to an industrial and urban country because growth was reinforced by the construction of roads, housing, factory jobs, and others elements of infrastructure.

In my opinion, this is the same process that China is undergoing at present. China has been growing at a rate of 9.5 percent in the last twenty years and it is also a rural country depending on self-consumption and agriculture. However, it is going from a very primitive agriculture of self-consumption to no longer an industrial stage, but rather this new civilization that we are experiencing.

[China] is already a country that is giving its people a great deal of education. It is a country that is rapidly absorbing the technology of this new civilization and that is making substantial progress at a very fast pace, however with a very long-term vision. In other words, they are not thinking about the last twenty years or even the next twenty years, but rather about many years to come. Out of a population of 1.3 billion, seventy percent or nine hundred million people are still living in disadvantageous circumstances; however, there are four hundred million Chinese who are already living in the urban world, are better educated, and who participate in a more modern and prepared society, and this is what creates the country's tremendous strength. It is to be expected, though, that China's process will still take many years.

In Mexico, this process was interrupted by the excesses of the administrations of the 1970s and 1980s, which experienced very high deficits in spite of growth. There were tax deficits; they spent the money borrowed from the well-known petro-dollars. I am not sure if you have heard about those. There was an oil boom and the oil countries did not know what to do with their oil money. They gave it to the banks, the banks recycled it, lent it to countries and the countries spend it irresponsibly, just like the bankers lent it.

So, somewhere around 1981 and 1982, not only were they in debt, but interest rates jumped to twenty-one percent. Can you imagine paying interest rates of twenty-one percent or twenty-two percent? Countries fell into an enormous crisis. The large crisis of 1982 was a terrible one; it was a crisis of external debt that not only affected Mexico, but also many other countries and Latin America in general.

Adjustment programs followed that crisis. One of them was called the Washington Consensus, which gave rise to the well-known model that has been followed to a certain degree but in fact continues to be an adjustment program. So, for the last twenty-three years our per capita growth has been practically zero. In other words, the number of Mexicans each year grows by maybe 1,700,000 or 1,800,000 and the economy by almost two percent. So, the difference is very small between economic growth and population growth, and not only was growth small but also irregular. Growth was suddenly good and then crises such as that of '95, '94, etc. occurred.

Two percent economic growth in twenty-three years

For twenty-some-odd years, we have had no per capita growth. In other words, the economy has grown at a rate of two percent in twenty-three years, which is insufficient for countries like Mexico.

Fortunately—or rather fortunately and unfortunately— there has been a very important escape valve, namely that 400,000 or 500,000 Mexicans go to the United States each year in search of work.

Mexico has many regions and the inhabitants of the rural regions that used to be able to find work in the cities now have to migrate to the United States to work; they send a great deal of money back to Mexico. So we are talking about maybe ten million people who have left Mexico in recent years and who are sending back US$18 to 20 billion. These are very large figures and the positive effect is actually double, since half-a-million people find jobs on the other side of the border and are able to send remittances.

However, at the same time it is sad that we have been unable to generate employment here, retain our citizens and give them opportunities to come back and find local jobs. We already have a twenty-three-year long serious problem of scarce growth since the crisis of '82. During this period, there have been good years and bad years intermittently, with the country growing at about the same rate as its population, in spite of many Mexicans having left. If those half-a-million people would have stayed in Mexico, growth per inhabitant would have practically been negative.

This is the outline of those twenty-three years, which has lead to serious problems, since there are no job opportunities, there is no growth, people have to go elsewhere to find work, and marginalization and lag have continued to worsen.

So, in our opinion, what we have to do is to go from adjustment plans to development plans, and reach agreements collectively as Mexicans. History has taught us that, when we have not been united, there have been many problems. For instance, after Mexico's Independence, for fifty-five or fifty-six years there were fratricide wars; then came the Revolution that was also fratricide, in which we destroyed, were invaded by other countries and lost half of our territory. The results have been fateful when we have been disunited. It is very important to have low inflation. Having a zero or balanced tax deficit is equally important, although they are merely means and should not be seen as national objectives.

We know that problems are neither attacked nor solved with agreements or laws; actions need to be taken to solve them and these are some rough ideas. Meetings and seminars need to be held and specialists need to be consulted. In this regard, the universities can help us a great deal.

We know that Pemex is essential; it is the most important company of Mexico by far and of Latin America, although it operates within the public budget. Here we said that legislating was necessary so that state-owned companies can be run autonomously. This means that they would manage their operations independently, as large companies—which they are—without political interference and split off from public budgets. That is to say they would not be part of the balanced budget in which revenues plus expenditures equals zero. So, what happens is that Pemex cannot make investments, nor can it be operated transparently by professional government bodies. A Board of Directors would be appointed whose intent is on maximizing national wealth, reinvesting profits and fostering the preservation and development of the company. Independent board members will appoint and remove the CEO, will make investment and compensation decisions, and when an investment has to be made, they will not have to ask the budget or the public treasury for permission and they will not be allowed to make investments that are not within budget. These investments are so important that it would be crazy not to make them. Pemex should operate with a Surveillance Committee and an Audit Committee and should have the obligation to pay taxes as any other productive company, including production taxes, taxes on services and other dues that have to be paid.

The new civilization

What is happening in this new civilization? During the agricultural civilization—and I am going to discuss some religious topics here—Christian doctrine was very generous, very advanced and well ahead of its time. Since two thousand years ago, society required slaves, needed to exploit mankind, and needed to treat men like machines; the only interest then was to exploit mankind and the planet. This agricultural society needed hard-working people who consumed little so that there would be as much as possible left over. This is why there were slaves. Slavery is inherent to an agricultural society. Thus in those days, it was very important to plan ahead, contemplate and be charitable.

Nowadays, however, things are very different. Everything has changed and I have spoken about today for many years. What we have not realized very well though, perhaps since World War II, is that there has been a very important change. Neither the economy nor society is interested in exploiting labor, exploiting mankind; the convenient thing to do now is to make sure that our neighbors, society, that everyone is well and that they consume more. In other words, it is no longer important to have uneducated and strong people to exploit their physical work twelve or fifteen hours a day. Now it is better for people to work with more knowledge, for them to be prepared, for them to work less time and for them to be able to have the satisfiers offered by civilization, to have time to become cultivated, to read, be entertained, do sports, travel, consume, etc.

The appealing and interesting aspect of this new civilization is that what used to be an ethical problem or a problem of social justice is now an economic need. Hence, the progress of China which is increasingly incorporating its population into the economy. This is not our case, which explains why we have not grown. Lag and lack of growth prevail among us because we have not incorporated a large portion of our marginalized population into today's modern society and economy.

Thus, the fight against poverty is the best investment, from an economic point of view, incorporating this marginalized population into society and into the economy. For it to become part of today's modern economy, for there to be educated people, people who participate in the social productive apparatus and who can produce more for society in general.

Society benefits from those people having the capacity and time to buy things and pay for services, and I am not just talking about goods. What are these services? To receive an education—higher learning—for them to enjoy entertainment, to go on vacation, to have a home of their own and to buy goods because this fosters growth.

Growth is encouraged and sustained by the wellbeing of others; this is very important. In this new technological civilization (it is called technological, but is actually a service-oriented society. If you recall, the previous stage was the industrial society, in which most of the population was engaged in industry, before that was the primary sector, farmers, etc. We are currently in a service-oriented society, in which most of the people are engaged in services, since machines can easily produce goods and large numbers of people are no longer needed to work on the machines), development is an accelerated process which takes place in very few years.

We no longer have to say, "We have to sacrifice this generation for the next ones or we have to sacrifice two generations." At present, this is an accelerated process which can take place in very few years and which feeds upon itself when shared; this is very important.

Mexico can and has to enter into this virtuous process, as other countries have already done, and it is here that we wish to underline other countries of diverse cultures and different continents. It is not that the Chinese or the Koreans are all working. This is also the case of Europe: the progress of Spain, Ireland, and others, as well as Central Europe, which had fallen behind. You remember this, don't you? Since 1989 with the fall of the Berlin Wall, in only fifteen years, many countries have been rapidly joining this new civilization.

What matters here is that we can join this new civilization and we will not require many generations or years to achieve it, because it starts, it receives feedback and supports itself. It is not a matter of creating wealth and then spending it; it is a matter of creating wealth. What is distributed is not the wealth per se, but rather the fruits of wealth, namely income.

If tomorrow wealth were to be handed out among the entire population, if, for instance, Pemex were to be distributed, people are not interested in having one thousand Pemex shares or ten thousand; what they want is the income. So, what the population needs is income to have a better living standard and well-paid jobs.

Fight against poverty

There is something else: well-paid jobs bring families and society together, and if families and societies are united, governability becomes easier. However, the opposite also breaks up families and society and complicates governability.

So, from every point of view—whether social, political or economic—the fight against poverty is essential. How does this fight come about? I believe that aid and charity only alleviate poverty temporarily. What has to be done is to ensure health, nourishment, education and employment. In other words, the best way to fight poverty is by creating better sources of employment. In order for these sources of employment to be better, education for the formation of human capital is paramount.

As mankind becomes civilized, it makes technological progress

Civilization has been making progress for many years. However, if we focus on let's say the last eight thousand to ten thousand years, from being hunters, nomads and gatherers who discovered valleys rich in fauna and flora, to the Ice Age, it was then that civilization began to flourish at an accelerated pace.

Mankind, as it becomes civilized, progresses technologically to make its life more productive, more effective, and to make its existence on this Earth easier. At the same time, this also makes it possible for more people to live in society. Most likely, ten thousand years ago, the total population was eight million or perhaps ten million. But to make things easier, let's say there were six million. Now there are six and a half billion, meaning that the population has increased a thousand times during those years. I think there were about one hundred million people two thousand years ago, meaning that the population has grown sixty times since then, and towards the end of the eighteenth century, there were one billion inhabitants.

Now there are six and a half billion of us. This progress has allowed the Earth to sustain the life of six and a half billion people and the story seems to be unending. Why? Because first, fire was invented, then the wheel, irrigation, windmills and then fertilizers. These were the great advances in agriculture. Then industry largely increased production capacity. Industrial development is what caused society to no longer be agricultural and to become industrial, to no longer be rural and become urban. It is during the industrial civilization that high-productivity machines began to be invented, allowing ten people to do what it used to take one hundred people to do, as a result of which the remaining ninety can do other things.

Nowadays, this is also a fact: now there are robots, equipment, fast machines and the like, allowing for goods to be produced easily and at great profits. Consequently, what has to be done is to lead society so that those workers who were displaced can perform different activities. Normally, what is happening in the world is that the people who used to produce goods, that is to say industry workers, are now engaged in the field of services.

If we watch movies from fifty years ago, almost everyone was linked to industrial work. At present, farm workers in the United States account for two percent of the economically active population. Out of one hundred percent of the population, forty percent is considered active; I believe that about ten percent works in the industry sector. Perhaps the construction industry occupies somewhat more, but the remaining eighty percent is engaged in business, education, health, federal employment, the financial sector, banking and entertainment. Why? Because a lot can be produced with very little.

Economic activity needs to be generated

What has to be done is to absorb this twenty-five percent of the population that lives in rural areas, that is still dependent on self-consumption, is marginalized and has to migrate to the United States; make the fields more productive; find sources of employment for them not within the industry, but basically in the service field. For instance, tourism and infrastructure construction services. If we are really serious about this, health and education need to be fostered. Therefore, we will have a lot of fields in which we will be able to generate economic activity.

Directing the economy outwards is good in terms of generating currency, but it is not good if the economy's internal sector is neglected, that is to say the domestic economy.

Internal economy needs to be addressed with the development of human and physical capital, which would provide substantial help. But how? Well, 850,000 houses need to be built each year, many highways need to be constructed, a lot of ports need to be developed, drinking water needs to be properly managed as well as sanitized, the sewage system needs to be treated, and airports, schools and hospitals are also required.

And of course, substantial amounts should be invested in forming human capital and providing education in the fields of science, technology and development.

Finally, here is the budget, and I wish to compare ... December of 2000 and 2005. The need for a tax reform was discussed earlier to have resources to invest. However, during those years, income from oil and the price hike in electrical power have accounted for 4.8 percent of Mexico's GDP, which is a lot of money.

This 4.8 percent translates into US$110 billion. Financial expense also declined significantly, but since interest rates went down and the GDP grew, this is why it was said that there was a favorable downward trend in interest rates, another 0.8 percent of the GDP. In this regard, there has been an income of 4.8 percent and a 0.8 percent savings in financial expenses, accounting for a 5.6 percent increase in the Gross Domestic Product as a percentage of the GDP during those years, whereas investments only increased 0.7 percent. What you can see is that there are so many social and political pressures, the idea of a paternalist government, etc., that I think that some efforts, actually some great efforts, have to be made because social assistance is very important. However, this assistance should focus on employment and investments.

So, in spite of this increase, investments have only gone up 0.7 percent, which is not enough. More than any other reform, what we need to do is to combine public resources, public investment with private investment. With this, we feel that the cap and brake on investment possibilities and domestic growth will be removed.*

Thank you very much.
 Slim Helú

Carlos Slim with Prince Charles.

PHILANTHROPIST AND PATRON
Mighty Gentlemen…

Possessing a multifaceted picture and a powerful magnetism, which attract both admirers and critics alike, Slim is not immutable to either criticism or praise. He takes advantage of his celebrity status to support causes like stopping global warming. When the Secretary General of the United Nations Ban Ki Moon invited Slim to form an advisory group on climate change, he eagerly jumped aboard.

It is unnecessary to list the amount of frivolous magazines that make satisfactory accounts of entrepreneurs and their wealth. As others have said, when one measures success in terms of money, it's boring and tiresome.

Slim's fortune is equal to six percent of Mexico's GDP thus making him the richest man in Mexico and among the world's wealthiest men. Although he has donated about a quarter of his fortune, he said it makes him uncomfortable to be thought of as Santa Claus.

"Problems are not solved by handing out donations. Charity doesn't consist in giving, but rather in doing and resolving," he said. "Poverty is not eliminated with donations, but with education and employment. We have to do things in life and prove to be efficient, compassionate and responsible with the management of our wealth. It does not interest me to construct a monument in my honor nor to be given awards for what I do. My concern is not being high or low on the *Forbes* list. My concern and my occupation is that my companies are efficient, that they develop, and have appropriate strategies that can compete with anyone."

Throughout his life, Slim has been surrounded by friends. But then again, everyone wants to be friends with such a powerful man. Some of people want to make their friendship with Slim known. Writers, poets, painters, singers, businessmen or politicians; all of them want a chance to say they know Slim. Presidents of all latitudes seek him out. Statesmen of America and Europe solicit his presence. The world's most important businessmen meet with him. The rectors of public and private universities ask him to give seminars "to enlighten" people, and forums invite him to present his vision of Mexico and its present and future reality. Several winners of the prestigious Nobel Prize have been entertained in his home. Characters from all corners of the world surround him.

Fortune has been kind to Slim in every way. In spite of it or because of it, the engineer continues to greet his employees and partners with the same taste and appreciation. He is interested in their lives and listens when time allows for it. He has very close friends from all walks of life.

The concept of friendship is an interesting one. In the early history of human civilization, people were called friends by way of their honorable treatment of pharaohs, kings and court officials. There weren't "friendships" as we know them. People who intervened in a friendship could be punished with death. Perhaps the most symbolic tale of friendship is that of the patriarch of Judaism, Abraham with God. The conqueror Alexander the Great, who by twenty-five had traveled throughout Europe, Asia and half of Africa, built his empire alongside his seven major friends, whom he called "generals." There is also the example of two great thinkers of the mid-nineteenth century, Karl Marx and Frederick Engels. Despite not seeing eye-to-eye in terms of philosophy and history the first time they met, after spending time in a German tavern, they became great friends and together they made history in the realm of political science.

Thus in the life of every successful man; friends are a cornerstone. For Slim, friends are a basic necessity.

His character, nature, vision and business acumen have not only impacted countless characters, but he has done so by way of selfless vocation. His multifaceted personality has dazzled men of power. The most powerful presidents (Bill Clinton, George W. Bush, Barack Obama) and political leaders such as Felipe González, the legendary Mikhail Gorbachev and Fidel Castro have all praised him, as have high-flying intellectuals and writers like Gabriel García Márquez, Carlos Fuentes and Octavio Paz. Journalists are no exception (some of whom claim to speak only with presidents) like Julio Scherer Garcia, who became a partner in Proceso.com, subsidiary of *Proceso* magazine. His nature is charismatic. Since Slim was very young, he worked with old legends and symbols of wealth such as Carlos Trouyet and Manuel Espinosa Iglesias. He has rubbed shoulders with the Rockefellers and Bill Gates, and he is friends with an infinite number of political and noble personalities such as Prince Charles. Every year, he is on the list of the one hundred most influential men in the world.

His power to attract attention is fascinating. Both left- and right-wing personalities are drawn to him as though he were a charismatic leader or an imam.

He is not infallible however; malice finds him. Some critics tried to link him to the controversial former president Carlos Salinas de Gortari,, but Slim denied any such partnership. The sharpest journalists have set it straight: Salinas and Slim share a name (Carlos and Charlie) but that is all.

Columnists have called him a survivor because of the crisis of the eighties. In addition to King Middas, he has also been called a patron of intellectuals, a bargain shopper, an art hoarder, the best representative of capitalism, a monopolist, a figurehead, a beneficiary of Salinas, an ambitious speculator, the Conqueror and many other adjectives. But he has also been the strong suit of the government when it has been necessary to explain the crisis in major financial centers or to negotiate credit for the country.

A counterpart of business and money, Slim's alter ego is immersed in culture, sports and philanthropy. Collector, philanthropist and patron, politicians of all stripes praise him. He is friends with priests and atheists, a lover of filmmakers; he is a scholar and has published articles like other economists. As a lover of the so-called "king of sports," baseball, he is erudite and has published articles using the game as an example of how he sees parenting and the positioning of heirs. He also has a love for boxing and boxers, most of them world champions. Many Olympic athletes receive scholarships from his foundations to support their development. The same is true of academics and intellectuals, many of whom come from various countries attending the *Centro de Estudios Carso* (the Carso Study Center). Here, they can do specialized research, accessing the invaluable collection of over 80,000 documents and nineteenth-century books on the history of Mexico.

The advisory board of the study center is composed of Enrique Florescano, Teodoro González de León, Patricia Galeana,

Miguel León Portilla, Carlos Martínez Assad, Enrique Krauze, Carlos Monsiváis, Fernando Solana Morales, Enrique González Pedrero, Ricardo García Sainz and Manuel Ramos Medina, among others.

For decades, Slim has had contact with many of the most important intellectuals in order to promote the study of the history of Mexico. Slim has a special affection for the historian José Ezequiel Iturriaga Sauca, whom he simply calls "Don Pepe." Another character with whom Slim has great affection is the humanist Ernesto de la Peña. "A friendly person with a great soul," Slim calls him.

In the eighties, when he began to project himself as the guru of business, Slim's circle attracted the most diverse intellectuals and he forged an intimate friendship (which later became estranged) with the journalist and writer Fernando Benítez. He met Benítez at his brokerage firm Inverso Bursátil. The tycoon had received a coded gift from a friend and was intrigued to understand its contents. Benítez helped decipher it and so began their friendship.

It was Benítez who introduced him to Carlos Fuentes, Hector Aguilar Camín, Carlos Monsiváis, and Carlos Payán. All of whom were attracted to Slim, as was writer Guillermo Tovar y de Teresa, the historian Enrique Krauze and the Nobel Prize winner Octavio Paz.

Slim was one of Octavio Paz's few friends. "They were very close friends; they truly cared for one another," said painter Juan Soriano, suggesting that Slim was "perhaps the poet's best friend." In December 1997, when at the age of eighty-three, the poet was confined to a wheelchair because of illness, he spearheaded an austere ceremony with President Ernesto Zedillo to announce the creation of the *Fundación Cultural Octavio Paz* (the Octavio Paz Cultural Foundation). Slim was one of the first to financially support the institution and along with another group of large employers like Emilio Azcarraga Jean, Alfonso Romo, Manuel Arango, Antonio Ariza, Bernardo Quintana, Carlos González and Fernando Senderos Zalabagui, among others, gathered in the Alvarado House on the street named for Francisco Sosa de Coyoacán.

When someone asked the writer Carlos Fuentes why Slim seeks the company of intellectuals, the author of *Where the Air is Clear* said that Slim "does not search us out; we enrich each other. We are attracted by his freshness and spontaneity."

Of his relationship with former Spanish president Felipe González, Slim said they never dealt with matters of business, "It's not our thing." Their friendship is more intellectual and spiritual. Slim recognizes him as a statesman: "Felipe is a universal type." Whenever they meet, they talk about new society and the paradigms of the new civilization. "One of the things that interest us is the challenge of how to solve our country's problems," Slim said. "These are the issues Felipe and I talk about."

Fernando Benítez told a story about his friend's simplicity when the two drove the Mayan route of southeastern Mexico. They both had to improvise in Yaxchilán, where they found some tents and slept on the floor.

In 1996, Benítez wrote an article in the newspaper *La Jornada* entitled *Slim*. In it, he extols the virtues of the billionaire:

> *More than twelve years ago, I met Slim and since then we have been friends. A few months in, Carlos, with the greatest*

tact, gave a large sum of money to Guillermo Tovar y de Teresa, José Iturriaga and me. Slim knew that we were master researchers of our history, always poorly rewarded for our work so he helped us in our endeavor.

Carlos was a remarkable entrepreneur and art lover. We took an unforgettable trip to the ruins of Palenque, Yucatán, Yaxchilán and the palace painted by the Lacandon[17] people. We spent beautiful moments together.

Carlos, along with other partners, bought the old golf club in Cuernavaca, which was about to be divided into many plots and was the only real green space in the city. He admired the way I cared for trees, especially the ahuehuetes[18] that were at the point of extinction, and he dug a small lagoon to save them. He told me: "If we did the same in Chapultepec, then the wonderful trees would not die."

At noon we ate at tables decorated by delicacies provided by his wife Sumy. At night we talked in the club lounge where General Calles played poker. It was on one of these nights that we read the magazine Forbes, which included Carlos. When I saw that he had two or three billion dollars, I yelled, "I never thought I'd be friends with such a rich man!"

Last Sunday, I was surprised to see that Carlos conceded to be interviewed by the magazine Proceso. The reporter, Carlos Acosta Córdova, is very astute and unforgiving. Carlos appeared on the cover with a title that read: "Salinas is Your Partner?"

"I have no political associates ... I do not need any," answered Slim. The city is full of rumors and uncertainties.

Carlos Slim is rumored to have made his fortune in times of Salinas; rumored on Colosio, Ruiz Massieu, Muñoz Rocha, the Attorney Lozano Gracia and from the tragic moments in which we live. The rumor is very old and sometimes dangerous. In the cafés they are always talking about candidates and who would be the next president or nominee.

Hardly anyone knows that Carlos was born rich. His father had a prosperous business near the National Palace and he sometimes bought old colonial houses that were worth more for their land than for their architecture. Carlos studied to be an engineer and with his inheritance, he built a multi-story building in which he lived in an apartment with his wife and children. Extraordinary financier, he began buying several businesses and factories.

Some Mexicans criticize him without knowing the Teléfonos de Mexico system. The modernization of the company demanded the termination of many employees, but Carlos did not fire anyone. Instead, he exercised a mandate to teach them new systems that would bring them up to the new standards. He does not fear competition though there are two more long-distance companies in the world: ATT and MCI. They operate in large cities, but are not interested in the villages and towns in Mexico. Instead, Telmex phone has taken 22,000 villages in Mexico.

Carlos criticized Proceso for attacking him. The reporter said he had collected opinions from various sources, including Cuauhtémoc Cardenas. Carlos said that the reporter tried to insult him due to his ignorance or bad faith.

Though I am not very familiar with the economy, I will

quote some of the concepts that Carlos said in his interview with Proceso:

"It is remarkable that six years after the privatization of Telmex, when the competition had begun, a mass of criticism started up against me, and mainly against Teléfonos de Mexico."

Denying that it was a spontaneous idea, he said, "The Grupo Carso started in 1965; in 1976 we already had Galas, which in the previous twenty years was a major advertising company in the country. Since 1981, we acquired Cigarrera La Tabacalera Mexicana (CIGATAM), which is certainly very important: it produces Marlboro cigarettes, Delicados, Lights, Benson, Baronet, and Commander. Then, in 1984 we purchased from Manuel Espinosa Church one of their packages of bank assets, which included 100 percent of Seguros de México, worth US$55 million. It was odd that a stranger could make a purchase of US$55 million, no?

"We do not have political partners. The Grupo Carso did not have nor will ever have political partners. That is clear and always will be.

"My relationship with [Carlos Salinas de Gortari] was cordial—I saw him four times. [He was] very respectful as secretary and as president, but regarding favors, [he did not grant me] even one. An example: in the late sixties, early seventies, I bought some land in the foothills of Xitle. During the Salinas government, they expropriated it from me and to date, I have not finished paying it off. I was never given any favors and in the businesses that I do, I don't need any

favors.

"I think the employer should work in their businesses and be oblivious to plans and projects of political concern. I do not belong to any political party nor do I want to belong to one.

"My personal image or that of Grupo Carso does not concern me. In the case of Telmex, its image is important for the time being given our competition with large corporations. With each falsity that is claimed, they are looking to discredit Telmex so that the transnational companies can penetrate our country.

"Among the wealthy as well, what matters is not how much you have, but what you do with what you have."

Carlos does not care about wealth, but how it should be spent. He dislikes talking about the doctors he enlists for poor patients or the 12,000 college students to whom he has given awards and scholarships (5,000 of them earn a minimum monthly salary and have a computer with Internet access). Among many other charities, Slim provides funding and financial aid to prisoners—prisoners who are incarcerated for being poor, not delinquent—and can't pay their way out of prison. He also helps healthcare institutions, as well as centers for research and prenatal care. He promotes feeding programs for low-income mothers and supports the training of physicians. He also supports museums and book production. He continues such funding with about MS$120 million annually.

I will end with the last question the reporter asked Carlos Slim: "What underlies all this seeming generosity? Any slope in consciousness? Because you could easily not do any of this social work."

To which Carlos answered, "No, nothing of that sort. I have total and absolute conviction, without a doubt. I am convinced that we must do it. I like it and want to do it. Also, I think when you leave this world you can't bring any of your material possessions with you. So, in some way, I am like a temporary manager of my wealth because I won't be able to bring it with me to the afterlife. You can have whims and commit mistakes, but in the end of it all, what for? Therefore, I believe we must do whatever is important during our lives because you can't do it after."

The concept of philanthropy is not a new one. The Roman Flavius Claudius Julianus, who invented the concept of charity, coined the term "philanthropy" with religious use by imitating the Christian zeal to paint paganism as a Roman religion. Now, this phenomenon is referred to by some as "philanthropi*capitalism*." To be the richest company in the world, or the richest man, you are managing the "profitability" of said wealth and you must make millionaire contributions.

In countries like the United States and Spain, there is a long tradition of philanthropy. Boston College will soon have a Study Center on Wealth and Philanthropy, and Madrid has established the Spanish Association for the Development of Corporate Philanthropy.

In Mexico, some millionaires also invest in poverty. Given the growing social polarization between the mega rich and the poor, some have focused their activities on those who are less fortunate, including the creation of the Mexican Center for Philanthropy. Universidad Iberoamericana, which also receives funding from magnates, created the head of the department of philanthropy aimed at researchers and developers who want to devote their research to this subject. Other institutions like the *Fondo para la Asistencia, Promoción y Desarrollo*[19] I.A.P. (FAPRODE) created the MIRA project with the aim of articulating a culture of philanthropy among broad sectors of Mexican society.

Since then, there have been those in power who have sought to benefit from philanthropy, as happened with Vamos México; created by the initiative of former president Vicente Fox's wife. Marta Sahagún invited Slim to join as an honorary member along with other employers, including Roberto González Barrera, Fernando Senderos, Alfredo Harp Helú, Ricardo Salina Pliego, Emilio Azcárraga Jean, Roberto Hernández, Lorenzo Zambrano, Manuel Arango Arias and María Asunción Aramburuzabala.

Slim invests millions in philanthropic activities annually. He said he does not act out of vanity, neither does he hope to claim that his name remains on a plaque generation after generation, but rather that he constantly seeks concrete solutions for education, health and combating poverty.

His name stands out among the leading philanthropists in the world next to Warren Buffett, Bill Gates, George Soros and the descendants of Sam Walton.

As a benefactor of the National Autonomous University of Mexico, Slim has belonged as a UNAM Foundation Board member since its inception. Among other members are the rector José Narro Robles, Rafael Moreno Valle Suárez, Alfredo Harp Helú, Bernardo Quintana, María Teresa Gómez Mont, Luz Lajaous Vargas, Abedrop Dávila, Cesar Buenrostro Hernández, Julia Carabias Lillo, José Carral Escalante, Alfonso de Angoitia Noriega, Juan Francisco Ealy Ortiz Martínez, Juan Diego Gutiérrez Cortina, Jaime Lomelín Guillén, Guillermo Ortiz Martínez, Fernando Ortiz Monasterio de Garay, José Octavio Reyes Lagunés, Francisco Rojas, Olga Sánchez Cordero, Salvador Sánchez de la Peña, Federico Tejado Bárcena, Jacob Zabludovzky, José María Zubiría Maqueno, Alfredo Adam Adam, Raúl Robles Segura, Francisco Suárez Davila and Araceli Rodríguez Fernández.

When Francisco Barnés de Castro was rector, the highest seat of learning, he publicly acknowledged Slim and honored him with a medal for his support of the UNAM Foundation. He had previously awarded grants totaling MX$40 million. "I wish there were more Slims who would donate generous grants to financially support more students," the rector explained.

The universities that make up the Corporación Universitaria para el Desarrollo de Internet[20], A.C. (CUDI), headed by Slim's Teléfonos de México and other telecommunications and technology firms such as Nortel Networks, Marconi Communications and Cabletron Systems have donated high-speed networks worth tens of millions of dollars to promote higher education in the country.

Slim also donated refurbished computers to Technology Museum of Federal Commission for Electricity for the benefit of students in public schools who come daily to take advantage of the computer lab.

With the support of his businesses, the Grupo Carso mogul gives thousands of scholarships to students. Through the Telmex Foundation, he awards thousands of computers each year to a large number of trainees. In addition, in order to prepare his Telmex employees, he created the Instituto Tecnológico de Teléfonos de México[21] (Inttelmex).

After Slim bought Teléfonos de México, his wife Soumaya Domit, along with the labor union at the company, created the Fundación Telmex[22], whose social activities have provided support to victims of natural disasters and assistance to disadvantaged students across the country. In the support of medicine, he created an organ bank in Mexico. His son Marco Antonio Slim Domit chairs the board of the National Transplant Council (CONATRA), which has a Web site and a phone line that provides information about transplants. The Board of this institution, at its inception, consisted of the young entrepreneurs Olegario Vázquez Aldir, Alejandro Soberon Kuri, Michael Aleman Magnani, Emilio Azcarraga Jean and Lili Domit.

Since his wife Soumaya undertook the task of social assistance, with support from the Telmex Foundation in the years 1996-2011, emphasis was placed on these achievements (only a few of many): 6,781 organ and tissue transplants, 629,965 surgeries, and 242,486 student scholarships. They have donated 256,864 bicycles to students from rural zones with poor resources and more than 127,750 eyeglasses to people with vision problems. In addition, they have contributed to humanitarian aid and financial support in natural disaster zones. From 2007 to 2009, the Foundation made possible 2,391 new organ transplants, particularly kidney, cornea, liver, heart, skin and lung.

Since 2007, the support of the Carlos Slim Foundation and the Telmex Foundation has grown exponentially to the degree of around US$10 billion for altruistic purposes in health, education, sports, culture, environment, social finance, justice, support for social institutions, the NGO's restoration of the Historic Center of Mexico City, and funds for possible natural disasters.

Soumaya and son Carlos Slim Domit are also members of the board of the National Institute of Medical Sciences and Salvador Zubirán Nutrition.

In its national fundraising, the Mexican Red Cross was a beneficiary of the Telmex Foundation. Support was given in the form of an advertising campaign in mass media and the donation of US$500,000 along with ambulances for extremely poor and unprotected zones.

Slim created the Fundación Carso[23], A.C. (originally under the name *Asociación Inbursa, A.C.*), in June 1986. The group's principal activities are to start, promote, sponsor, fund, or establish and maintain libraries, newspaper libraries, museums and exhibitions, conferences and congresses, support hospitals and orphanages, as well as help people in need. He has encouraged donation because since 1989, all donations are tax deductible. In order to increase his capacity to support the association, he has reinvested the surplus of financial resources in Mexican securities. Irrevocably, income from donations and the proceeds generated by their investments have been earmarked for social, cultural and charitable organizations.

Slim was instrumental in the creation of the Museo Soumaya in 1994. Since its founding, a number of cultural and social projects have benefited from the financial support of Carso, A.C. Among them are the Mexican Red Cross, the Mexican Association of Aid to Children with Cancer I.A.P., the Association of Friends of the Metropolitan Cathedral of Mexico, A.C., the Music Academy of the Mining Palace, the Mexican Health Foundation, the Mexican Center for Writers, A.C., and UNAM Foundation, S.C., and the Children's Hospital of Mexico Federico Gómez.

In 1988, a year before her death, Soumaya Domit was awarded the Philanthropy Award for her social work with marginalized groups.

Through the justice program of the Telmex Foundation, intercessions were made for the release of unjustly imprisoned indigenous people, as happened with sixty Zapatista prisoners in Chiapas who were accused of various crimes. Each year, the foundation supports nearly ten thousand people who commit petty crimes or who are victims of the abuse of power.

This program is operated by the Telmex Foundation in collaboration with the Fundación Inbursa. The main purpose of this program is to support poor people who are accused of committing a criminal act and who are deprived their freedom in different prisons in the country. In order to be granted their freedom, they must pay the bond or guarantee to repair the damage, but they cannot access the funds because they do not have the necessary resources. Fundación Telmex works in conjunction with the Office for the Development of Indigenous Peoples of the Presidency of the Republic.

Slim also participates in the Chiapas Fund along with other business groups in the country to boost economic recovery and contribute to reconciliation of the state. "There is no better investment than fighting poverty," Slim said.

From his very personal perspective, Slim said of the problem of marginalization:

> *There is no doubt that in addition to moral or ethical connotations of trying to eliminate poverty, there is also a fundamental economic sense that we should all consider. There is no better fight than the one we are fighting against poverty; it is the best investment one can make in society (or even neighboring societies). To eliminate ignorance is to strengthen markets, develop domestic demand, and improve living standards. This is what I pointed out in Europe, where the countries that are lagging behind are supported by those that are far more advanced. At the moment, Mexico can resolve this problem fairly quickly, and our growth will be fuelled. We must start with a mother's nutrition during pregnancy, care of children at birth, infant feeding in the early years (a time when the brain grows four times its size), child health, and education. They are the fundamental elements. When speaking of this new civilization in which it is much easier to create wealth, it is paradoxical that there would be more poverty. No doubt one of the needs of any country is to bring its population into the economy, to modernity. Poverty*

is a social, political and economic burden. When I talk of addressing the domestic economy, I mean that which I just explained.

Slim acknowledges that the funds given are not sufficient to eradicate poverty. That is why he has made alliances with companies and groups from other countries to support poor people with micro-credit. For example, the Slim Foundation and Grameen Trust (a not-for-profit NGO), an international affiliate of Grameen Bank, signed an agreement to provide credit lines to people in the poorest areas of Mexico who are excluded from the international banking system and the support provided to them is made with interest rates well below any bank.

This project began in late 2008, with a capital of US$45 million driven by Slim and Professor Muhammad Yunus, with the Grameen Bank. They jointly received the Nobel Peace Prize in 2006 for their work against poverty around the world.

He has done the same by supporting the Clinton Foundation. Slim joined with Frank Giustra, a businessman from the mining industry in Vancouver, Canada, and each agreed to contribute US$100 million to the program named the Clinton Initiative for Sustainable Growth. To a large extent, Slim's contribution to this project will target Latin America. Through his role as former president of the United States, Bill Clinton has launched several campaigns, including one for AIDS and another to fight childhood obesity.

His philanthropy goes beyond any border. Slim has devoted more than US$2.5 million to the actions of Impulsora del Desarrollo y el Empleo en América Latina[24] (IDEAL). IDEAL's foundation aims to address the poorest families in the region with particular emphasis on problems of malnutrition, maternal and child health research and the environment.

His philanthropic work has not gone without recognition. For example, in a ceremony headed by President of Mexico Felipe Calderón, the Panamanian First Lady Vivian Fernández thanked Slim for his philanthropic support of her country and all of Latin America. She described him as "a human being that is above material success."

But not all that is said about him is praise. Slim has been criticized for the way in which he exercises his monopoly. For example, a dissenting voice on Slim's work is Denise Dresser, a contributor to the magazine *Proceso*. In an article entitled "The Two Faces of Slim," she wrote that while his philanthropy should be applauded, we should be suspicious of his motivation. She writes that we should question what inspires the tycoon to seek to "appear as a virtuous man at a relatively low cost." Slim's philanthropic efforts, Dresser asserts, are to "clear his name through a legacy that no one could question," especially when his efforts led Bill Gates to donate US$31 billion of his personal fortune and create the Bill & Melinda Gates Foundation and led Warren Buffet to also donate US$27 billion.

Dresser maintains that Slim is a conditional philanthropist. "Philanthropy for profit that runs counter to what he supposedly seeks to promote: altruistic donations and selfless contribution. To develop oneself based on philanthropic work would be the exact opposite of what has made Bill Gates who he is," she wrote.

"Gates donates shares of Microsoft to the foundation he created and relinquishes control of them so that his donations are not tied to the Gates Foundation, to the performance of his company, or to obtaining government contracts. He donated money to polish his reputation. There is nothing wrong with that because he never used it to advance himself or his business. His philanthropy has never been linked to the return for more money. And he never put together a philanthropic scaffold in which generosity depended on the government's willingness to let him venture into other areas of economic activity. Slim aims to give, however, he stands to gain even more."

In a completely different light, former President Bill Clinton lends the following as his perception of Slim's philanthropic spirit as founder of Carso. "Slim is one of the world's most important philanthropists even though most people have never heard of his humanitarian activities," Clinton said. "He owns stock in more than two hundred companies that employ more than 200,000 people in Latin America and beyond. He has used his resources to help develop the communities where his businesses are located. In his own country, Mexico, he has personally supported more than 165,000 young people in attending university, paid for numerous surgeries, provided equipment for rural schools, and covered surety bonds for 50,000 people who were entitled to their freedom but could not afford it. He recently created the Carso Institute for Health and designed it to provide a new approach to health care in Mexico. He has US$4 billion of investments ready to be spent towards the promoting of education, health and other great challenges, and has recently announced an additional US$6 billion investment in several programs, including his Telmex Foundation."

Juan Antonio Pérez Simón, collaborator and one of Slim's closest friends, exalts the qualities of the philanthropist and patron. "It is always important to know what your limits are, because you can have a foundation and say yes to everything. I think that Slim has done very well. There are many foundations that do charitable acts, but they will always reach their limit," he said. "But when it comes to charity, support should be endless. Carlos has been charitable in a very organized way and that is how he always does things. His biggest concern has always been social problems. He is a man of constant work and he is brilliant, but it is his consistency that is the formula for success. Another of his virtues is his honesty, which is not easy to find. He is an honest man, dedicated to a mythical business to which he devotes all his time. For him, honesty is consistency. It goes beyond what you perceive; it is transparency. Moreover, he is also a great scholar and researcher; he can learn or take a lesson from anywhere. Carlos will not issue an opinion of value if he does not have a deep knowledge of the subject. He must conduct interviews with fifty people or read two-hundred books before he will deliver judgment on the matter."

When Salinas de Gortari took office as president in the midst of challenges that portrayed him as an "impostor," his special guest, Fidel Castro, was dazzled by Slim.

Salinas was the second youngest president in the history of Mexico, only after General Lázaro Cárdenas, who came to the first legislature of the country at thirty-nine years old. Salinas came to power amidst allegations of election fraud of massive proportions.

Slim met Fidel Castro with other politicians, intellectuals and academics while enjoying his stay in Mexico City for a meeting with wealthy businessmen. The legendary commander was interested in the character of whom many spoke so highly. The meeting took place in the Lomas de Chapultepec at a dinner that lasted until dawn. The host Enrique Madero Bracho, president of the Mexican Business Council for International Affairs, invited a select group of businessmen. Slim Helú was there and attracted the attention of the Cuban Revolution leader. Between toasts, Madero Braco did not hold back emotion and praise and lavished his special guest. He said, "Commander, if you were in Mexico, you would be a great entrepreneur. You have the talent to be."

To which Castro replied, "Well, boy, I am an entrepreneur, but of the State."

Slim, who was already a celebrity, addressed the issue of external debt and captured the attention of the commander. Castro listened without blinking. Slim seduced him with his chatter. The tycoon discussed the need Mexico had to keep its credit abroad and support the modernization of the country. Castro interrupted his interlocutor by bluntly saying, "Do not repay the debt. It is unpayable and uncollectable." The Cuban's argument was that the country had an excess of interest, which they considered a tribute to the US Empire and so there was no justification to continue to pay the capital.

One of Slim's comments was that Mexico, in order to resolve much of its debt, had ventured into a new strategy: to exchange debt for shares of Mexican companies. Through this system, it was buying cheap debt because the market was at half its value. As examples, he gave the cases of some Central American countries that had paid their debts to Mexico through swaps.

This pattern made sense to Castro, who seconded Slim's notion and accepted that several governments were already following such a strategy.

Similarly, Slim has attracted leftist representatives like Andrés Manuel López Obrador, Pablo Gómez, Rolando Cordera Campos, Cuauhtémoc Cárdenas and Porfirio Muñoz Ledo.

Other prominent intellectuals have also succumbed to the tycoon's seduction. Many of them have been dazzled by the money shown at Slim's parties, like with the wedding of his daughter Soumaya Slim Domit, at which the following were all in attendance: former Spanish President Felipe González, General Enrique Cervantes Aguirre, Miguel de la Madrid and his wife Paloma Cordero, Liébano Sáenz, Epigmenio Ibarra and his wife Verónica Velasco, David Ibarra Muñoz, Héctor Aguilar Camín and his wife Ángles Mastretta, Monsiváis, Iván Restrepo, Payán Velver, Rolando Cordera, Emilio Azcárraga Jean, Jesús Silva Herzog, Santiago Creel, Rafael Tovar y de Teresa, Ricardo Rocha, Germán Dehesa, Gerardo Estrada, Luis Yáñez and Adriana Salinas, Antonio del Valle Ruiz, Lorenzo Zambrano, Juan Antonio Pérez Simon, Fernando Lerdo de Tejada and his wife Marinela Servijte, Tania Libertad, Fernando Solana, Porfirio Muñoz Ledo, Juan Soriano, Manuel Felguérez, María Felix and Cecilia Occelli.

When Slim acquired Teléfonos de México, the senator Cuauhtémoc Cárdenas Solórzano contested the operation with Porfirio Muñoz Ledo, another leftist politician and one of the founders of the PRD. The PRD even presented a complaint to the Attorney General's Office on this very fact. Cardenas said that never in his life had he dealt with Slim and therefore could not speak of personal grudges. But his differences with the tycoon were diluted when the PRD politician Andrés Manuel López Obrador invited Slim and businessman Emilio Azcárraga Jean to participate in economic projects for the nation's capital.

The Federal District's plans consisted of the creation of industrial parks, the restoration of the Historic Center Alameda-Reformation and the Basilica Cathedral, the expansion of the transport network, and the promotion of emerging environmental markets through a multi-million dollar investment.

The Italian architect Francesco Bandarín, technical manager of the International Campaign for the Conservation of Vienna, said that the Historic Center of Mexico City (classified as a Cultural Heritage Site by UNESCO in 1987) suffers a severe degradation and requires "a global conservation policy."

The recovery of the Historic Centre was initiated by Slim and Pepe Iturriaga. Andrés Manuel López Obrador was interested in the Reform Promenade and invited Slim to invest, but the employer insisted that for him, the priority was the Historic Center as long as President Vicente Fox would support the project. With or without López Obrador, Slim was determined to rescue the Historic Center, which finally happened. He was appointed coordinator of the Executive Committee in which the Cardinal Norberto Rivera, journalist and historian Jacobo Zabludovsky and historian Guillermo Tovar y de Teresa all participated, and with whom Slim had spoken of the urgent need to carry out this project long before getting involved. López Obrador ended up recognizing that Slim's presence on the committee was important because it would guarantee the participation of other entrepreneurs in the hotel industry as well as others who wanted to invest in parking lots or in housing projects. They would immediately become active in the revitalization of the Historic Center, and only then would people return to populate the area that for years had become depopulated. For López Obrador, no one was more influential than the Telmex tycoon in promoting the regeneration of the area.

On April 4, 2002, the *Diario Oficial* published news of the granting of fiscal and administrative facilities for those willing to invest in the recovery of the Historic Center in zone "B," as President Fox announced during a working trip to Mexico City where he accompanied the prime minister, Andrés Manuel López Obrador.

The resolution for zone "A" was conducted in October 2001. As for zone "B," its limits were the streets of La Merced, Abraham González, Reforma, Zaragoza, Ferrocarril de Cintura, Herreros, Ánfora, Labradores and Doctor Liceaga, to name a few.

According to data provided by the trust to rescue the Historic Centre, zone "A" consisted of avenues such as Lázaro Cárdenas, Izazaga, Juárez, Hidalgo, and also the streets of Perú, Chile, Paraguay, among others.

The great challenge would be the construction aspect. Before December 31, 2002, the first town made up of thirty-one blocks comprised of the Eje Central (Central Axis) and Donceles to Venustiano Carranza. It was to be built by February 5, requiring the investment of MX$500 million that would be broken down as follows: MX$100 million in public safety, MX$25 million in rearrangement of mobile vendors and MX$375 million in public works.

The purpose of this project would be to reorder the economic and social activities of the Historic Centre, which is comprised of 668 blocks, as well as restore and reconstruct buildings in keeping with historical, architectural, monumental and urban importance of the area. The decree issued by the Federal Government established the following incentives for properties that are within zones "A" and "B" of the Center:

- Investments in real estate may be deducted immediately and up to one hundred percent.
- Investments in property repairs and adaptations involving additions or improvements to fixed assets shall enjoy the same benefit as they increase in productivity, life, or allow the property to be used differently than what had originally been provided.
- Paperwork is given for immovable property when it is disposed of for rehabilitation or restoration, with respect to the fact that the transferor may be treated as an acquisition cost for updates of at least forty percent of the amount of the transfer.
- Fiscal stimulus is given in asset tax for taxpayers required to pay on the real estate that is owned and is being rehabilitated or restored.

Slim, from the beginning of the project, contemplated that the recovery of the Historic Center would encourage new family life and economic and social development in an area where there are sixty museums and over three thousand cultural events each year. They found that the palaces, buildings, shopping areas and neighborhoods all had immense valueand should be used for work and fun and to enjoy the rich history, and to walk safely and sleep peacefully.

Many street vendors were removed and a new security strategy was implemented. More than a hundred fifty high-definition cameras were installed and such efforts began to bear fruit. Thanks to technology and surveys that were conducted every month, stronger security was achieved.

The restored old mansions became homes for than five hundred families who became the newest tenants in the Historic Center. Traditional restaurants that closed with the seizure re-opened and began encouraging others to open their doors. Some corporations that had their headquarters in Santa Fe installed part of their business in the Latin American Tower. In Juárez, in front of the Fine Arts Museum (which was once the headquarters of Financial Approvals, now Banca Serfin), a department store opened, the largest in the Federal District, accompanied by restaurants and other businesses. This complex attracts the attention of more than a million and a half visitors who cross the Central Axis and Madero daily. Banamex-Citigroup also reopened in the refurbished Palacio de Iturbide.

Slim bought the old Mexican Stock Exchange building on Calle de Uruguay 68 where he worked as a stockbroker and where he was once not allowed to enter because he didn't bring a tie. There, he set up an entertainment center.

One of the first records on the recovery of the Historic Center was the initiative of historian José Iturriaga, who was worried about the deterioration of the area. He proposed a work program to then-

President Adolfo López Mateos to restore buildings of Hispanic heritage and restrict street vendors. Iturriaga proposed to improve the Zócalo, the streets of Moneda, Santísima, Guatemala, Rodríguez, Puebla, San Ildefonso and Belisario Domínguez, along with the squares Loreto, Santo Domingo and La Concepción. The project included loops without traffic and created overpasses, as well as creating a company with capital of US$1.5 million. Although he mustered the interest of several bankers, the plan did not prosper because of political pressure from then-head of the Federal District Ernesto P. Uruchurtu and his threat of resignation to destabilize the presidency of López Mateos. To calm political spirit, in 1964 he decided to appoint José Iturriaga ambassador to the USSR. Upon his return, Agustín Legorreta, proposed the creation of a company, México Antiguo, S.A., which would buy buildings for the restoration and recovery project of the Historic Center.

After contributing to the restoration of the Historic Center, Slim's attention moved to another neglected area of Mexico City. In the municipality of Nezahualcóyotl, on area of 600,000 square meters (646,000 square feet), he transformed the former landfill Xochiaca into the Telmex Center for Bicentennial Sports. The project proved to be an ecological rescue and a successful fight against marginalization and poverty.

At its founding, Nezahualcóyotl had less than half a million people, most from the country's poorest states (Michoacán, Guanajuato, Oaxaca, Puebla, Hidalgo, Jalisco, Veracruz, Tlaxcala, Guerrero, Aguascalientes, Morelos, Querétaro, Chiapas and Zacatecas, including the same settlers of the State of Mexico).

Anthropologists and sociologists referred to Nezahualcóyotl as the Calcutta, India, of Mexico. The city stands in stark contrast to the opulent neighborhoods of Mexico City like Polanco, San Ángel and Las Lomas. These districts were seen as a haven when the country lived the idyllic Mexican Miracle and members of Mexican high society traveled to American shopping centers and malls in search of *fayuca*[25]. In South America, the wealthy Mexicans were offered special packages, credit cards, bilingual shopkeepers, and special credit lines to support their industry of pleasure and consumption.

Though this period was called "stabilizing development," it was marked by uneven progress in which a small, middleclass segment of the population, highly protected by government policies, grew richer. However, their increased spending was not enough to redeem or meet deficiencies of the marginalized people. This trend paved the way for the first steps of Mexican unionism. In short, it was the model of development for a few Mexicans, but the inhabitants of Neza were excluded. Since then, Neza was a collage of poverty, a ghetto in an area of 62.4 square kilometers (twenty-four square miles) with borders marked by social strata rather than physical or political boundaries. The unsavory trademarks of this poverty-stricken district included alcoholism, drug addiction, death by malnutrition, unemployment, and violence.

Until two decades ago, schools in Neza saw seventy-five percent of primary school children drop out before completing six years of compulsory education. The illiteracy rate exceeded twenty percent and functional illiteracy reached thirty percent.

Sociologists summarized it as the decade of the defeated. According to surveys published by the journal *Unidad y Línea* of the Popular Education Services (SEPAC), the ideology of men in Nezahualcóyotl disaggregated as follows:

- Fatalism: "There will always be poor: they are poor because they are lazy and drunkards."
- Impotence: "I am unable to do anything."
- Masochism: "I must suffer on this earth to gain heaven."
- Individualism: "I have to improve myself in order to be better, with work and perseverance one becomes rich."
- Skepticism: "Nothing can change anyway. At best I will lose what little I have."
- Reformism: "We have to change things gradually, without violence, without haste."
- Consumerism: "It is most important to get things."
- The technocrat "One must have titles and deeds to have anything at all."
- The machismo: "I am the master of my house."

The municipality of Nezahualcóyotl, considered one of the poorest in the country, was named in honor of the king of Texcoco. Ironically, the poet and emperor of the Aztecs was distinguished by grandeur. For example, when they celebrated the centennial of the founding of Mexico-Tenochtitlan, they built a grand castle at the foot of the hill of Chapultepec. Texcoco (where Neza now sits, but once part of its jurisdiction) had several shining moments, even in the nineteenth century after the founding of the State of Mexico. Texcoco was appointed residence of the Supreme Powers of the State in January 4, 1827. However, over time it entered into a process of decay. In 1963, when a municipal decree formally entitled Nezahualcóyotl to its own government, its growth was marked by lawlessness.

The first generation of Necenses (people of Neza) emerged under the stigma of being born to lose. Many lived in half-built, cardboard or wooden shacks among endless rows of water tanks where the haze of dust storms mingled with the smoke of burning garbage. In an incipient city with long, monotonous streets and neglected green areas where few trees languish under the heat, anguish, bitterness and hatred festered. Adding to the failure of schools were the required "contributions." Official primary schools charged twenty dollars on average for the registration of each child even though this practice violated the right to education ensured by the constitution. The collection of these contributions funded a wide array of supplies and services: glass, seats, paint, janitorial services, delivery receipts, certificates, tests and extra-curricular activities such as dance classes. However, teachers did not give official receipts for their fees.

So dismal was the picture of this emerging area that the company Televisa planned to install a cable system free of charge for economically disadvantaged urban areas. Televisa would provide Nezahualcóyotl with thirty simultaneous channels of transmission to provide "information and guidance for proper handling of a more immediate reality, individual, family and community development, and to provide roots and love for the area they inhabit." However, Televisa fell short on their plans and left everything in the pipeline.

Nevertheless, Nezahualcóyotl has grown by leaps and bounds. Urbanization continues to progress as well as the development of infrastructure.

Slim undertook the ecological rescue of an extremely important zone, an area in which there were a thousand tons of garbage and which generated serious pollution. The waste was compacted and covered with several layers of soil, eliminating vermin, falling particles and airborne bacteria as well as reducing the pollution of groundwater from the putrefaction of organic waste.

What was once the Board of Xochiaca is now a shopping mall, two universities, a technological research center and a hospital zone, collectively known as the Bicentennial Garden City. The Telmex Bicentennial Sports Center is also self-sustaining. Its four ecologically sound lagoons gather up to five million liters (over one million gallons) of water per year and provide five thousand permanent jobs.

The sports facilities are quite extensive and offer free facilities for recreation with twenty-five soccer fields, four tennis courts, four basketball courts, four volleyball courts, two football fields, and two baseball fields. The complex contains a stadium with a capacity for over three thousand, a playground, tennis aerobics, cycling, squash, a gym, landscaping, parking and a helipad.

To inaugurate the sports facilities, Slim invited the star player Alex Rodriguez from the New York Yankees, named the best baseball player in the Major League in the 2007-2008 season.

One of Slim's little-known interests is his fondness of sports. He is a friend of Edson Arantes do Nascimento (Pelé) and many baseball stars. Though baseball is his favorite sport, this does not stop his companies from supporting and advertising their professional soccer teams in the first division. Though on the board of the Condors, A.C., he has donated to American football teams. He enjoys playing American football himself.

However, baseball is Slim's greatest passion. When the slugger Mark McGwire set a record for homeruns, the mogul wrote an article in *Letras Libres*, a magazine run by Slim's friend and historian Enrique Krauze, where he displayed his knowledge by placing emphasis on the diamond statistics.

> *Baseball, whose Mexican supporters seem to have woken up after long periods of half-empty stands, is a spectacular sport that much depends on the abilities and technical skills of its practitioners—but also, the deployment of intelligence. Hence, the best games are those known as "pitching duels," close games that are usually determined by good fielding or the solo homerun.*
>
> *In baseball, like no other team sport, the numbers speak, memory is activated, and legends are forged. Unfortunately, it is impossible to reconstruct, in this sense, the statistics of the American Negro League (ANL) since the majors adhered absurdly to the "color barrier" (broken in 1947 by the second baseman for the Brooklyn Dodgers, Jackie Robinson).*
>
> *Those leagues—like those that Mexico could benefit from, importing outstanding figures in the time of businessman Jorge Pasquel—along with Cuba, boasted teams of legendary players. The memory brings to mind, and in no particular order, the names of Josh Gibson, Martin Dihigo, Roberto Ortiz, Ray Mamerto Dandrige, James Cool Papa Bell, Leon Day, Theolic Smith, Burnis Wright, Cristóbal Torriente,*

Silvio García, Ramón Bragaña, and Luis Olmo. What fan who knew of these star athletes could escape the seduction of their legend?

In the Dominican Republic, at the beginning of the Great American Depression, the dictator Trujillo took great players from the Negro Leagues, causing chaos in this country and instilling in the people a greater love and enrichment of a tradition whose fruits they enjoy today in the Major Leagues.

The numbers speak for themselves: think of the great exploits of pitchers like Nolan Ryan, who served for twenty-seven seasons. There was also the black pitcher Satchel Paige, who played in the big leagues for forty-two years. He won six games and lost only one in his first season, and Paige was almost a sexagenarian [by his final game]. Among the pitchers is a group that can be considered as the Big Five including Paige, Christy Mathewson, Walter Johnson, Grover Alexander and Cy Young. After them, many characters have graced the mound, people of yesterday and of today, and their memory brings us happiness.

I quote in non-chronological order: Whitey Ford, Lefty Grove, Vic Raschi, Sandy Koufax, Sal Maglie, Warren Spahn, Nolan Ryan, Ed Walsh, Three Fingers Brown, Adie Joss, Steve Carlton, Gaylord Perry, Tom Seaver, Allie Reynolds, Bob Lemon, Bob Gibson, Bob Feller, Don Drysdale, Early Wynn, Sam McDowell, and the rescuers, some still active: John Franco, Dennis Eckersley, Randy Myers, Jeff Reardon, Rollie Fingers, Jeff Montgomery, Doug Jones, Rick Aguilera. These men come to the rescue when the ball is hot. Though they sit in on more than a thousand games, on average they play less than two tickets per occurrence, and are winners or losers in the game twenty-five percent of the time. The closers are pitchers with good control, very mild nerves, and good punchers. Among active starters, one can't forget Roger Clemens (who has won the Cy Young Award five times for best pitcher) Greg Maddux to Dominican Pedro Martinez (a new important figure) Tom Glavine, Dave Cone and output, Orel Hershiser and Dwight Gooden.

On the pitch there are brands that seem insurmountable: the 7.355 entries drawn by Cy Young, the 511 victories achieved by this hero of the squadrons of Cleveland and Boston; the clean sweep by Ed Walsh (1.81); the percentage of wins and losses at Ford (690); the number of strikeouts by Ryan (5.714); the rate of strikeouts for Randy Johnson (once per nine innings); the number of wins for Jack Chesbro (41 obtained in 1904); the strikeouts per game Sandy Koufax achieved during his career as shortstop for the Dodgers (an average of 9.28, just below the 9.55 of Ryan and of course the 10.6 that keeps Randy Johnson on top, now playing with the Arizona Diamonds).

The numbers speak and myths flourish also among hitters. For me, the top five of the century have been Babe Ruth (who built Yankee Stadium while consolidating the magic of the sport), Ty Cobb, Roger Hornby, Ted Williams and Lou Gehrig, without forgetting Honus Wagner, Eddie Collins, Joe Jackson, Ed Delahanty, Tris Speaker, Billy Hamilton, Willie Keeler, Nap Lajoie, Al Simmons, Stan Musial, Joe DiMaggio, Mickey Mantle, Jimmie Foxx, Mel Ott, Hank Greenberg,

Ralph Kiner, Jackie Robinson, Willie Mays Frank Robinson, Harmon Killebrew, George Sisler, Harry Heilmann, Roberto Clemente, Rose Peel between assets and Tony Gwyn, Wade Boggs, Cal Ripken, Rickey Henderson, Ken Griffey Jr., Mark McGwire, Sammy Sosa, Barry Bonds, Larry Walker Frank Thomas, Albert Belle, Juan Gonzalez, Jose Canseco...

The numbers speak for themselves: Babe Ruth's 714 homeruns were hit within fewer times at bat than those of Hank Aaron (755). The frequency of his big hits has never been surpassed.

McGwire, meanwhile, has five seasons with fifty or more homeruns. Only ten batsmen have ever overcome that barrier: Ruth (60 in 1927), Roger Maris (61 in 1961), Foxx (58 in 1932), Greenberg (58 in 1938), Mantle (54 in 1961), Wilson (56, 1930), Kiner (54 in 1949), Mays (52 in 1965), George Foster (52 in 1977) and Mize (51 in 1947). Among the assets they have McGwire (which reached 70 in 1998), Sosa (66 in 1998), Griffey Jr. (56 in 1997 and 1998), Cecil Fielder (51 in 1990), Greg Vaughn (50 in 1998), Albert Belle (50, 1995).

Playing with astonishing numbers, McGwire would have exceeded eight homers had he played twenty-two seasons. Griffey, with fewer shifts, exceed the rate set by Aaron. In 2001, McGwire will be the fourth-best homerun hitter in history behind only Aaron, Ruth and Mays. He will most likely be close behind Bonds, Canseco and Griffey Jr., though he will exceed five hundred homeruns. In 1927, Ruth hit a homerun on average every nine times at bat. In 1998, McGwire did it every 7.27 times.

The numbers speak in an infinite diamond: the memory, imagination, and the creation of legends. The renewed enthusiasm for baseball once again plays with intelligence.

Slim's addiction to baseball is so great that he has a consortium with Ogden de México. With sixty-six percent US capital and the remaining thirty-four percent Mexican, he is one of the main operators in the management of stadiums and arenas in the United States. He managed the sports facilities where the Sacramento Kings and the Chicago Bulls played as well as other centers in Chicago, Baltimore and Philadelphia. Slim was presented with a project to build a professional baseball stadium on the land that he occupied for many years with his cousin Alfredo Harp Helú of Banamex, Red Devils team owner. However, Slim denied the rumors that a major league franchise would play in Mexico stating that he does not want to make his hobby into a business; he just likes to enjoy baseball.

Carlos Slim with New York Yankee Alex Rodriguez.

THE COLLECTOR
Art, a Symbol of Wealth

Extravagance is quite common in the world of the wealthy. There are those who collect the most unexpected things and there are those who squander fortunes in bulk. For example, the American millionaires Dennis Tito and Gregory Olsen, and South African Mark Shuttleworth have each allegedly spent US$20 million to travel to space as "tourists." A regular on the *Forbes* list of the world's richest, Warren Buffett sells his time. By sharing a meal with a stranger, he takes in a little over US$2 million. Zhao Danyang, a Chinese businessman, paid that amount to dine with Buffett in a luxurious New York restaurant. The money Buffett raises for these meetings is assigned to a foundation that helps the poor and homeless.

A mega-rich man from Russia acquired a mansion built on an area of 11,000 square meters (120,000 square feet) on the Cote d'Azur near Monte Carlo for US$900 million. The "Leopold Villa," known as the world's most expensive house, belonged to King Leopold II and has been owned by Bill Gates, the Agnelli family, owners of the Ferrari and Fiat automotive brands, and Edmond Safra, the billionaire businessman of Lebanese origin.

Slim lives outside this type of fairytale. His time is shared between his businesses, foundations, grantees and his family. When a reporter asked why he did not live in a bigger house, Slim told him that he has lived in his house in Las Lomas de Chapultepec since he was thirty-two years old; it is where some of his children were born. "I have not changed and will continue [to live] there until they take me out front, feet-first," he said. "It is a warm place to meet with my children and friends. My parents' house was better than mine, by far. Larger, more spacious, more valuable, but when one looks for materials, they are going the wrong way."

His empire is made up of more than money. Slim said that when he dies, his greatest legacy will be his family. However, the mogul also belongs to the breed of collectors whose transactions amount to tens of millions of dollars each year in the select international art market. His main hobby is acquiring high-quality works of painting and sculpture. While the rich and powerful have art for fashion or as a form of investment, Slim's objective is to have an artistic heritage at the level of the best museums in Europe. He is among the top ten art collectors in the world and owns the "collection of collections" with more than 70,000 pieces.

With the purpose of exposing the public to his growing collection, he opened the Museo Soumaya in 1994. Located in the Plaza Loreto in the south of Mexico City, the institution was conceived by the tycoon's late wife and is now directed by his daughter, Soumaya Slim Domit. The museum also hosts works that have traveled from museums in the United States, Europe and Asia.

Slim follows in the steps of eccentric billionaire Jean Paul Getty, who in 1953 opened a small museum in his Malibu home to show his art collection to the public. After nearly five decades, his museum has grown to become one of the most vital art institutions in the world.

Slim's collection is priceless; it includes the second most important private collection in the world of sculptor Auguste Rodin with one of the twenty versions of "The Thinker." His eldest son,

Carlos Slim Domit, is also referred to as "The Thinker" because he dedicates an hour a day to reflection. Some pieces of Slim's collection are superior to those in the Palace of Fine Arts. Jacques Vilain, director of the Rodin Museum of Paris, was surprised at the richness of Museo Soumaya when he visited Mexico. However, in the austerity of Slim's office is where one can admire a replica of "*La Piedad*" ("The Mercy") by Miguel Ángel. The sculpture has been certified by the Casa Buonarroti and even has a papal blessing. In the Grupo Carso boardroom, only two framed items have a fixed place: Slim's professional qualifications, signed by the reader of UNAM Ignacio Chávez in 1964, and a small watercolor by his father Julián Slim. In his office, Slim displays some works by the American landscape artist Conrad Wise Chapman. He took advantage of the floor space to install a museum gallery for his guests to enjoy.

Mexico boasts at least twenty of the two hundred top art collectors in the world. Most are businessmen and others are politicians. Among these Mexicans who own works of art worthy of the best museums in Europe and the United States is Slim, although he doesn't usually appear in *Art Review*, the glamorous publication run by American art dealer Larry Gagosian, curators Nicholas Serota and Glenn D. Lowry and collector Eli Broad. Nor has he been noted in *Art Review* magazine's annual "Power 100" list, which features the most important figures in the contemporary art world. Before Slim, the art world was limited to Europe and the United States. His stock is of such great importance that a new Soumaya Museum was built in 2011 in the north zone of Mexico City. It is an expansive building that boasts over 50,000 art pieces, including textiles, folk art, colonial art, European antiques, coins and sculptures by Auguste

Rodin. They also installed one of twelve copies worldwide of *La Pietà* by Michelangelo.

Slim's multifaceted collection includes sketches, paintings, watercolors, tempera, murals, sculptures, photographs, invaluable books, Baroque and Hispanic-American art, caste and religious paintings, Marian titles, hardware from the sixteenth century, Mexican portraits of the eighteenth and nineteenth century, old engravings and modern European paintings. Slim also has the same portraits and landscapes of the work of Maurice de Vlaminck, one of the largest representations of Fauvism, works by Tamayo, Siqueiros, Rivera, José María Velasco, Dr. Atl, John Correa, Miguel Cabrera, Cristóbal de Villalpando, and valuable sculptures and paintings by European artists such as Camille Claudel, Pierre Gibran, Auguste Renoir, Edgar Degas, Emile-Antoine Boudelle, Giorgio de Chirico, Picasso, Dalí, Monet, El Greco, Van Gogh, Paul Gauguin, Matisse, Maillol, Miró, Ernest, Carpeux, Carrier-Belleuse, Daumier, Rubens, Murillo, Cranach, Brueghel, Tiziano, el Tintoretto, and Toulouse-Lautrec and Rouault.

When the Soumaya Museum first opened, it displayed five patriotic exhibitions. The first room showed a collection of paintings from the eighteenth and nineteenth centuries, which were part of the selection of "A Portrait of Mexico." The second room contained a series of works under the title "Mexico as Seen by Mexicans and Foreigners." The third room had works grouped under the concept of "Mexican and Latin American Baroque Art." The forth room housed a collection entitled "Decorative Arts of Mexico and Spain."

In this museum, as with some of his companies, buildings, or various Sanborns restaurants, one can admire Slim's collectables.

Much of his artistic heritage was gained via catalog from the comfort of his office. However, he personally reviews each acquisition even though he has specialists, curators and art conservators at his disposal. They integrate the collections and preserve them for public enjoyment, as happened with the legacy of the Lebanese poet Gibran Khalil Gibran, who died in 1931 after being excommunicated from the Maronite Catholic Church and exiled by the Ottoman government. In 2008, the Soumaya Museum and the Centro de Estudios de Historia de México Carso[26] acquired Gibran's collection of oil paintings, drawings, illustrated books and first editions, and a rich body of original manuscripts and copies of his personal library. These are the legacy of Khalil Gibran.

In his memoirs, Michel Laclote, emeritus director of the Louvre Museum, wrote, "In any collector there is an irrational side that is maniacal." He was referring to the compulsion of some magnates to buy art works and to continue enlarging their collections.

Discussing the whims of Kurt Gitter's, one of the most important collectors of Japanese art, another collector asked how he goes about buying a work of art while relaxing in a hot tub in Tokyo.

"I look at the painting in question and I close my eyes," the collector said. "I compare that picture with a stack of bills. Finally, I decide which one I prefer to have. The painting always ends up winning."

According to experts, many Mexican collectors buy works of art as a form of investment, gathering cultural goods more for business than for pleasure. Some wealthy Mexicans acquire works of art as a commodity-investment, stored in safes in their homes or in banks, hoping that the price increases. Many art specialists consider this as a hindrance to enjoying or admiring the aesthetic value of art. They see such collectors as mere merchants who often generate fictitious value. Inexperienced collectors who to speculate on art have broken down the price of works much like a stock market speculation.

The art specialist Rodrigo Lake argues that as art became fashionable as a form of investment, it created confusion between the concepts of value and price.

Everything that glitters is not gold. And the unfortunate thing in our times is that, as Oscar Wilde said, "People know the price of everything and the value of nothing." Rodrigo Lake said, "The Mexican colonial area, which is one of my specialties, is a strange phenomenon accentuated among the millionaires of our country who are dedicated to acquiring works of art as fruitful future investments, which is acceptable, even greater for preventing the migration of wonderful pieces, but whose counselors, generally consultants of Hispanic origin, reject the advice of knowledgeable Mexicans, risking that they will be taken for a ride for their money … The Legend of Quetzalcoatl is still alive in our subconscious.

"I recall a funny anecdote that perfectly illustrates the unfortunate choice of many wealthy Mexicans who are surrounded by 'consultants' that advise them on which pieces of art to buy and not buy … The important antiquarian Sir J. Duveen and an expert named Bernhard Berenson were responsible for the existence of almost all major US collections created in the inter-war period. They sold a lot of pieces to the famed billionaire J. P. Morgan; the antiquarian sent him the piece that Berenson authenticated. The fact is that one day Duveen met up with Berenson and told him that night that they would go to Morgan's house to discuss the sale of a magnificent painting. Berenson responded that he had not been announced, but Duveen said they would go together regardless. Upon arriving at the meeting, they found that J.P. Morgan had a second expert at his house of European origin, who, upon being interrogated on the subject of the art piece, said that he would have to think about it. At that moment, Duveen took the piece off the wall; he shook Morgan's hand and walked out of the house. Amazed, J.P. Morgan asked why he was going. To which Sir J. Duveen responded, 'Pardon me, but if your expert needs to think, it is because he does not know. An expert does not think, he knows!'"

Under the premise of investing in art, the majority of Mexican collectors have formed an important historical and cultural heritage.

Unlike art millionaires, Slim can boast that he is not only a tenacious collector, but a piece of art as well. He unveiled his figure in the Wax Museum of Mexico City where it appears alongside prominent world leaders, artists, singers and athletes. The creation of the statue took four months of photography and modeling (the glass eyes had to be placed in the exact position and each hair of the correct shade applied one by one). The body has Slim's exact dimensions and Slim gave personal items like a black suit, white shirt and green tie to dress the figure. This was the first time that a wax sculpture of a Mexican businessman was made as a tribute to his historic and global significance.

The visual artist Agustín Portillo is dedicated to characterizing the most important personalities. In the American and Mexican series,

Portillo combines expressionism with art and portrays celebrities and people of high society, but in a very irreverent way; distorting the image to convey the person's essence. The painter's fame has transcended the borders of the United States and Mexico, and his work is generally characterized by movement, colors, elements, and poses that aim to create reactions in the viewer. The artist has been commissioned to interpret characters from Spanish and British royalty.

Slim has also been used as a character for such writers as Carlos Monsiváis, Cardinal Norberto Rivera, Margarita Zavala, María Asunción Aramburuzabala, Paulina Rubio and Gaby Vargas, among others.

Another one of Slim's passions is books. He is a voracious reader and is always carrying books with him in the trunk of his car. He knows every title of the nearly four hundred books crowding the bookshelf in his office.

His passion for reading and for history has led him to acquire the Center for Historical Studies of Mexico Condumex (now Center for the study of Mexican History Carso), which has been a part of Grupo Carso since 1992. Grupo Carso has provided continuity to the project and a new wave of diffusion.

The purpose of this school is to acquire, preserve, catalog and disseminate books and records relating to the history of Mexico. Its main objective is to facilitate its collection for researchers interested in studying and propagating national history.

The library consists of over 80,000 books specializing in the history of Mexico. With great pride, the institution first housed the colonial collection, one of the richest of its kind, American incunabula books, religious and civil chronicles, legal arguments, sermons, novenas, indulgences, biographies, and so on. The other specialty of the library is nineteenth century books, from 1821 to the Porfirio Díaz era. The collection of books from the twentieth century relates to volumes of the first half of the century and is considered rare by domestic and foreign libraries. The center is particularly known for housing these rare books. The archive includes journals, newspapers and magazines from the eighteenth and nineteenth centuries. It dates back to the first Mexican newspaper and very rare publications of the late nineteenth century.

The archives in the center are extremely varied. Prominent among the oldest documents is one signed by Queen Isabella, dated in Valladolid in 1491, and an Ordinance of Christopher Columbus in 1493, the only one of its kind in all the Americas.

The center includes documents from the colonial period, the War of Independence, the proclamation of Agustín de Iturbide as first emperor, much of the government of Porfirio Díaz, and the Mexican Revolution. The documents are of various kinds and are brought together by various acquisitions and specific collections of main characters, such as Lucas Alamán, Enrique C. Creel, Porfirio Parra, Francisco León de la Barra, Venustiano Carranza, Pablo González, Manuel W. González, Félix Díaz, Federico González Garza, Luis Montes de Oca, Antonio Carrillo Flores, Luis Chevez Orozco, Juan Sánchez Azcona, Roberto Montenegro and the Guadalupe sisters, María and Rosa Narváez Bautista.

In 1997, the center acquired important archives from José Yves Limantour, Secretary of the Treasury during the Porfirio Díaz regime. In addition to said documents, the center also has a library that houses various collections such as those of José Mendoza, Federico González Garza, Pablo González, the Cristero Antonio Ruis Facius and the actress Dolores del Río (her collection reflects the cultural and artistic life of Mexico).

The building that protects the center's invaluable archives is an old estate dating from the late colonial era. After passing through the hands of several prominent lawyers and a religious college, it became the Center for the Study of Mexican History. Slim acquired the property in it 1992, further enriching the historical heritage of this institution as well as modernizing the system. The documents have been cataloged and archived, some of them already published on CD, allowing for rapid retrieval of the documents to better facilitate research. Today, they also have three microfilm readers with photocopying services for immediate playback of documents and books.

THE MIRROR OF KING MIDAS
The Multiplication of His Fortune

Slim's fortune has grown faster than any other in the world, according to the influential *The Wall Street Journal*. The magazine has followed the Mexican tycoon's every step. The most important people in the world see him as a symbol of a new era.

There is nothing new about the interest shown by the international press. The significant fact is that Slim became the richest man in Mexico, and from Mexico has established an empire that spans more than twenty countries on various continents.

His business expansion in recent decades has bestowed onto Slim the picture of a postmodern emperor. He is powerful and as any true businessman, he is forceful in expressing his ideas. In Europe he is seen as a "conqueror." Even though he does not know the exact number of his companies, what is clear is that after Petróleos Mexicanos, the country's largest industry, he is the country's biggest taxpayer. Each year, he brings around $10 billion to the Treasury. One company of his vast empire, Telmex, has a market capitalization of more than MX$15 billion and along with other companies, represents about 30 percent of the Mexican Stock Exchange.

Those who admire Slim see him as the wizard who holds the "secret" to turn everything he touches to gold, but critics have insisted that his empire is the product of speculation. For many, it is incompressible that the son of a Lebanese immigrant and a self-made multimillionaire has accumulated wealth in a country that has never been considered a land of opportunity.

Some have tried to discover how he succeeded, but the common explanation is that Slim was simply "in the right place at the right time."

In June 1994, at the close of Salinas de Gortari's government, Slim developed a document called *The History of Grupo Carso* in which he tells the origin and development of his companies:

After discussing it with my family and several friends, I collected and wrote some notes on the history of Grupo Carso. The result seems incipient to me, although it fills some of the sought-after objectives, such as establishing its chronological development and the disclosure of certain personal and family history. But beyond the story, I also wish to relate, in general terms, how it operates and how it evolved financially. I believe that this exercise of individual and collective memory may be of interest to my children, friends, family, and colleagues to businessmen, journalists, investors, and students.

It is my intention to continue these notes later to deepen and broaden the group's history with other specific data combining subjective concepts, such as the principles and foundations on which Carso operates and develops.

Slim explains that the foundations of his empire came in 1911 when his father Julián and thirteen-year-old brother José established a corporation named after his place of origin: the Eastern Star. His capital was MX$25,000, with each of the proprietors owning fifty percent of the shares. The reason for its commercial success was simple: vocation, talent and hard work. His advice on professional issues, moral, and social responsibility was very clear. The report continues:

The gestation of Grupo Inbursa and Carso began in 1965. It was then that I acquired the bottling company Jarritos del Sur and began building several businesses like Bolsa Inversora Bursátil (Stock Market Investment), Inmobiliaria Carso (Carso Real Estate), Constructoria Carso (Carso Construction), Promotora del Hogar, S.S.G. (Housing Promotions), Mina de Agregados Pétreos el Volcán (Stone and Volcano Mining), Bienes Raíces Mexicanos (Mexican Roots) and Pedregales del Sur (Stones of the South).[27] I established Inmobiliaria Carso in January 1966, three months before my marriage. The name comes from the first letters of Carlos and Soumaya.

Inmobiliaria Carso acquired some properties like the 65th Guatemala Street, corner Correo Mayor, August 19, 1970, Isabela la Católica corner of Mesones, on November 14, 1970; Palmas 1730, August 16, 1971; and also many other areas in the west and south of the city. The aforementioned acquisitions were complex negotiations involving nearly one hundred farms and constituted an area of over 1.5 million square meters (over sixteen million square feet). To purchase some of these properties, Inmobiliaria Carso mortgaged all of its property at an annual rate of eleven percent and paid interest and credit with the flow of rent.

In relation to real estate, it should be noted that some land south of the city, acquired in the early seventies, was expropriated in 1989 for ecological purposes, constituting part of the city's green belt. These lands were only partially cleared and at a value of ten percent of its market value.

Also, Flornamex, a company established in 1981 for the cultivation and export of flowers, had to close shortly thereafter due to various errors and problems.

The chart on the next page shows Slim's first investments:

	EL ESPEJO DEL REY MIDAS					
DATE	COMPANY OR INVESTMENT	%	INVESTMENT (PESOS)	DOLLARS	LIABILITY	RECOVERY (PESOS)
1965	Jarritos del Sur	40	600,000	240,000	--------	2,000,000
1970	Jarritos del Sur	40	800,000	320,000	--------	57,000,000
1965	Inversora Bursátil	34	340,000	27,200	--------	(Dividend Dec. 1982)
1967	Inversora Bursátil	66	660,000	52,000	--------	7,000,000
1965 – 69	Condominio del Bosque	100	3,400,000	272,000	2,400,000	(Sale 1967 - 69)
1966	Inmobiliaria Carso	100	3,000,000	240,000	--------	--------
1966	Inmobiliaria Carso	40	400,000	32,000	--------	1,000,000 (1971)
1968	SSG Inmobiliaria		1,200,000	96,000	--------	--------
1969	Bienes Raíces Mexicanos		1,000,000		80,000	Expropriated in 1989, US$3.5M
1972	Pedregales del Sur					Expropriated en 1989, US$1.81M
1970 – 71	Inmuebles		4,500,000	360,000	3,000,000	Credit paid in rent
1969 – 73	Terrenos y Poniente Sur		20,000,000	1,610,000	5,000,000	From the South approx.

	Expropiados					US$6M
1969 -73	Galas de México	60	10,000,000	800,000	--------	
June 1976	Cigatam	10	26,000,000 (aprox.)	1,050,000 (aprox.)	--------	Dividends 1982 - 84
August 1981	Cigatam	39.60	214,000,000	8,620,000		54,000,000 (paid in dividends)
August 1982	Cigatam	5	39,000,000	260,000	--------	350,000,000 Dividends 1985 - 94
1982 – 83	Anderson Clayton	3.5	10,000,000	66,600	--------	1.860,000 Sale and dividends
1982 – 83	Reynolds Aluminum	17	12,300,000	82,000	--------	--------
1982 – 83	Hulera El Centenario (Firestone)	23	23,800,000	158,600	--------	
September 1983	Sanborns	4.27	161,500,000	1,076,000	--------	
June 1984	Sanborns	8.65	673,750,000	3,800,000	--------	
June 1985	Sanborns	33.57	7,210,000,000	22,270,000	--------	
1982 – 84	Moderna	40	860,000,000	4,456,000	--------	35,000,000 in sales January 1985

Under the principle, "Don't act now thinking that what once happened will happen again," Slim continued with the business evolution of Carso and Inbursa:

During the four years of 1981 to 1984, we made many large investments and acquisitions including the purchase in 1984 of bank stock shares, originating in the repurchase of significant bank assets.

In June 1976, we acquired sixty percent of Galas de México in the sum of MX$10 million through a capital increase of said society, and in 1980, we formally established the company that is currently Grupo Carso with the aim of acquiring Cigatam (Cigar Tabacalera Mexicana). Grupo Carso was then the Group Galas. Having bought about ten percent of Cigatam for approximately MX$30 million during 1981, on August 11 we acquired Cigatam for 39.6 percent with an additional MX$214 million. The acquisition of this company turned out to be of enormous importance to the group as the significant cash flow enabled us to engage in other investments. Since the introduction of Cigatam to Grupo Carso, it became a company with the lowest cost of production and operation in the world and was the lever and the motor that helped develop Grupo Carso. The group spent about MX$20 million over the course of twenty-five years. Its market share increased in this period, from twenty-eight to sixty-three percent.

In those years, and considering the fact that many major domestic and foreign investors did not want to keep their investments, it was feasible to acquire several companies at prices far below their real value, including "Mexicanizing" some of them. Among these companies were Reynolds Aluminum, Sanborns, Nacobre and its subsidiaries. Later, we Mexicanized and operated Luxus, Euzkadi, General Tire, Aluminum and thirty percent of Condumex. Another way in which we Mexicanized companies was by selling them to other Mexican companies like the case of Penwalt Chemistry in 1983 and the Moderna in 1985.

During the second half of 1982 and the beginning 1983, the value of companies was even more irrational than people's pessimism. In those years, some companies were worth less than five percent of their book value. Currently, several companies are trading at more than five times their revalued equity. Although a product of our own environment, these two situations are not alien to the international environment. Indeed, in the early eighties the interest rate in international markets was greater than twenty percent and US inflation was in the double digits. At the end of the eighties, with an inflation rate of three to four percent, the interest rate was reduced substantially to levels of two percent (negative return in real terms). For that reason, they revalued fixed assets in the United States. By converting US investment funds to the Mexican stock market since 1991, Mexican companies gained more than ten times the value by the applied US investment parameters (multiples, performance, growth). This reassessment has led several Mexican companies to turn to these markets to capitalize in an important way and in favorable conditions.

THE MARKET VALUE OF SEVERAL COMPANIES IN THE MEXICAN STOCK MARKET

	December 1982		December 1984		June 1994	March 1995
	$ in M	Pesos	$ in M	Pesos	$ in M Pesos	$ in M Pesos
Anderson Clayton	281	1.9	9,312	47.8	123.0	58.3
Celanese	1.722	11.8	18,867	96.8	1,431.0	1,097.8
Cementos Mexicanos	3.9	26.0	20,750	106.4	7,820.0	2,391.4
Firestone	109	0.7	2,772	14.2	----	----
Kimberly Clark	4,075	27.2	19,106	98.0	3,698.0	1,675.6
Loreto y Peña Pobre	212	1.4	692	3.6	150.0	70.6
Hulera Euzkadi	7.59	7.9	40.5	186.1	65.1	
Moderna	724	4.8	13,716	70.3	2,870.0	1,297.5
Reynolds Aluminum	86	0.6	348	1.8	----	----
Sanborns	3,451	23.0	19,580	100.4	690.0	440.0
Segumex	----	----	8,520	43.7	980.0 (including the split)	449.6 (including the split)
Telmex	25,809	172.1	61,777	316.8	29,445.0	15,245.7

The eighties marked a milestone in our history. Grupo Carso established itself as a group of large companies, a conglomerate. This was a critical stage in the history of Mexico in which most lost confidence in their own future. While others refused to invest, we decided to do it. The reason for this decision was a mixture of trust in ourselves, trust in the country, and trust in common sense. Any rational or emotional analysis told us that to do anything that was not an investment in Mexico would be an outrage. You can't educate and train our teenage children (or anyone at any age) with fear, mistrust and bribery. The conditions of those years remind me of the decision my father made in March of 1914: during the time the country was in the midst of a revolution, he bought his brother's fifty percent of the business, risking all their capital and their future.

Between 1982 and 1984 we made several investments in various companies, as was the case of Firestone with twenty-three percent, 3.5 percent of Anderson Clayton and 21.6 percent of Sanborns. In the same year we acquired seventeen percent of Reynolds Aluminum, and significant stakes in several other companies.

In 1984, we concentrated on various controls. We acquired the "Group 2 Package" of Bancomer, in August of 1984 at MX$11,238 million (US$58 million), including one hundred percent Seguros de México (Insurance of Mexico), before Seguros Bancomer (Bancomer Insurance), plus thirty percent of Anderson Clayton and several other important investments.

The acquisition was carried out as follows:

DATE	INVESTMENT	AMOUNT		ACQUIRER	
		PESOS	DOLLARS		
AUG. 23, 1984	Anderson Clayton	2,800.0	14.5	Cigatam	
				Inversora	
AUG. 28, 1984	Segumex	5,100.0	26.4	Bursátil	484.5
				Majority	2,805.
				Shareholders	5
					1,810.
				Public Offer	0
AUG. 29-Sep. 7, 1984	Highway Investment	1,645.0	8.5	Segumex	
AUG. 29-Sep. 7, 1984	Highway Investment	200.0		Inversora Burstil	
AUG. 29-Sep. 7, 1984	Highway Investment	948.0		Grupo Carso	
AUG. 29-Sep. 7, 1984	Value sold on the market	545.0		Various	
		11,238. 0	58.1		5,100. 0

With these acquisitions, we formed the Inbursa Financial Group, comprising of Bolsa Inversora Bursátil, Seguros de México, and Fianzas la Guardiana (Guardian Financial). In 1981, we founded the fund, which in the last thirteen years has yielded approximately thirty-one percent in dollars annually and in which we invested proceeds from the sale of Venustiano Carranza.

By 1983, the equity of the Bolsa Inversora Bursátil was MX$3,000 million and had paid MX$57 million in dividends.

In 1985, Grupo Carso acquired control of Artes Gráficas Unidas (United Graphic Arts) and Loreto y Peña Pobre, Porcelanite, and most of Sanborns, and its subsidiary, Denny's.

In 1986, we acquired Minera Frisco, Nacobre and their subsidiaries, and we still maintain an important role in Euzkadi.

From these acquisitions, we sold various minority purchases that we had previously acquired without corporate interests, including forty percent of the company Empresas de Moderna, already mentioned above.

All companies above-mentioned constitute part of Grupo Carso from the referred-to dates and until 1986. We didn't acquire the majority of the company until 1992.

In its statutes, Grupo Carso maintains exclusion clauses to foreigners that prohibit them from becoming shareholders. Excepted are the investors who, since 1991, participated through the trusteeship Nafinsa with exclusive patrimonial fines.

As of June 18, 1990, we made Grupo Carso a public company through a primary share offering to those who followed the fusion with other companies within the group, an augment in capital, and with two other primary international public offers. Before the offer in June 1990, Carso was a private company with few partners, all working together in collaboration with the group even though several controlled companies were public and had numerous investors.

In late 1990, Grupo Carso with Southwestern Bell, France Telecom and several Mexican investors won the bid to privatize Teléfonos de México. They acquired 5.17 percent of the company through the purchase of Class AA shares at a price twenty percent higher than the stock value of Classes A and L. Despite the group's solid financial structure, the important companies that formed it, the viable accelerated investments, and the use of the resources generated in the operation of its subsidiaries, to maintain a sound financial and operational position and address this important payment, they achieved diverse public offers in order to finance the acquisition. The first was in June 1990, after registering on the Mexican Stock Exchange. They made a public offer for an amount equivalent to US$100 million; a bond issued in June 1991 of MX$500 billion and two other subsidiaries with MX$550 billion in May and July to consolidate liabilities. We conducted a second public offering of shares of Grupo Carso and gave MX$140 billion to the Mexican

Stock Exchange and US$214 million in international capital markets. Investment in the purchase of our interest in Telmex was US$442.8 million, our public offerings were about US$360 million of capital and US$165 million in liabilities. This is to say, we captured through these offers US$100 million dollars more than the investment of Telmex. It is noteworthy that our Mexican partners (including Segumex) acquired the remaining five percent of the Class AA shares of Telmex, even though they were forced to maintain their long-term investment to pay above the market and buy shares of the control (Class AA) that they cannot sell.

Given the importance of the company, its lag, and the enormous changes and investments in the sector on worldwide level, it was necessary to establish an aggressive investment plan to grow and modernize a program to accelerate the training and begin a process of cultural change and reconstruction outside the old network to improve services. It was also necessary to perform the painful removal of cross subsidies, greatly increasing the local services to reduce that of long distance services.

In February 1993, and to continue their development plans, Grupo Carso made a third public offering—also primary—for approximately US$352 million in order to remain a healthy and strong group of companies capable of competing with powerful international companies.

Following the acquisition of Class AA shares of Telmex, the band continued its policy of total reinvestment of profits, mainly in the sectors of construction, auto parts, consumer products, communications and commerce.

From 1992 to date, we have acquired foreign companies such as Pirello, Alcoa, Continental, Condumex enterprise, Aluminum and General Tire, of which we were key partners with thirty, forty-eight and ninety-nine percent, respectively. With the latter two cases, we were responsible for the operation. With Continental, we maintain a technical assistance and marketing agreement.

Despite the great achievements in almost three decades of work, we have had numerous difficulties. During these twenty-nine years of business, we have had problems from others' brands (Jarritos, Hershey's, Reynolds, Goodrich, Sugus, Toblerone) that we have had to develop to the point of expropriation (1989), free trade, illegal entry of products passing through operating permits, denied land use, land invasions, unaffordable prices of mining products, depletion of mines, monopoly problems, labor problems, dissociation (Constructora Carso, Minera Real Ángeles), unexpected changes in technical assistance, obsolete facilities, pollution or consumption of too much water (Planta de Celulosa de Peña Pobre, Loreto, Euzkadi in the Federal District) and bad business (Flornamex). Negotiations have been swift and cordial, like that of Frisco and Condumex, or long and difficult.

Although all companies involved required a great individual and collective effort, we have had very difficult professional and financial challenges, which are, from a professional point of view, Galas and Telmex. Galas, upon purchase, presented very difficult conditions in 1976: a

158

strike, too many products, obsolete equipment, high debt, customers inconvenienced by the strike, suppliers that did not work for non-payment, outstanding debts with banks, leasing companies and suppliers, as well as conventions of taxes, with more limited industrial social insurance. Fifteen years later, in 1991, Teléfonos de México, with its large gaps in service, an outdated equipment plant, a deteriorated exterior, a large unmet demand, and cross-subsidies of painful adjustments, had significant impact on the social and economic life of the country.

Integrating the Mexican group was difficult for the amount and timing of the investment (five to ten years) and the negotiation was especially arduous with our technology partner, Southwestern Bell and France Telecom. However, after reaching agreements, we have had no problem for nearly four years.

No doubt, the more you discuss and define the conditions of an association, the fewer problems the company will have later on. The Grupo Carso investment, although very large, was funded with relative ease through chirographic obligations of MX$500 billion, a public/private offering of MX$307 billion, an increase in capital of MX$500 billion, and an international public offer of MX$794 billion. Subsequently, we made a second international public offer of MX$1,094 billion in January 1993.

On top of the large capitalization of Grupo Carso, thanks to the three primary offerings, we continued to reinvest the profits of the group and divesting minority stakes, allowing Carso to have very healthy finances to continue its development.

The following is a summary of the business history of Grupo Carso and Inbursa after four decades of having laid the first foundations of the empire.

Companies

Slim spent more than half his life building and running Grupo Carso. Although he has left the majority of his companies to his board of advisors, he still plays many roles within his company. He is head of the Board of Directors of Impulsora del Desarrollo y el Empleo en América Latina (Fostering Development and Employment in Latin America OR IDEAL). He is also head of the Board for Carso Infraestructura y Construcción (Carso Infrastructure and Construction or CICSA), a company the size of ICA, which Slim took two years to develop while its competition took half a century. Slim is president of the Telmex Foundation and the Fundación Slim (The Slim Foundation). He is the acting chair of the Executive Advisory Council for the Restoration of the Historic Centre and of the Historic Centre of Mexico City Foundation.

He remains actively involved in his businesses although his main focus now is on education, health and employment in Mexico and throughout Latin America through his foundations. His three sons, Carlos, Marco Antonio and Patricio Slim Domit run his businesses.

His leadership style is very practical. Grupo Carso doesn't have corporate "staff." Rather, each company has its own structure.

His first company was founded in 1965 with the acquisition of the bottling company Jarritos South and the establishment of several companies such as Casa de Bolsa Inversora Bursátil (Stock Exchange and brokerage Firm), Inmobiliaria Carso (Carso Real Estate), Carso Construcción (Carso Construction), Promotora del Hogar (Housing Promotion), S.S.G., Mina de Agregados Pétreos el Volcán (Stone and Volcano Mining), Raíces Mexicanos (Mexican Roots) and Pedregales del Sur (Stones from the South), as well as a company that buys, sells and leases construction equipment.[28] Inmobiliaria Carso was established in January 1996.

In the late sixties, he bought about two million square meters (twenty-two million square feet) of land south of Mexico City, which was expropriated in 1989.

In June 1976, he acquired Galas de México. In 1980, the conglomerate that is now known as Grupo Carso was formally established with the purpose of acquiring the majority of Cigatam, a partner of Philip Morris, who owned twenty-nine percent.

The beginning of the eighties marked a milestone in the history of Grupo Carso. In 1982, the same year that Mexico was in a debt crisis and the banks were increasingly becoming nationalized, Carso began investing in an intense and active way.

Between 1981 and 1986, Slim succeeded in several investments and acquisitions of businesses small and large, among them Citagam, which was the first and most important for their cash flow. In twenty-five years, they gained an average of 1.5 percent of market shares each year. Other companies that he acquired were Hulera el Centenario (Firestone) with twenty-three percent, and also Bimex. During this period he also attained Reynolds Aluminum and Aluminum, Inc.

In August 1984, Slim concentrated on the purchase of Seguros de México (Insurance of Mexico) with a thirty-three percent equity stake worth MX$55 million. Inbursa Financial Group was composed of Casa de Bolsa Inversora Bursátil (Investment Securities Brokerage Firm), Seguros de México (Insurance of Mexico) and La Guardiana.

In 1985, Grupo Carso acquired control of Artes Gráficas Unidas (United Graphic Arts), Papel Loreto y Peña Pobre (Paper mills), and most of Sanborns and its subsidiaries, including Denny's.

In 1986, they acquired the company Minera Frisco and Nacobre Enterprises and its subsidiaries and the control of Euzkadi tire company, a leader in the market, and later in 1993, most of General Tire. In 1991, he acquired the Hotel Calinda (now Ostar Hotel Group), headed by his nephew Roberto Slim Seade.

In 1990, Grupo Carso joined Southwestern Bell, France Telecom and several other Mexican investors, and he won the bid to privatize Teléfonos de México. Grupo Carso bought into the privatization of Telmex with 5.8 percent of the company, which had a twenty-five year run of successful business experience; Southwestern Bell acquired five percent and an option for another five percent, France Telecom bought five percent, and a group of Mexican investors had 4.6 percent stake. Since 1981, along with Cigatam, all companies that are part of Grupo Carso were made public. Consequently, its history can be accessed, as it is now public information.

Grupo Carso has sold several companies in part or in their entirety, such as tissue paper manufacturers, tire companies, several hotels, printing and packaging business, parts of Cigatam, El Globo,

Química Flour (Chemical Flour) and Porcelanite, among others. The companies in the group generate more than 220,000 jobs.

Carso's growth has been possible thanks to Slim's philosophy of constantly reinvesting the profits of the companies to continue producing goods and services while creating jobs for Mexicans. Grupo Carso re-invests their profits s into the most dynamic sectors, in medium- and long-term vehicles as well as maintaining flexibility and speed in decision-making.

Grupo Carso is purely a Mexican-based and Mexican-owned company that has demonstrated the ability to successfully manage all the companies under its umbrella, which operate in highly competitive markets, both nationally and internationally.

Telmex

In 1990, Grupo Carso and other Mexican investors acquired 10.4 percent of Telmex shares, five percent of those associated with SBC along with the option of another five percent, and five percent of France Telecom. Since 1990, Telmex has fostered a culture of work where training, modernization, quality and customer service are priorities. Over the last nineteen years, Telmex has developed a world-class technology platform that has not only enabled the optimization of processing, but has strengthened the corporate culture, which has greatly improved service levels and commitment.

In 1991, Telmex operated with obsolete infrastructure such as electromechanical, analog, and many other forms of outdated technology. Telmex has since been upgraded and now boasts a fiber optic network of more than 68,000 miles across the country.

Telmex operates with the belief that all people should have access to telecommunications, even if there are no profit margins or subsidies available. The company has the most extensive industry network in the country.

Public telecommunications has been an important part in facilitating the access to the population. In December 1990 there were 69,025 public telephones (payphones). By December 2007 there were 715,000.

Since its privatization, Telmex worked to meet all the telecommunication needs of its customers by offering the most advanced products and services with the highest standards of quality and the best prices. Telmex is the leading telecommunications company in Mexico.

Telmex is a conglomerate formed by Teléfonos de México, S.A.B. de C.V., its subsidiaries and affiliates. It was created to provide telecommunication services in Mexico. Coverage of services includes, among others, the operation of the most comprehensive network of local and long distance telecommunications. It also offers services such as connectivity, Internet access, collocation, hosting and interconnection services to other telecommunications operators.

Competition

Telmex is the only telecommunications company in Mexico that has invested time and money to ensure that the communication needs of all socioeconomic sectors of the population are met. Their focus is to give a boost to rural telecommunications and provide Internet access in hard-to-reach areas across the country.

Telmex, in the business of landlines in Mexico, competes with operators who are focused primarily on high-income segments, A and B. Telmex's commitment to provide telecommunications services has led them to be the only land-line operators with a presence in the homes of socioeconomic segments C, D, E and the prepaid segment of the country, with one hundred percent market share. In a market of approximately 19.6 million fixed lines, Telmex has a market share of between sixty-three and seventy-eight percent of public, prepaid and landlines. As of June 2008, the overall market share (landline and mobile) of Telmex was nineteen percent.

DEALER or CONCESSIONAIRE (May 2008)	TOTAL NUMBER OF COMPANIES
Local Tele.Comm.	12
Long Distance Tele.Comm.	15
Long Distance Marketer	10
Local Tele.Comm. with Cable	30
Public Tele.Comm.	106
Suppliers of ISP	443
Suppliers of Private Networks	25
	640

Investment

Since its privatization, Telmex has invested more than US$30,000 million alone in Mexico while the total investments in the telecommunications sector between 1990 and 2007 was US$45,818 million. Telmex's investment accounted for more than sixty-five percent of this.

Eighty-two percent of the investments in landlines during this period came from Telmex.

América Móvil

In September 2000, Telmex split their business between their cellular phones and the majority of their international investments to create the new company América Móvil.

The decision to make this split was, among other things, motivated by the advantage of making them independent companies that competed. They focused on business and financial flexibility in order to cope with different strategies of Telmex and América Móvil.

Since February 7, 2001, when it first began trading shares on the Mexican Stock Exchange, New York and Madrid, América Móvil has grown to become the largest cellular company in Latin America and one of the largest in the world.

In June 2008, the mobile company had 165.3 million mobile subscribers and 3.9 million landlines in the Americas. By the end of March 2011, it had 231 million wireless subscribers, 13.6 million broadband accesses, 28.7 million landlines and 10.8 million PayTV clients, for a total of 284 million accesses.

Today, América Móvil has a presence in the following countries: Argentina, Brazil, Chile, Colombia, the Dominican Republic, Ecuador, El Salvador, Guatemala, Honduras, Jamaica, Nicaragua, Paraguay, Peru, Puerto Rico, Uruguay, the United States and Mexico.

América Móvil is a very good example of creating value for investors. Slim pioneered the prepaid system in 1996 and accelerated the development of another scheme that he was already working on. The "Hot Bill" service, which gave rise to the prepaid system Amigo de Telcel in April 1996, a solution that revolutionized the Mexican, Latin American and world market.

Telmex Internacional

The year 2007 was a milestone in the history of Telmex. On December 21, the General Assembly of Shareholders approved the strategic initiative to reorganize the corporate structure of Telmex into two independent companies. Telmex spun off its operations in Latin America and the Yellow Pages business. The new company was named Telmex Internacional.

With the split, it is expected:

1. To give each company in Mexico and abroad more efficient operation and adequate size, so that each operates autonomously in its administrative, commercial and financial sphere;

2. To improve the competitive position of each of the companies;

3. To expand the Telmex operation even more in the Mexican market of telecommunications, making the difference clear between their operations in the markets of medium and high income, where there is competition in low-income and rural areas, and where there is no competition; and,

4. Telmex International will operate in Argentina, Brazil, Chile, Colombia, Ecuador, Peru and Uruguay, offering a complete support structure for local and regional

opportunity and responds efficiently to customer requirements. It also operates in the United States and Mexico through the Yellow Pages.

5. On June 10, 2008, the price of Telmex Internacional was initiated on the International Stock Exchange in New York, Madrid and Mexico.

IDEAL

One of today's challenges is to encourage the development of Latin America and fight against its lag through the training and development of human and physical capital. This can be accomplished through a company like Impulsora del Desarrollo y el Empleo en América Latina (IDEAL), which is engaged in the development of physical capital, acting primarily toward cost-effective investments as well as supporting training and development of human capital not-for-profit.

Currently, Grupo Carso is divided into the following holdings:

1. Carso Global Telecom holds the majority of the share control of Telmex and Telmex Internacional.

2. América Móvil, a leading provider of wireless services in Latin America and abroad.

3. Grupo Carso has operations in commercial areas of industrial services and consumer goods through CICSA, Condumex, Nacobre, Frisco, Sears, Sanborns, Ostar Grupo Hotelero, and Promotora Musical.

4. Grupo Financiero Inbursa includes Inbursa Bank, Seguros Inbursa, Casa de Bolsa Inversora Bursátil, Afore Inbursa and Operadora Inbursa, among others.

Fostering Development and Employment in Latin America (IDEAL) is a company focused on identification, feasibility studies, financial structuring of projects, and the implementation and operation of long-term infrastructure. IDEAL does not take construction risks and is organized to generate physical and human capital through the development of roads, ports, generation and distribution of energy, processing, collection and distribution of water, among others activities. The infrastructure firm is also working on a project to develop a shopping center, schools and a hospital in Mexico City. Many of these large projects are carried out through Carso Infrastructure and Construction.

Carlos Slim with Brazil ex president Luiz Inácio "Lula" da Silva

THE CONQUEROR
Futurist of Globalization

If the English author Daniel Defoe had known Carlos Slim, he would not have written the novel *Robinson Crusoe*. Slim's ancestors came from the Middle East region that is known as the cradle of human civilization. It was in this region that "metal money" first appeared between 3,000 and 2,500 BCE, when the Mesopotamians began to use ingots of precious metals as legal tender, replacing barley. Later, its use spread to Egypt and Babylon in the surrounding parts of the Middle East. In the seventh century, Greece began the minting of coins to replace the weight of precious metals. Paper money is a Chinese invention and we have been aware of its existence since the ninth century. Before the invention of printing, the Venetian explorer Marco Polo was amazed to discover that the Mongols had replaced the use of precious metals with paper. In his book *The Travels of Marco Polo*, also known as *The Book of Wonders* or *Million*, he wrote that perhaps they had discovered the philosopher's stone with this invention.

As many have marveled at these stories, many others around the world have been impacted by the Slim's career; some believing he is a modern sorcerer or King Midas because everything he touches turns to gold.

The success of Slim's business has left many wondering. His foray in several countries has caused a stir. In the last decade, his companies have invested sixty million dollars worldwide. According to World Bank figures, Slim's business groups have made the most investments on the planet in the last ten years. These investments have had a direct effect on the economy and the domestic markets of Mexico and sixteen other countries. These resources have been directed to various areas such as telecommunications, industrial and commercial conglomerates of Grupo Carso, the construction of roads, oil platforms and undersea cables as well as their participation in the launch of the satellite Starone.

Journalists in South America have been stunned by the Mexican tycoon's fortune. The Argentines have written that Slim's money could upholster the whole of his country fourteen times over if covered with dollar bills. The Chileans have gone further: with Slim's personal fortune, they say, they could build bridges with dollar bills or make thirty round-trips to the moon. The truth is that his empire has spread like the Big Bang.

Shakespeare wrote that money guarantees friends and neutralizes enemies. Slim has been very clear that his money has been a tool of power. His money holds influence and power over others.

Although it has been argued that political entrepreneurs have no right of veto, Slim and some of his peers have described how his voice can be used to assert himself. His economic power has given him a very special aura. Many see him as a financial guru; a business leader who believes that money can solve everything.

In Mexico, some entrepreneurs have taken advantage of loopholes in the financial and political system to enhance their business. Slim argues that, in his case, this is false even during the Salinas de Gotari government, from whom he was accused of receiving favors. He has always rejected political ties, but he came to recognize that presidential campaigns do provide some resources.

In any case, Slim made a discretionary use of economic power under the rules of the system.

He boasts of his ability to swim against the current and affirms that this is how he built his empire. In the nineties, he was declared the richest man in Mexico and throughout Latin America. He argues, "The best business for an entrepreneur is that poverty should not exist." However, he has been criticized for having made his fortune in a poor country, where five percent of the population accounts for over sixty percent of the wealth. On the other hand, people admire him because he has shown that one is able to create an empire from Mexico.

His business is top-ranked and brings in the highest incomes; he tops the list of the main generators of employment (Telmex, Grupo Carso, América Móvil and Inbursa employ 250,000 people); his assets, together with the hundred leading businessmen, are equivalent to sixty percent of the GDP; he is on top of his group of businesses controlling a little over thirty percent of the Mexican stock market and contributing over US$10 billion to the treasury annually.

In 1997, *Time* magazine's Global Corporate Reporting identified Slim (along with the Brazilian entrepreneur María Silvia Bastos Marques) as the only Latin Americans among a dozen "key players" of globalization in the world of business. *Time* has often praised Slim for his decision "not to shrink" in front of the big US corporations and to challenge the giants of communication in the United States like AT&T and MCI in his own playing field.

Since appearing on the international list of *Forbes* magazine, Slim has stayed within the group of the world's richest. His fortune was estimated in 2001 at US$10.8 billion and in 2007, he reached the top of the *Forbes* list when he was attributed to be worth around US$60 billion. The magazine has kept him in the top three of the ten richest people on the planet until he became the richest man in the world in March 2011.

In November 1999, the newspaper *Reforma* put Slim at the head of the top twenty most influential men in Mexico of the twentieth century. The list included business leaders, economic advisers, academics and journalists specializing in economics and business. Specialists elected the magnate of Lebanese descent above the likes of Treasury Secretary for Porfirio Díaz; José Yves Limantour; Manuel Espinosa Iglesias, founder of Bancomer; Emilio Azcárraga Vidaurreta, founder of Mexican radio and television; Manuel Gómez Morin, director of the Bank of Mexico, and founder and ideologist of the National Action Party and chancellor of the UNAM; Alberto J. Pani, founder of the Bank of Mexico; Rodrigo Gómez, banker who was deputy director of the International Monetary Fund and director of the Bank of Mexico; Eugenio Garza Sada, a prominent businessman from Monterrey, and founder of Monterrey Technology; Jesús Silva Herzog, an economist and historian, and founder of the National School of Economics and professor emeritus at the UNAM; and others like the banker Antonio Ortiz Mena, the creator of the Mexican Miracle or stabilizing development.

Unlike *Forbes* who called Slim "the Conqueror" for his growing business empire, *Business Week,* the influential Wall Street magazine, wrote a critical portrait of the man who stood in the "protected plutocracy" of the Salinas government. The Salinas government, meanwhile, was identified as responsible for putting a real "gold mine" in the hands of a billionaire by giving him ownership of 5.16 percent of Teléfonos de México and its operational control.

Business Week editors spoke of the rewards Slim made from his supposed friend Salinas. "Rumors and allegations of cronyism hover around the privatization process. In response, the government is doing everything possible to create an impression of impartiality," they reported. "For example, in the cabinet meeting that decided who the new owners of Telmex would be, the three bidders were named A, B and C. But everyone knew who was who."

Slim benefited from the stock market boom in the eighties and increased his fortune in the nineties. He acquired six percent of his Televisa shares, the leading Spanish-language television network in the world, and invested in telecommunications companies in South America and the United States, consolidating his empire with interests in telecommunications, mining, and the financial sector.

A powerful and calculated mind, he is considered among the top men of power and money due primarily to his charismatic personality. He became a modern King Midas because of his incredible ability to consistently sniff out money during the worst economic crises in the last five decades.

As Bill Gates' associate, one the world's richest men, Slim has on his side two of the most renowned futurists: Alvin Toffler and Nicholas Negroponte.

Author of *Changes in Power* and other works such as *Future Shock* and *The Third Wave*, Toffler began to venture hypotheses in the eighties that no academic would dare to consider and that men with a sense of the future such as Slim know how to decipher.

As the driving point of his dissertation, Toffler adopted the idea of knowledge about information, super-symbolic language as he calls it, and developed *The*sis that has effectively created change in economies. This model has a large capacity for adaptation and generation of newness, replacing an open economy in collapse with another under construction.

For business futurists like Slim, ways of making wealth are totally dependent on the communication and dissemination of data, ideas, symbols and symbolism. Although, to avoid monopolization of growth in this super-symbolic economy, and in order to socialize, democratize and generate a general well-being, and new ways of life, social and political intelligence are required.

The management of these high technologies makes it so the production process is being taken over by small businesses that are more flexible and agile.

In the field of production, the need to bring down inventory and reduce financing costs, insurance and storage has pushed suppliers to meet the "right now," therefore forcing them to develop and prepare their final product for what may dictate a two or three month turnaround time.

The organization of a firm changes due to continuous learning, unlearning and re-learning. An environment where the knowledge of consumer change is the most valuable, the feedback of preferred lifestyles offers information and insight to the production chains in the market.

In this generating revolution, a new economy and new policies recognize the value of ideas.

In the twenty-first century, the source of economic prosperity and power is found in the production of new goods and services, scientific research and technological development of human resources, specialized software, advanced communications, organization and flexibility specialties, e-finance, knowledge and information.

The merger of the media was a feature in those years. Ubiquity and the interaction with the viewer are the great gifts of the media. Connecting the PC to a phone or television is a novelty that has great potential.

This new heterogeneous and innovation-oriented society advocates freedom of expression in its amazing intellectual partnership between managers, communicators and industry: the coalition of interests ensures the intellectual and economic progress of the new era.

To meet these challenges with foresight, Slim has used the advice of futurists. In *Future Shock*, Toffler discusses the process of change and how it affects people and organizations. *The Third Wave* focuses on the approach of change while *The Change of Power* addresses the control of changes that must occur: who will shape them and how.

Toffler's central argument is that humanity faces a profound social change. Humans face a future that is quickly approaching and for which neither they nor institutions are sufficiently prepared. In the pages of *Future Shock*, he systematically explores the effects of accelerating change that is affecting humanity, which came from the late-second millennium. The main issue he discusses is not only the process of change itself, but it is the acceleration of this change that brings on de-structuring and makes it difficult for the individual to assimilate.

For Slim, the future is already here. Globalization is not an alternative but a reality and it is communication that implements globalization. The tycoon has also reached out to Nicholas Negroponte, architect and professor of media technology who founded the Media Lab at the Massachusetts Institute of Technology in 1985.

In early 2000, Walter Bender, director of the Media Lab, worked on a project for the Carso Group, whose main objectives were research and development of new information technologies appropriate for Latin America as well as the training of specialists for the development and transfer of digital literacy.

In this context, Slim and Bill Gates have joined forces to launch a telecommunications program in Spanish through MSN T1 (today Prodigy) to dominate the Latin American market as the beginning of an empire that now extends to Europe and the US Prodigy was later acquired by Slim, making his telecommunications company the largest ISP in Mexico and one of the largest in the United States.

Toffler is one of the world most inspiring celebrities, even getting the attention of the controversial British actor Orson Wells who created a film based on his book *Future Shock*. Toffler was a renowned journalist who served as a White House correspondent. He was also a civil rights activist and fighter. He discovered Marxism and served as an industrial worker, emerging as a fierce political activist, and then moved on to become a respected essayist, writing on social and technological issues.

The author of a vast work on the process of changing humanity, he has spared no praise for Slim. In 2008, he wrote this glowing piece for *Time* magazine's Top 100:

> *No one needs to be convinced of Slim's business acumen. But less known are his intellectual interests, ranging from the origins of our planet to contemporary literature. Sharing dinner with him, my wife Heidi and I have also been face to face with writers like Gabriel García Márquez and Carlos Fuentes. We might discuss our most recent book with him or ask about the future of the cell-phone industry or the role of remittances in the Mexican economy.*
>
> *Once during a weekend visit to his beach house, Heidi woke up very early and went to the kitchen to get some coffee. Carlos was already sitting at the table, reading what looked like a school notebook. "I've been up for two hours writing," he said. "I like to stay in bed. [I] think and write in my notebooks." He had sketched out detailed ideas for remodeling a slum neighborhood in Mexico City, which would involve building low-cost housing, schools and a community hospital. All but unknown are Carlos's contributions to infants in need of highly specialized surgery, to young people seeking higher education and to adults in Mexico's equivalent of what amounts to debtor's prison.*
>
> *Although he has been harshly criticized for his wealth, Carlos , 68, belies simplistic characterization. Even a super billionaire can love and honor his spouse, treat women with respect, pursue wide-ranging intellectual interests and, in his own quiet way, support social reform.*

Slim's vision of the challenges Latin America faces in the emergence of the new civilization was exhibited in 2007 at a seminar in Punta del Este, Uruguay, where he addressed the businessman's role. The following is the text presented by Slim:

I would like to offer on this occasion some ideas that can define the present and give us some insight for the future; and also understand the deep crises we have been through in the twentieth century, and those we will face in the twenty-first century.

As we all know, 10,000 years after the ice age was over and civilization started, the first societies were agricultural, with very clear paradigms. Some of them still survive now, but in general they were displaced in the nineteenth century, mostly by industrial societies in countries that are now developed. In the last fifty years, these societies have turned into technological, knowledge or digital societies. To make it simple, we could say that the agricultural society was primary; the industrial society was secondary and the technological or service society would be tertiary.

In this society, most of the population provides a service, which generates an important change in the society as a whole. Obviously, this new society has far different paradigms from those of the agricultural society.

This change was provoked undoubtedly by the technological advancement, which derives a change in productivity and totally transforms society by simplifying the production of goods and services, mostly goods.

The agricultural society ended in the eighteenth century as the steam engine appeared. The most significant manifestations of change were seen in transportation (the railway engine, sailing) and in machinery, both industrial and heavy production (tow trucks, tractors), which increased productivity and quickly transformed society. That was the first stage in the industrial society.

A second stage started by the end of the nineteenth century and early on in the twentieth, with the internal combustion engine and electricity. That was the modernization of the industrial society that took place in the twentieth century and totally transformed it.

If we observe the agricultural societies, we clearly see their characteristics, very different paradigms from those in modern societies, among which we can mention little social mobility and class division. The authority is monolithic and political power is integrated with religious, economic and military power. It is not coincidental that the Egyptian Pharaoh descends from divinity as well as the Mexican Tlatoani and the Japanese emperor.

It also happened in the colonies. The social immobility prevailed for the need to have the people working in specific areas, or to implement the monarch's decisions, laws or edicts.

That was the reason for slavery: servants were inherent to the agricultural society.

The agricultural society is also a society in which the economy is, in general, a zero-sum economy. They have to work a lot, produce the most and consume the least. The printing machine, then, had limited effects because people did not know how to read. I think that until the seventeenth century or even later in the nineteenth, just a few could read or write. Some of the main characteristics of that society included the land, the servants, the tributaries, and the conquest wars. The military force for defense or to conquer was very important. It is curious, but as great disadvantages as this situation may have had, it was also ethnically helpful to keep a relation between people at great distances, because as you know, one or two hundred years ago, people were born, lived and died in the same place.

There are great transformations during this period, great technological advances (from the wind mill, the plow, and the wheel, which was used in a very significant way, except in America where there were no traction animals). Bronze was found and then steel, which were both great technological changes. At the time, the business part was very limited and it was centered in the formation of certain middle classes, generally in commerce.

By these years also, thousands of years ago, globalization started mainly in the Mediterranean with navigation. By then, what provoked globalization were the communications (now telecommunications). The Phoenicians globalized all over the Mediterranean not only with the commercial activity, but also with a cultural change. The business activities were limited, the economic force was concentrated, and there were important commercial activities (for example, the silk route, the Mediterranean commerce) and of course, the beginning of banking and a different type of economic activities. But power was monolithic and what they sought was power through conquest, looting, and slavery, gaining territories and demanding tributes. Sovereignty is later defined with some characteristics that are different today. What used to be military wars now are economic wars, competition for markets. In a certain way, it has been mentioned here in passing, the modern armies are the cross-border companies, the economic activities of the countries. The present sovereignty is then basically culture and market.

This has provoked many changes. The industrial society already has other paradigms. In the modern industrial society of the twentieth century, there are many advances in productivity and technology. The great transformation comes also during the twentieth century with the new knowledge society, which is also called the service society. When this society globalizes, it is integrated as a result of switching the horse and the sailboat or the train and steamboat, to the speed of sound and light, which makes our world smaller and form a very important part of it. But the paradigms of this new civilization are different and started showing since the eighteenth century with the French Revolution. They were stronger in the nineteenth and in the twentieth where they were established.

Now, which are the new paradigms for this new civilization? This civilization is a product of a radical change in which the people are no longer dedicated to produce primary goods, not even secondary, only tertiary. In fact, I think it is the change in the relation of exchange terms. In the industrial society the exchange terms for primary products were lowered. In this society, the exchange terms are lowered for industrial products. However, primary products started improving because of the population growth, which started participating in the modern economy, while stopping self-consumption, which is mostly the case in China, Asia in general. India is as well in a very important manner; a little less and hopefully soon in a significant way, through the incorporation of the population that was sidelined to the modern economy of Latin America.

So, I think these new paradigms are very clear and make reference to democracy, power division, freedom, human rights, environment, plurality, diversity and in matter of economy they make reference to concepts like competition, productivity, innovation, technology.

Globalization, in my opinion, is simply a feature of this new society. It is not the change and it is not the paradigm.

I differ a little from what Espinosa Iglesias said that we need total openness. I think we need to be open but in an intelligent way, just as China has done, or like Brazil is doing. But each country is different, a country with two million people has to be very open; a country with one billion can be more closed but without losing the advantages of openness, globalization and technology.

What is very sad is that the civilizing changes have not been well conducted by the ruling authorities, the politicians and by all of us.

Today, education is essential—quality education, middle and superior education. We are behind in this regard and we have to work hard on it as soon as possible.

In the twentieth century there was a change in society in which fear of change, ignorance of change, and not knowing how to conduct it provoked both world crises and wars, as well as political and economic social experiments, which may be as bad as world wars that led to many hundreds of millions of people living in all types of dismaying conditions for many years because of the lack of possibilities to progress in life.

*But this new civilization, in contrast to the agricultural, which was a zero sum civilization, is developed and sustained in everybody's welfare. This means that everybody is interested in others wellbeing, forming part of the economy, the market, having time and being able to buy services, goods, etc. For that reason, the best investment is to fight poverty. It is no longer just an ethical or moral problem or a social justice problem. It is an economic need. Developed countries have done it because they have been incorporating better-remunerated activities to its population, thus a larger purchasing power. I have no doubt that poverty has been seized in the wrong way. In the agricultural society, charity, donations and health care were reasonable. Nowadays, charity, welfare and social plans help a little, but poverty is only reduced with health, education and jobs. **The solution to poverty is not charity, welfare or free food.** Education and health are very important and they should be of high* *quality and public so that the people can grow in them and gain great social mobility, which is one of the paradigms of this new society.*

What we need for sure is health, education and jobs. Now, the government can open positions to work at their offices, or maybe have large armies, can make aggressive programs and maintain social order, but at the end, jobs are what we need and jobs are given by employers and usually they are businessmen. And those who grant more jobs are small and medium businesses and those that have intensive manpower force.

So, it is very important that the governments create an adequate climate for business development. As much as infant mortality has decreased, let's reduce business mortality, especially for really small businesses. That can be achieved with less regulation or no regulation at all so that there are no impediments for them to develop and get the financial resources to operate.

I think that even the Chinese proverb about "not to give a fish to a man, but to teach him to fish" is then obsolete. To teach to fish will keep them in a self-consuming situation; they are going to eat fish for a lifetime. We need to teach them to trade or commercialize that fish. That is when social changes come. When a community was born, lived and died in the same place, self-consuming was fine. Today, all this has changed very significantly.

I would like to finish by establishing that today, the businessman's role goes beyond investment, reinvestment or traditional business activity, tax payment and personnel training, but that the businessman's role is different from the role of the business itself.

Further than the traditional characteristics, businessmen must change their activities beyond the business responsibility; a social activity that contributes to the reduction of backwardness. In other countries, there have been jealous politicians who do not like that the businessmen come near or enter those fields. I believe that is in the past. In the last years, I have noticed a greater openness for a more participative civil society and the performance of the businessmen is very important. I think that when we businessmen manage our resources effectively, we can make with one coin what others make with two, we can provide strong leadership within organizations, we can offer a long-term vision, knowledge, and strategy, as well as the ability to operate things effectively. This type of management will reverse backwardness, meaning a lack of progression especially in job generation, education and health.

When progress is stalled, there is an opportunity for investment, jobs and growth. We do not need to invent warm water; we only have to look at what all other developed countries have done, which is having economic activity, creating human capital, and creating physical capital. The development and formation of human and physical capital is essential to any country, even in agricultural societies. There is no country that has been developed and did not have big constructions, infrastructure, and formation of human capital, even for war as well as for other issues of lesser importance. Also, we need to do what others have already done, what has been done in China and India. What these countries have done is remarkable, even though it gets us a little envious, because Latin America has taken twenty-five years since the '82 crisis to develop new, proper economic models. David Ibar calls it "stabilizing standstill." We need another thing: development plans, economic activity and as Felipe González said, "not to confuse instruments with objectives."

The objective is not a well-balanced macro-economy or a fiscal deficit; that is an instrument, conditions that are necessary but not sufficient. We need to make clear which are the objectives. We have seen Spain, which is the best example in the last twenty years. Under Felipe Gonzalez, the GDP growth rate grew from .02 percent to 5.5 percent in six years. And it has been in just one generation. We don't need to sacrifice one to get the other. On the contrary, it is not by sacrificing, but by incorporating most part of the population to the modern society, welfare, economy and high-level jobs, just as China is doing with forty million people every year.

I think China already reached the critical mass; they are educating their people and they already have high technology, which is very important. In our country, Mexico grew 6.2 percent during fifty years because it passed from being an agricultural and rural society to an industrial and urban society. Today, China is passing from being a very primitive, from a thousand years of being an agricultural and rural society, to a society not only industrial and urban, but a high technology society, a knowledge society, a highly modernized advanced society, in an accelerated process. And while we were growing during fifty years at 6.2 percent back then, they have been growing at ten percent. The Chinese have done it, they have done it also in Singapore and in Korea and they are still doing it. The Germans and Japanese did it to rebuild, and Central Europe is doing it. Spain did it. We have to do it in Latin America.

Very distant from the Chinese experience, Mexico is increasingly incapable of making the leap out of underdevelopment. In early November 2009, in a business summit in Monterrey, Slim directed the spotlight of the media onto the absence of an explanation from the authorities about the depth of the Mexican crisis. The magnate was very specific: "Government and business have to invest more since Mexico has missed four clear chances to get out of underdevelopment."

The first opportunity was in the seventies, with the increase in oil prices. The second in late 1989, when external credit reopened and they couldn't go to the capital and money markets. The third opportunity that was missed was the dynamism of world economies in the late nineties. Finally, the fourth opportunity was when oil prices reached nearly US$150 per barrel after the crisis of 2000. So it was from 2003, when oil prices rose dramatically and terms of trade improved in developing countries, that the economy resumed its expansion.

SMART MONEY
Carso: A Model to Defend

With technocrats coming into power in the eighties, businesses grew in the country. The barons of wealth emulate the characters in the book *Gog*, by Giovanni Papini, author of *Don Quixote of Deception*. In this work, the Florentine author wrote:

This month I bought a Republic. A costly caprice, but one that will not have imitators. It has been a desire of mine for some time and I wanted to liberate myself from it. I figured that owning a country would be something I might like.

The opportunity was good and the matter was settled in a few days. The president was up to his neck in water: his ministry, composed of his clients, was a danger. The Republic's coffers were empty and new taxes would have been the sign of the collapse of the whole clan that was in power, perhaps a revolution. There was already a general who was arming bands of regular people and promising positions and jobs to the first comers.

An American agent who was at the scene told me the Minister of Finance rushed to New York; in days we agreed. I advanced a few million dollars to the Republic, assigned a President and all the ministers and their secretaries and doubled the emoluments received from the State. I have the collateral—without the people knowing—from customs and monopolies.

I'm just the incognito king of a small Republic in disarray, but the ease with which I managed to dominate and the evident interest of all initiates to preserve secrecy makes me think that other nations, perhaps more extensive and important than my Republic, live, without realizing it, in a similar unit of foreign sovereigns. Still needing more money for my acquisition, instead of a single owner as in my case, I will try trusts - a syndicate of businesses, a small group of capitalists or bankers.

But I have grounds to believe that other countries are run by small committees of invisible kings, known only by their trusted men, who naturally continue reciting the legitimate role of chiefs.

In a very similar fashion, on May 28, 1984, two days before he was killed, the journalist Manuel Buendía wrote about the creation of a company incorporated under the acronym LESA of C. V. (Libre Empresa S.A. de C.V.)[29] in his column for the *Red Privada*. It would be headed by Emilio "The Tiger" Azcárraga and other conspicuous representatives of the Mexican plutocracy who had been named in it, including billionaire Carlos Slim Helú, Roberto Servitje, Abel Vázquez Raña, Antonio del Valle, Antonio Madero, Xavier Autrey, José Luis Ballesteros, and Juan Diego Gutiérrez Cortina, among others. They would buy all the government enterprises and create an anonymous society for it, with capital formed with an initial contribution of MX$25 million from each of its members.

Encouraged by the neo-liberal policies of Miguel de la Madrid, entrepreneurs everywhere sought to acquire all public sector enterprises controlled by the state. LESA was a sign that he had private investors.

During the cycle of technocrats in power (Miguel de la Madrid, Salinas de Gortari and Ernesto Zedillo), the largest privatization process in the history of the country took place.

Among waste and political interests, MX$10 billion was allocated to the Solidarity Program. A total of MX$35 billion was raised from the sale of public sector enterprises and financial institutions, as stated in a report from the specialist firm White and Case (Wac). During the period of 1982 to 2000, the government sold 75,000 state enterprises and banks.

For some analysts, this policy served to contribute to the improvement of the economy and financial and social investments. From the perception of the trade publication *Tribune Desfosses*, "For the Mexican government, privatizations were a crucial axis of its policy of economic restructuring (which ended the fight against inflation) and external debt reduction."

During the Salinas administration, the largest number of privatizations occurred, which in financial terms was equivalent to eighty-nine percent of International Reserves of the Bank of Mexico.

The extraordinary income obtained through the process of divestiture of non-strategic public entities or of priority, including those derived from the liquidation of the FICORCA (Trust for Hedge Funds), was more than MX$30 billion.

These resources helped to strengthen the country's financial assets. The income generated from the sale of companies and banks allowed the government to avoid wasting the Bank of Mexico's reserves.

With the privatization that took place in these six years, the process of concentration and capitalization of financial groups accelerated. The number of industrial and commercial groups grew significantly as well as "financial groups" composed of a majority of banks, brokerage firms, insurance, bonding, money exchange, and stock market trading. Of these, only six financial groups came to control eighty percent of the country's financial assets. These groups also established economic ties with the ten most powerful industrial and commercial groups, which by the mid-eighties were already concentrated to about sixty percent of the loan awarded nationally and ninety percent of international financial flows.

All of this was possible thanks to the takeoff achieved during the administration of De la Madrid. Under his leadership, the government injected a stream of funding channeled by the bank into the economy and multiplied the private sector.

Entrepreneurs resurfaced, as did the privileged elite thanks to economic and financial reforms promoted by the government. This shift radically changed the economic conditions in the country.

Later, in the administration of President Carlos Salinas de Gortari, the corporate sector was consolidated, leading to a true plutocracy.

The Salinas reform ensured that shareholders maintained control of their capital, even with investments as small as 5.16 percent. With Telmex, Grupo Carso won fifty-one percent of the vote. In the case of financial groups, they assumed control of investment banking institutions from five to twenty percent, on top of achieving an international scale by strategically partnering with foreign capital.

Government support was crucial for entrepreneurs. Thanks to the new economic policy on debt, business groups arranged special support through financial subsidies to big business consortiums by the FICORCA or were acquired by the state. Meanwhile, public sectors with severe financial problems were reorganized and then privatized. This trend continued with the governments of Ernesto Zedillo and Vicente Fox, excelling in the latter case due in part to the expropriation of sugar mills.

In Mexico, the elites of power and money have a basic agreement that guides economic policy. As a consequence however, businessmen did not accept the policies of the government and politicians. The government meanwhile demonized the entrepreneurs by deeming them disloyal to the country.

The period of greatest tension came in the government of President Luis Echeverría when a more open political activism arose on the part of employers. The most explosive case happened with the bank expropriation during the government of President José López Portillo. Until then, social balance was the main problem faced by the government, arising from the Mexican Revolution.

Beginning under President Miguel de la Madrid, international economic changes started to add up while internal economic changes promoted by the new governance group led to a national financial oligarchy. The oligarchy had direct involvement in decisions about economic policy that effectively changed the direction of the nation.

During the government of de la Madrid, there was a major shift in national life and the governance of the country. With the new government, the rules of the game changed and the pattern of economic policy consisted of postponing social engagements. The reorganization went deep and the state was subjected to a rigorous diet to shed some weight, starting with the re-privatization of banks and the sale of public sectors. For businessmen, this new economic project in the country was almost paradise. With the change, the privileged benefited at the expense of the rest of the population.

During the administration of President Carlos Salinas de Gortari, economic transformation of the country responded exclusively to integration in the US economy, leading inexorably to Mexico's absolute dependence. In his six-year administration, President Ernesto Zedillo continued this policy but sought new markets for increased economic viability of this new model in order to attach it to the trends of the global economy.

Prior to the expropriation of the banks, four brokerage firms controlled forty percent of the shares traded on the Mexican Stock Market. And before the 1987 boom, they controlled 65.4 percent of the shares until the bubble burst, leading to the historic collapse of the exchange in autumn of that year. According to experts, it stemmed from the speculation of thousands of inexperienced investors who were attracted to the illusion of strong returns. Within days, the Mexican Stock Market lost MX$35 billion (US$2,792,164,973.39). That figure represented twice the amount for payment of annual interest on debt, or a quarter of the value of production in the country. It also represented the equivalent of oil exports for one year. However, in a more general environment, those who profited from trading were the owners of brokerage houses. They were also the owners of major companies listed on the Mexican Stock Exchange and resorted to the commercial financing through the issuing of shares, bonds and commercial paper in an amount equivalent to fifteen percent of all lending by commercial banks in that year.

During this period of transformation, various business groups emerged such as those belonging to Slim. They were able to decipher the codes of the economic project of technocrats. The tycoon attributes the origin of his empire to common sense, or knowing how to buy during a crisis.

For example, even before the eighties, Slim already controlled a consolidated industry and one of the nation's largest enterprises, though not as a magnate with a dynasty like those of Garza Sada or Azcárraga. At the time, he had a high percentage of Cigatam (seventy percent), Mexico's largest cigar company, which he had acquired in the midst of the six-year Lopez Portillo economic crisis; a time when the big businessmen had overtaken the country's capital.

During the "lost decade" of the eighties (from 1981 and 1986), Slim knew how to seize the moment amidst the crisis and started buying up companies. In doing so, he fully repeated historical cycles by great investment masters like Paul Getty and the investor Warren Buffett to amass great fortune.

For Slim, the difference between an investor and a speculator is very clear. In his view, "The investor seeks to do business when it conveniences him, and the speculator makes a shorter term investment, like a sort of financial Rambo." In Slim's practice, he was able to take advantage of his ability to sniff out major investments, even during a time of crisis.

During the crisis of the eighties, Slim bought the banker Manuel Espinosa Iglesias's business out of the blue.

In his memoir, *Bancomer, Achievement and Destruction of an Ideal*, Espinosa recounts that he was stripped of his assets by a "business decision" made by President José Lopez Portillo and Miguel de la Madrid. Espinosa Iglesias tells that when the crisis blew up in the hands of Lopez Portillo, in his desperate desire to save his presidency image, he ordered the expropriation of banks:

> *It didn't matter to him to attribute responsibilities to the private bank that he didn't have, nor to destroy the work and reinforcement of many people over many years of work.*
>
> *In my case, as I have said, it was the sum of work of my whole life. Perhaps this is why they stole from me more than anyone else. I cannot yet fully understand how he could let this happen.*

Espinosa did not have a good relationship with De la Madrid. As an ex-banker, he was a nobody. In one excerpt, he notes that he proposed, in a fair and reasonable way:

> *To distinguish money that was the bank's, separate them from businesses and banks; refresh the latter to their original owners and forget the value that the primaries could obtain. Only this was the solution I proposed to Lopez Portillo before his term ended, De la Madrid and his officials refused to recognize its merit and decided to spoil it.*
>
> *As I reflect on the distress and anguish that seized me in those days, I've come to realize that there was another factor that contributed to the worsening thereof: I could not help feeling that the money I had received in compensation was bad money, ill-gotten. How could I enjoy that shareholder capital while hundreds of minor shareholders were worse off*

than me? In that sense, I found myself in a unique position, because unlike other directors who participated in the negotiations, I personally knew the majority of shareholders who were provincial advisors or bank employees. I had a duty to worry about them and defend them, but outside of the proposal I made to López Portillo, and that De la Madrid rejected, I could not do anything else.

The sum of these two emotions—to feel that I could not do anything and that I had in my possession a capital that I didn't have full rights to—led me to sell companies in the group, two to the engineer Carlos Slim, and three to Roberto Hernández. As I wanted to get rid of them, I sold them at the price at which they would buy them. These groups are not comprised only of Bancomer and Bancomer Brokerage Firm, but many other important companies. Given my mood, I sold everything without paying attention to detail. For a couple of years, I only retained companies of the first group, chief among them the mining FRISCO, and made it the starting point to form a major mining group. My efforts, however, were met once again with refusal and rejection.

In effect, Espinosa admits that he had the disaffection of Miguel de la Madrid against him, who had ordered him not to sell any mines. Espinosa Iglesias recounts, "Slim was once again the buyer of FRISCO, who besides being the owner of the brokerage firm Inbursa, also owned Cigatam and in turn Marlboro and some shares of Sanborns. By then, he also owned other companies I had sold him. Slim is an extraordinarily capable businessman, and I am very pleased that at least part of what I sought to do with my work ended up in the hands of a capable man."

The acquisition of companies of what was once the emporium of Espinosa was consolidated by Grupo Carso as a giant project undertaken by the mega-rich Slim.

The old guard of the business community had somehow been learning from Slim, who raised his fortune immeasurably since the nineties. The richest man in Mexico, he had begun to build his great capital in the stock market boom of the eighties. So, while many of the industrial families were entrenched in the crisis and had to restructure their debt and sell their shares when the market was down, Slim devoured cheap companies and established his control.

The creation of the Grupo Industrial Carso is linked to the brokerage firm Inbursa, founded in 1965, which over the years became a pillar of Grupo Financiero Inbursa under the direction of its largest shareholder, Carlos Slim Helú.

Grupo Carso is a piecemeal conglomerate that was formed by amassing like companies. For instance, Cigarros la Tabacalera Mexicana is dedicated to the manufacturing and sales of cigarettes and boasts the highest consumption of such products in the country. It includes brands like Marlboro, Benson & Hedges, Baronet, Commander, Dalton, Elegant, Delicate, Faros, Parliaments, Philips Morris, Virginia Slims, Cambridge, Merit, Saratoga, and Sanborns (which operates a chain of more than one hundred full-service shops that combine retail with restaurant and bar). In Marlboro, Slim started with eight percent of the shares. Years later, he sold his tobacco company.

Nacobre Industries, a manufacturer of copper products and alloys (largest in Latin America), covers much of the needs in construction, automotive, refrigeration, electricity, electronics and the power generation industries.

Other subsidiaries of Grupo Carso are Frisco Enterprises, which controls five other miners that extract mainly copper, silver, gold, lead and zinc.

In financial services, Grupo Financiero Inbursa includes Seguros de México Inbursa. In the hotel business, he has Real Turismo, acquired by Cantabria property, which is the group that operates Calinda hotels.

Researcher Carlos Morera Camacho, a specialist in the study of Grupo Carso at UNAM, refers to the consortium as the new financial capital in Mexico. It is closely related to Inbursa since it is the axis of the reunification of churches and former bankers Espinosa and Cosío Ariño, who were the main shareholders of Banamex. Slim has also become an intrinsic part of government support and his strategic partnership with other major capitals, national and abroad.

In other words, referring to Inbursa and Carso is talking about a complex set of new economic relations of production and power that existed prior to the nationalization of banks.

As a conglomerate, Grupo Carso has investments in sectors of the Mexican economy as follows: 24.9 percent in telecommunications (Telmex as a partner); 8.3 percent in mining (Frisco); forty-four percent in the manufacturing industry. The manufacturing industry is further broken down as follows: 7.1 percent in the production of cigars (Cigatam); 36.1 percent in the production of machinery and equipment (Nacobre, 14.4 percent, including 21.75 percent Aluminum Corp., 13.9 percent of Condumex and 7.9 percent of Industrial Llantera, which acquired one hundred percent of the shares of General Tire of Mexico, and 50.1 percent of the Euzkadi Rubber Company). Grupo Carso also invests 1.8 percent in the construction industry (Porcelanite and Cementos Moctezuma, associate company); 11.7 percent in trade sales at stores retail (Sanborns, Denny's, Discolandia, Mixup); 5.5 percent Inmuebles Cantabria (including Club Racqueta de Cuernavaca); and 12.63 percent in financial services (Seguros de México S.A. de C.V.). With the exception of Cementos Moctezuma and Telmex, which is a major Carso partner, all others are part of the Grupo Carso.

Unlike Slim, who has demonstrated a keen insight to enhance his pruned business, the vast majority of employers turned to the support of the Trust for Hedge Funds (FICORCA) created under President Miguel de la Madrid.

Specialist Jorge Basave Kunhardt, author of *Capital Financial Groups in Mexico*, describes how entrepreneurs squeezed FICORCA by forming triangles with State support:

> *The FICORCA program was successful in terms of the objectives for which it was designed, but its economic and social impact can't be evaluated solely on their stronghold. Resources for the federal government to absorb the changes of the exchange rate thereafter increased the private external debt from 1982 (because of a sharp devaluation in 1987, and the downslide of the peso) were obtained with the critical increase of its domestic debt.*

The debt was repaid with high interest rates against the capital invested by individuals and private companies whose cash surpluses were freed from paying their external creditors.

With the expropriation of the banks, it seemed that Mexico had experienced a new division of financial duties between the public and private sector that altered what had persisted for over fifty years. It happened only partially.

There was a level of control ceded to the private sector, which represented a capital growth space that conformed to the new conditions of the crisis. In financials, their returns exceeded considerably against the performance of business production. It became the stock market operated by the brokerage firms. Until then it had been a market virtually underutilized and highly concentrated. But from that moment on, its level of concentration was simultaneously converted into the axis of investing the funds of the Treasury. The release of businesses because of FICORCA, along with the internal finances of the country, became the center hub of political-economic power, which had little concern over the disappearing of a private banking system.

It seems that by giving complete control of the stock market to brokerage firms, the state provided for two possibilities (or a combination of both).

The first was that the surplus of cash that was part of the FICORCA groups. This cash would be directed to productive investment, which also brought with it an increase in tax revenues in the short term.

The second is the investment of these surpluses in Treasury Certificates (Cetes) to cover urgent needs for government funding, among other things, due to the implementation of FICORCA and its own external debt.

The State had high expectations for productive investment hence the initial periods of amortization of FICORCA were planned for six to eight years. By 1986, one year before the crash, the price index and prices had risen 321 percent. That year, four brokerage firms (Acciones y Valores de México, Inverlat, Operadora de Bolsa and Inversora Bursátil, the latter owned by Slim) controlled sixty-five percent of the stock market.

According to Basave Kunhardt's research about the extraordinary profits of these financial clans, he affirms that:

Most of the cash resources of the groups that were invested in the stock market went to money markets, mainly Cetes.

To a lesser extent, they invested in the stock market. In this sense, speculative investments directly by the companies were very small in relative terms. The real advantage of a stock market overvalued by the companies was exploited through the most direct and effective approach, represented by the rise of primary issues in a context of high prices.

The plethora of purely speculative investments should have been placed in the sale of unrealized shares (for capital gain) by entrepreneurs as individuals and by brokerage firms for their own profit. In this regard, it should be added that besides the higher market situation, the growth of inexistent adequate law and controls about the use of confidential information was taken advantage of.

With the support of FICORCA, business groups in Mexico ended up implementing a financial investment strategy that produced huge profits. They then decided to drastically abandon productive investment with the consequent delay in their levels of productivity.

Morera Camacho, author of *Financial Capital in Mexico and the Limits and Contradictions of Globalization*, established that "the creation of FICORCA boosted the stock market and with that, the financial speculation of the major groups, whose purpose was to reorganize the most indebted groups by converting public and private debt and through the implementation of adjustment programs to society as a whole."

Thus, during the early years of FICORCA (1983-1987), Morera Camacho shows the beginning of the internal fortification of Grupo Carso through the acquisition of the brokerage firm Inbursa, the instrument that allowed the appropriation of five of its seven subsidiaries.

One of the most significant indicators in this period was the volume of profits earned by Inbursa. Its strategic position as a broker-dealer allowed it to take over the ownership and control of the issued shares of Frisco, Cigatam, Loreto, Euzkadi, Nacobre and Sanborns, and from there, access to the financial and industrial profits thereof. To understand the magnitude and the significance of this change, it is sufficient to note that in 1987, the value (financial and operational) was around MX$200 billion. Compared with earnings of Inbursa for the same years, presented 41.1 percent of the total profits of all brokerage firms. Among issued shares, Frisco deserves special mention, which had one-and-a-half times the amount of profits and nearly four times the operating profits of Inbursa.

The huge financial investments in this period of MX$2.305 million in contrast to productive investments in the same period, in the order of MX$609 million, paid off huge financial profits. Among the issuers that were expected to excel were Frisco and Cigatam, the first in 1987 when it had MX$290.3 million in financial profit, versus an operating income of MX$75.5 million; Cigatam, meanwhile, stood out in 1986, having gained a financial profit of MX$209.4 million against an operating income of MX$41.1 million. These huge profits allowed them to settle almost all their debts and offset falls in income from operations and considerably expand their scale of activity. The results yielded by the six issuers controlled by Inbursa during this period have been affirmed.

In order to illustrate from a holistic point of view the form assumed by the speculative element in the process of accumulation, it is necessary to explain that the financial gains were not incorporated in the calculation of the integral cost of financing. The surplus in stock, with the rest of the financial gains, price increases and currency exchange can be compared with operating profits.

The results observed between 1984 and 1987, which incorporated the effects of monetary and financial exchange, showed benefits for all the groups. In the relationship between Cigatam and Frisco, the results were positive in 1986 and 1987; for Cigatam, it varied from 2.40 to 5.09 times, and Frisco, in 1986 it ranged from 0.89 to 1.17 times and in 1987 from 2.07 to 3.85 times.

In the cases of Loreto and Peña Pobre, Euzkadi, Nacobre and Sanborns, the relationship was negative, because the financial obligations were greater than financial gain. However, in these cases the inclusion of currency exchange, monetary and speculative, allowed them to reduce the ratio in all years and in all cases, which amounted to Slim contributing until the group diminished its financial operations.

It is under these conditions that the brokerage firm Inbursa acquired Frisco, Citagam, Lypps, Euzkadi, Nacobre and Sanborns to benefit from the extraordinary financial gains obtained in these years, access to credit and the collapse of stock prices by the stock market crash in 1987. Major acquisitions were made possible from 1983 to 1989 because of the economic crises; several companies were acquired from 1974 to 1982. With the exception of Frisco and Sanborns, the groups faced a severe debt. The amount of the latter had grown from four to six times and this was particularly acute in cases like Loreto and Peña Pobre, Euzkadi and Nacobre, whose liabilities in 1950 rose 208 and 57 percent, respectively. As a result of falling sales from 1980, the years 1982 and 1983 suffered heavy losses.

A specialist in financial capital groups in Mexico, Dr. Morera Camacho has been researching the evolution of Grupo Carso for over a decade. He traces it from its formal creation in 1990 with the companies it acquired during the eighties and during the first three years of the nineties when Slim made equity investments of MX$427 million in new pesos (1992)[30]. That year, he bought 5.16 percent of the Class AA shares and five percent of all shares of Telmex, for which he appealed to the funding provided by the federal government (for an amount of MX$426 million, at an interest rate of 10.68 percent, and during a time period of six months).

With the award of the controlling company and the investment of five percent from its main partners, each one of his foreign technologist shareholders, France Cable et Radio and Southwestern Bell International Holding Co., Seguros de México (1.8 percent) and thirty-three Mexican investors to acquire 20.4 percent stake in Telmex (including Carso), represented by Class AA, shares would be awarded fifty-one percent of the votes of the shareholders. The amount for the transaction of sale of the controlling company, 20.4 percent of its capital stock, ascended to MX$734 million in Class AA shares. Of this percent, the shares purchased by domestic investors, equivalent to 10.4 percent of the company, were acquired through funding. Meanwhile, foreign investors bought in cash.

The acquisition of Teléfonos de México was the most important event in the history of the group for several reasons. First, it started with a form of productive investment in the telecommunications sector. This formed a new type of global investment partnership, which continued the new mode of foreign investment in Mexico corresponding to the globalization of the world economy. Second, in the history of the group, the socialization of capital and the centralization of control had never been so openly addressed by the capital management as large as its own and similar to the risk of socialization. Thirdly, in conjunction with the operation, internal oligopolistic market control was guaranteed until August 1996 by not giving any additional allowance for long-distance telephone service.

As for the Mexican financial capital as a whole, the new form of stock ownership and controls established in the country ushered in an unprecedented cycle that links all the forms of that capital (cash, production and sales). From this, the combination of the Carso and

Inbursa groups handled the process and gave rise to the phenomena where they financed seventy percent of the companies they acquired in 1992. In July and August of that year, they purchased Aluminum and Condumex.

But Slim's expansion of his group didn't stop there; in January 1993 he acquired 99.9 percent of General Tire of Mexico, which together with Euzkadi, formed the new subsidiary of the group called Corporación Industrial Llantera. In September of 1993, he authorized the creation of a bank with national coverage, which was integrated into Grupo Financiero Inbursa.

While the origin of Slim's business goes back to the seventies, it was not until the eighties that he became one of the most important financiers and business owners in Mexico. His big development has primarily been the result of the reorganization of groups since 1983.

The Grupo Financiero Inbursa was formally established in October 1992. However, its origins go back to the brokerage firm Inbursa, founded in 1965, and it didn't achieve a notable presence until 1983. Slim acquired insurance and bonding after the nationalization of the banking, and created the bank in 1993. Stockholders' equity of Grupo Financiero Inbursa was invested in Seguros Inbursa, Inversora Bursátil, Pensiones Inbursa, Banco Inbursa, La Guardiana (a general finance company), and Operadoras de Fondo.

How could this change, in less than three decades, have led him to own the most powerful financial capital group in Mexico? What role does the brokerage firm Inbursa and Grupo Financiero Inbursa play in this new power and what link exists between them? What characteristics does this phenomenon have? What was the situation of production and financial structure and modus operandi of the groups of which it consists today? What changes have occurred in connection with ownership and controlling shares in the old public and private groups of financial capital that ten years ago belonged to the old oligarchy and now make up the Grupo Carso and Grupo Financiero Inbursa in the figure of Carlos Slim?

In the development of Slim's companies as a major business group in Mexico, there have been two fundamental periods: 1983 to 1989 and 1990 to 1992. The first has to do with its origin and internal expansion from the brokerage firm Inbursa, which is the instrument that allowed the appropriation of five of its seven subsidiaries. During the second period (1990 to 1992), the conglomerate Carso was directly linked to the privatization of Telmex and the trans-nationalization of the group. As a brokerage firm, Inbursa is linked with the insurance and bonding company, acquired after the nationalization and the formation of Grupo Financiero Inbursa. Subsequently, the lessor and the bank joined his group.

One aspect of this group structured around Inbursa brokerage firm that contrasts with the vast majority of other brokerage firms is the high concentration of the share capital in the hands of one person, Slim himself. From the beginning, Slim has retained the majority stake. In 1986, he owned 61.9 percent of the equity of that brokerage firm. With this capital structure, Slim has been in a position to exercise important decisions since 1983 and has been permitted to energize the patrimonial centralization of this group. In 1991, with the appearance of the brokerage firm as a self-owned company, the situation prevailed in the fundamentals.

Slim began acquiring bankrupt companies in 1976 when he bought Galas de México. This company, a manufacturer of paper products, was restructured after its acquisition to form several companies directly related to the field and materially linked through Grupo Galas de México. The group then became a subsidiary of the brokerage firm house Inversora Bursátil. To increase their own capital, they issued shares of their various companies. Later, the group merged with others and acquired Artes Gráficas Unidas.

Another one of Slim's companies is Inver Corporación, S.A. of C.V., established to further the privatization of railways, petrochemicals and electricity.

During 1983 to 1986, Grupo Carso acquired the following companies: Fábrica de Papel Loreto y Peña Pobre, Hulera Euzkadi, Sanborns, Industria Nacobre and Compañía Minera Frisco.

Slim's inventory soared in the eighties, strongly positioning him in the manufacturing, mining, trade and services sectors. The group's great leap was made with the acquisition of Teléfonos de México. This was a highly sophisticated financial operation with the basis of strategic alliances with foreign and Mexican shareholders.

Slim's power has overtaken the country's borders. The tycoon is one of the few Mexicans who are part of the board of the multinational company Southwestern Bell, which is associated with Telmex. Slim was also invited to join the board of the multinational Philip Morris Corporation.

On the strength of immeasurable economic power, Slim heads up the twenty biggest proprietary families that own the major financial groups in Mexico and has decided to expand his empire to other latitudes. Among his purchases in recent years, he gained the Prodigy (MSN T1) in the US along with Bill Gates; Microsoft and SBC Communication (in partnership with Telmex); he bought one hundred percent of the chain store CompUSA; he acquired sixty percent of the shares of Conecel, a mobile phone company in Ecuador; in partnership with Bell Canada, he bought forty percent of the shares of the cellular company Techtel in Argentina, and Telmex was listed on the Labitex European market. Slim and Gates also raided Apple Computers; the Mexican businessman bought three percent of the shares and Gates made an investment of US$150 million.

Based on the projection of Internet users in Latin America and the likelihood that their activity would increase from twenty-two million in 2000 to seventy-seven million in 2005, through MSN T1, Gates and Slim acquired the totality of shares of Yupi.com (the Spanish portal), whose market counts one hundred million subscribers worldwide, for US$50 million dollars.

In New York, the Securities and Exchange Commission reported Slim's investment of US$52.8 million in the purchase of nine percent of the shares of CDnow, an online music store that was facing financial problems.

He also bought 7.5 percent of Office Max, an American chain of materials and office supplies with operations in the US and Japan. He also acquired 12.2 million shares in the New York Stock Exchange, or 5.9 percent of the total value of Circuit City, the second largest chain that sells electronics in the US

To his stock list, he added sixteen percent of the shares acquired from the department store chain Saks, Inc., owner of the legendary store Saks Fifth Avenue.

He had the luxury of recovering Televisa in 1995 from a financial crisis that was threatening to sell part of its capital to foreign investors. Slim, through the bank Inbursa, acquired six percent of the shares with voting rights, shareholding belonging to the Diez Barroso and Miguel Alemán Velasco.

He also controlled forty-nine percent of the shares of Cablevision and sought to sell twenty-five percent of his part to recoup his investment. He began negotiations to acquire forty-nine percent of the network integration company Consorcio Red Uno, a company that supports Telmex in the technological modernization in terms of data communication through Telcel, the largest subsidiary of América Móvil. Telcel operates in eighteen countries and has a list of about two hundred million subscribers, of which less than a third is in Mexico.

América Móvil is also involved with these companies: Dominican Telephone Company, Puerto Rico Telephone Company, PRT Long Distance; Communications Services in Honduras; Tractofone Wireless Inc. (Delaware); Americel; Claro, Telecomunicaciones de Guatemala, AMK Argentina, AMK Paraguay; AM Wireles Uruguay, América Móvil Peru and Panama.

Through Grupo Sanborns, Slim acquired eighty-five percent of the shares of the subsidiary México de Sears Roebuck and Company for US$103 million in cash.

In its report from 2000, *Latin Trade* magazine ranked Telecom Carso Global below the Brazilian oil company Petrobras. Telecom Carso Grupo, major shareholder of Telmex, is the second largest company with sales in Latin America, registering US$13 billion that year.

Many entrepreneurs in the financial sector, which analysts call representatives of Smart Money (those who know where the money is), were destined to benefit from speculation. Three months after Salinas took his mandate, he sent them a clear signal through the Secretary of the Treasury at the time, Guillermo Ortíz Martínez. The secretary reassured the "stock market boys" that, "from today on, we live in another stock market: there is no witch hunt, nor will there ever be. So here is the issue of alleged violations of the Securities Market Act. In this sense, the sheet has been folded."

Years after the Salinas dynasty, beneficiaries finished under the pillory Ernesto Zedillo. The "model" banker, Carlos Cabal Peniche, majority shareholder of Union Bank, was extradited and faced criminal charges for crimes of civil and business fraud for more than US$600 million. The neo-banker Ángel Isidoro Rodríguez "the Divine," former owner of Banpaís, faced charges of tax fraud and patrimonial suffering. When the transportation entrepreneur Roberto Alcántara Rojas failed to manage Bancrecer, the government had to inject about US$11 billion into the bank to rescue him. Banker by descent, Agustín Legorreta Chauvet led Multibanco Comermex to bankruptcy, which became Inverlat and purchased Scotiabank. Jorge Lankenau of Banca Confía and brokerage firm Abaco went from the top to ruins and was jailed for fraud. Adrián Sada González, who presided over Operadora de Bolsa Serfín bank, faced charges of money laundering. Cleaning up his bank cost the Institute for the Protection of Savings Bank US$12 billion. Roberto González Barrera of Banorte also received favors of millions of dollars from Fobaproa. Roberto Hernández, owner of Banamex, was the most favored because the Presidents Salinas, Zedillo and Fox protected him.

The abuse in the handling of privileged information seemed to be second nature for these entrepreneurs, but the CompUSA case brought out a scandal that sparked international outcry.

The influential *Wall Street Journal* revealed that during the first week of May 2001, the US Securities and Exchange Commission (SEC) filed charges involving shares of companies listed on the New York Stock Exchange.

According to the investigation, among the implicated were financial lawyer Alejandro Duclaud González, member of the firm, and Frank, Galicia, Duclaud and Robles, Slim's business consultants.

The defendants in the case allegedly began their negotiations on January 6, 2000, with the purchase of 325,000 shares of CompUSA for US$5.25 each. After, they acquired 546,000 additional shares in two sessions, January 19 and 20, days before the Sanborns Group and CompUSA had grossed nearly US$4 million.

The Duclauds used four offshore companies in the operations to appropriate the money. Those companies involved were Anushka Trust, Caribbean Legal Trust, Antares Holdings Investment Ltd. and Banrise Ltd. BVI.

According to the *Wall Street Journal*, "Allegations of insider trading have long abounded in Mexico, where family groups tend to own ninety percent of the shares of a company listed on the market, but are rarely punished."

The scandal over insider trading also caught the conspicuous Salinista character red-handed along with entrepreneur Claudio X. González, a member of the board of administration for Grupo Carso and ex-advisor on foreign investment for Carlos Salinas de Gortari and Ernesto Zedillo.

The influential New York newspaper said González bought stocks at 0.1 percent in CompUSA, months before Sanborns made a public offer for shares of US computer retailer. The entrepreneur then sold his shares of CompUSA after the company was sold to Sanborns, when the stock had doubled in value.[31]

Carlos Slim with former US President Bill Clinton.

POLITICS AS A HOBBY
Money: The Code of Power

In the Mexican system, politicians and businessmen are part of the same structure and therefore share power. After the expropriation of the banks during the López Portillo government, the moneymen assumed a more active role in terms of politics by entrusting the management of the state to the technocrats. They were also the ones who carried out the thinning of the state economy to spearhead the privatization of enterprises and banks that were in government power. At the basis of the decision to remove banks from the control of entrepreneurs, former President López Portillo said in his autobiography *Mis Tiempos*[32], "My fellow countrymen think I am bad and evil."

Technocrats followed in the footsteps of former US President Lyndon B. Johnson who argued that men of political power should co-opt the moneymen because they are more dangerous than opposition politicians. Johnson said, "It's probably better to have him inside the tent pissing out, than outside the tent pissing in."

The PRI's defeat in the historic elections of July 2, 2000 was the corollary of a complex struggle. On the one hand, the success of businessmen in politics overturned the rules of the game, but on the other hand, the technocrats were the bridge in the displacement of politicians to make way for the plutocratic elite.

Slimemerged as one of the most influential plutocrats in the new political system of the country.

During the Salinas de Gortari administration, Slim emerged as the richest man in Mexico. So, during his presidential campaign,

Luis Donaldo Colosio acknowledged him by inviting him as a special guest from the powerful Lebanese community. Colosio remembers President Adolfo López Mateos as, "the man who marked my life forever," and who wisely used to say, "whoever does not have a Lebanese friend, go find one."

Though he is always associated with Salinas, Slim denies his relationship with the ex-president. During the Salinas government, reporters identified them as Carlos and Charlie.

When the journalist Carlos Acosta Córdova asked Slim if Salinas was a partner, Slim said, "We have no political partners. The Grupo Carso does not, did not, nor will we ever have political partners. That is clear and always will be. My dad never had nor will my children ever have political partners — that is for sure. We have been immunized."

However, Slim and Emilio "the Tiger" Azcárraga Milmo were the two entrepreneurs who Salinas invited along on tours. Both were frequent companions of the leader inside and outside the country and were fully identified by the foreign press as friends of the president.

The privatization of Telmex was in Slim's favor and provoked some politicians to try to stigmatize him as a *Salinista* businessman, even though Slim had shown that he was a pragmatic businessman who adapted to whichever government came to power.

The truth however, is that his career launched in a massive way when his name began to appear on the list of major investors during Miguel de la Madrid's administration.

When de la Madrid named Salinas de Gortari as his successor, an important group of businessmen in 1988 joined the Finance Commission of the PRI.

Slim was one of them. Businessman Ángel Borja Navarrete presided in the committee in which the following employers appeared: Pablo Álvarez Treviño, Antonio Ariza Canadilla, Paul Brener, José Carral, Juan Elek Klein, Augusto Elías Paullada, José González Bailó, Roberto González Barrera, Ricardo González Cornejo, Julio Gutiérrez Trujillo, Antonio Gutiérrez Prieto, Kretschmer Smith, Eduardo Legorreta Chauvet, Antonio Madero Bracho, Enrique Molina Sobrino, Anuar Name Yapar, Peralta Quintero, Enrique Rello Vega, Ernesto Rubio del Cueto, Isaac Saba Rafoul, Fernando Senderos Mestre, Nicolas Zapata Cárdenas, Patricio Zapata Gómez and Slim.

Already in the midst of the presidential campaign, a group of businessmen, convened by Hank González, met at a dinner held in Professor Lomas de Virreyes' mansion to show their support for Salinas.

Halfway through the Salinas administration, the influential magazine *Business Week* caused a political scandal with the publication of a report in the July 22, 1991 issue. It was a description of the business elite in Mexico under the patronage of Salinas.

Then-senator and respected economist Ifigenia Martínez took the matter to the tribunal of the Standing Committee of the Congress to denounce the privileges and favoritism of the President of the Republic in the sale of public sectors.

Portrayals of the money barons appeared in *Business Week*. Among them was Slim:

The old guard of business is learning from Slim, a relative newcomer, who has given a lesson in money management. Like Roberto Hernández, Slim made his fortune in the stock market boom in the eighties. While many industrial families were entrenched attempting to restructure their debt to sell in a down market, Slim devoured cheap companies and established his control with minority shareholding. Slim converted his Grupo Carso into a giant with the financial support and advice of ex-banker millionaire Manuel Espinosa Iglesias.

From his foxhole in the stock market, he expanded by buying copper, tires, insurance, tobacco, packing companies and Sanborns, which consisted of a national chain store.

Astute strategy. However, all properties are small compared to Slim's new jewel, the phone company. In line with Slim's method, the government divided the giant telephone company in minority regulatory shares. That allowed Slim to buy the control with only five percent of the shares, a payment of approximately US$400 million. Along with the aforementioned, he controlled the block of Southwestern and France Telecom, along with investors from the old, rich families in Mexico. Later, the government sold the remaining shares in the Mexican market with a bid of US$2 billion in foreign Stock Markets.

Two years after the scandal caused by the *Business Week* report, *The Economist* made a lot of noise with report of a new episode between Salinas and the moneymen.

The newspaper described the details of a dinner at the home of former Secretary of the Treasury and former president of the Inter-American Bank of Development, Antonio Ortiz Mena. In attendance were the old and nouveau rich, highlighting Slim as the richest man in Mexico and Latin America.

Miguel Alemán Velasco, president of the National Finance Committee of the PRI, was in charge of the meeting promoted by Salinas de Gortari.

Among those in attendance were Lorenzo Zambrano, Adrián Sada, Roberto Hernández Ramírez, Gilberto Borja Navarrete, Jorge Larrea, Diego Gutiérrez Cortina, Bernardo Garza Sada, Manuel Espinosa Iglesias, Antonio del Valle Ruiz, Alberto Bailleres, Jerónimo Arango, Abedrop Dávila, Eloy Ballina, Alonso de Garay, Hank Rhon, Ángel Lozada, Raymundo Flores, Jorge Martínez Güitrón, Claudio X. González, Emilio Azcárraga Milmo, and José Madariaga Lomeli.

This gave Salinas a major ego boost. He said that these were triumphant men who are needed in order to "create and strengthen the assets of the PRI." He requested US$25 million from each one of his guests.

"This was all a mere cover up [to avoid public knowledge of] the diversion of public resources to the PRI," said the businessman Lucas de la Garza Monterrey, an advisor to Cuauhtémoc Cardenas. "I know them very well. They are so stingy they wouldn't even give water to a rooster who crows on Easter[33]."

López Portillo, who refused until the last day in office to reveal the list of famous *sacadólares*[34] alluded to in his sixth and final government report, questioned the attitude of the Salinas government to favor employers.

Any balance of the Salinas government would be truncated without regard. To a large extent, its management rested on the support it had received from the business class, especially a small group of businessmen who benefited from the neo-liberal-political-economic force of the early eighties.

The strategy involved strengthening the cooperation between the Mexican state and capital while seeking support from a fraction of Mexican entrepreneurs linked to transnational economic groups.

This meant carrying out a shift in the pattern of economic development in the country, which would reduce the government's involvement in the economy and continuing the process of privatization of public enterprises while opening the commercial industry to the outside.

The close association between the Salinas group and entrepreneurs linked to its management were the great stock market speculation; management of the country's economy by a few families, and a lot of business fraud.

Eugenio Clariond Reyes from Monterrey, one of the highest ranking representatives of money, acknowledged in a talk to students and also in an article published in the newspaper *El Norte*, how thanks to technocrats, businessmen were able to recover after the expropriation and the structural crisis of the eighties. "Thanks to FICORCA and its director Ernesto Zedillo, we were able to survive," he said. "No one in the political system in our country could seriously ensure the achievement of our economic and fiscal ideals with responsibility like Ernesto Zedillo."

The last year of the Salinas government, the *Forbes* list included twenty-four Mexicans among the worlds richest.

The presidents De la Madrid and Salinas began to open up the Mexican economy and reduce the number of state enterprises from 1,155 to two hundred. They signed Mexico up for the GATT and the Free Trade Agreement, generating more jobs and trade, and put the country in fourth place for billionaires behind the United States, Germany and Japan.

Slim first appeared on the *Forbes* list in 1992 with a capital of US$2.1 billon and then jumped a position in 1994 with a fortune of US$6.6 billion. Since then, Slim has sparked envy and some have thrown darts loaded with suspicion trying to stigmatize him as a mere business *croupier.*

While it didn't bother tycoons like Gilberto Borja Navarrete, Salinas and Claudio X. González to be associated with the twenty or so public and private board of directors, Slim cares very much for his image in that respect.

It is in that way that technocrats were identified and entrepreneurs established themselves as the new power elite.

When Zedillo served a year in office, representatives of the "smart money" showed their appreciation for the economic policy that had been designed especially for them by the previous administration. During a meeting in Los Pinos between thirty of the country's richest businessmen (called the Mexican Council of Businessmen) Claudio X. González, member of the board of directors of Grupo Carso, told President Zedillo, "We would not be risking and investing in our country if we did not believe in its viability, the potential of its domestic and foreign markets, and in all structural, economic, political and social changes that have begun."

Salinas inherited a country in crisis from his successor, which provoked the anger of some entrepreneurs who felt betrayed by the ex-president. They saw their capital at risk with the so-called "December mistake," a situation that provoked the Zedillo government to request an emergency rescue from US and international banks for a total of US$50 billion.

Slim's presence in New York placated the complaints from investors on Wall Street.

Slim's services were requested by the Zedillo government to accompany the officials of the Ministry of Finance seeking to calm the markets and to negotiate emergency aid. The support of the richest man in Mexico and Latin America was vital to President Zedillo.

The tricolor and blue-white presidents have always recognized Slim's power. In the election campaigns of 2000, Slim supported all candidates, including the Friends of Fox. Friends of Fox was funded by MX$18,750,000 that was channeled through the Trust for Development and Democracy, over which, Rojas Magnon presided.

When Senator Carl Levin, from the subcommittee of investigations, questioned the Cuban-American senate, Amy Elliot responded by saying the Salinas family has benefited from an increase in the value of the telephone company. Elliot was a private banker in charge of the accounts of Raúl Salinas de Gortari at Citibank and related to former President Salinas and Slim's associate in Teléfonos de México.

In early November 1999, the executive committee, which gained more than MX$60,000 in monthly commissions for the management of accounts for a small group of Mexican businessmen, had revealed that Raúl's money, which was deposited in Citibank accounts, came from legal investments from various Mexican companies, especially Telmex.

Slim immediately reacted against the statements. He called a press conference to "clarify" that "the control of the 'AA' shares, which have power of decision in Telmex, is [...] not related to Salinas de Gortari."

To remove any doubt from Amy Elliot's statements, Sergio Rodríguez Molleda, the attorney for Teléfonos de México, sent a letter dated November 12, 1999 to Elliot herself, vice-president of Citigroup Private Bank, with a copy to the President of Citigroup, John Reed, and engineer Julio A. Quezada, general director of Citibank Mexico S.A., and of Grupo Financiero Citibank, which stated:

> *The publication of the statements that you made a few days ago in front of the Senate Committee of the United States of America, in relation to potential investments and high returns in shares of Teléfonos de México, S.A. of C.V., the engineer Raúl Salinas de Gortari, has created doubt and misinformation that may harm our business.*
>
> *Several newspapers noted that you said quite vaguely that you believed that part of Mr. Salinas de Gortari's money came from investments he had made in Telmex. We ask that you please explain your statement due to the serious implications it can cause to the company.*

The answer to the demand of the Director of Legal Affairs of Teléfonos de México came a month later in a letter to Richards Spears Kibbe's office, where Linda Imes, the lawyer representing Amy Elliot, wrote:

Dear Mr. Rodríguez Molleda,

As you well know, I am Amy Elliot's legal representative. I understand that you need further explanation to make the information I sent in my letter from November 19th more complete, the letter relating to matters that have been attributed to Ms. Amy Elliot's articles in the newspaper relating to Raúl Salinas de Gortari and Teléfonos de México.

As I settled in my previous letter, during the visit or presentation to the Permanent Subcommittee on Investigations in the United States Senate on November 9, Ms. Elliot said that this information, among other details, on the welfare of the Mr. [Raúl] Salinas was that Salinas had investments in Telmex, a company that doubled in price in about a year and a half. Ms. Elliot heard that Salinas had purchased shares in Telmex. There would be no reason to believe that stocks or acquisitions were inadequate. It was the knowledge of Ms. Elliot, although she does not specifically recall how this information came to her, that Salinas purchased shares of Telmex in the open market. She has never said that Salinas purchased the "control market" or had a controlling interest in Telmex.

I hope this letter will clarify Ms. Elliot's situation.

The letter ends with the signature of the attorney Linda Imes.

"If Salinas won in the stock market, I do not know about it," said Slim, analyzing Elliot's claims from a legal point of view.

"With the company Galas of México, which was first connected with Luis Echeverría, then with López Portillo and also with the Lebanese President [Amin Gemayel] (who was my wife's cousin) as well as the former Secretary of State David Ibarra, chances are they will say I also had links to Zedillo," Slim said.

Despite the clarification from Slim's lawyers, Vicente Fox echoed the remarks of Amy Elliot and sued the Zedillo government to address the complaint regarding alleged irregularities in the privatization of Teléfonos de México. "They should investigate Salinas' shareholding, not only in Telmex, but in other privatized companies during his administration," Fox said.

Moving past the affair, Slim retreated to the trenches without leaving politics. He wholeheartedly supported the campaign of Francisco Labastida Ochoa and he was present in the headquarters of the PRI in the afternoon of July 2, when it was made known that the PRI candidate was defeated. Slim was supportive of Labastida, despite the fact that he had contributed resources to almost all parties in contention, including the National Action Party.

The entrepreneur Guillermo H. Cantú, close to President Fox, author of *Assault on the Palace: the Entrails of a War*, revealed that the three businessmen that supported the NAP candidate most, after having done so with Labastida, were Slim, Roberto Hernández and Alfonso Romo.

Álvaro Cepeda Neri, a seasoned Sonoran journalist, emphasized Slim's support of the presidential campaign of Labastida Ochoa in his column "Conjectures."

Under the title "Slim in the PRI and Cathedral: Two bankrupt companies?" Cepeda Neri wrote:

The raw post-election has prevented us from getting to the bottom of what really happened ... (the 1997 elections, the closure of the key federal funds for the branch thirty-three that kept millions of pesos flowing to states to "lubricate" the PRI machinery, etc.) and to examine other events. For example, that half of Carlos and Charlie, Slim Helú, was up to his elbows in Labastida's campaign, proving that even an employer lucky with money (our Latin American and worldwide pride, as one of the richest men) can make mistakes.

What characterizes Slim is that since he began to enrich the streets of Correo Mayor until now, as he rubs shoulders with Bill Gates and other billionaires, is to have a nose for sniffing out when a company is on the verge of bankruptcy. He arrives as the "savior" to buy all kinds of companies available to the highest bidder... This is how Slim has become the owner of service chains (all Sanborns are his), bakeries, factories, banks, television, newspapers, computers, and so on. Businessman and entrepreneur, Slim is currently the richest man in the country of the post-revolutionary era, and especially since the rise of liberalism.

The only thing that comes to mind is that Carlos Slim, interested in bankrupt companies, is at best already getting closer to the PRI, which is near bankruptcy (it seemed like a bank for the millions that ran the election, until Zedillo cut off the supply), and he had gone to place an offer to buy the old party. Others say that Slim got closer to the PRI to ensure that in fact what the media said (Slim is a partner of Televisa and some radio stations), was true and that Fox had defeated Labastida and Cárdenas. So they already knew the PRI, in the sense that if you sell the PRI you will have a buyer.

Slim was reintroduced into the spotlight when the Vicente Fox administration had just begun. In an erroneous and illegal manner, Fox made the decision to appoint four of the most powerful businessmen as members of the Board of Directors of Petróleos Mexicanos.

In political circles, this was interpreted as payment for favors done for Fox during his campaign. As critics of the NAP president, they warned of the risks that businessmen could misuse information about PEMEX to gain strategic benefits.

Violating the Organic Law of PEMEX and public-sector entities, Fox appointed Slim, Alfonso Romo, Lorenzo Zambrano and Rogelio Rebolledo to be advisors of Pétroleos Mexicanos.

His decision provoked the disapproval of the Standing Committee that reprimanded the President of the Republic, citing that he had exceeded his powers.

Raúl Muñoz Leos, director of PEMEX and the transnational executive of DuPont, was the one who made the proposal that entrepreneurs join the board of directors.

The technocratic ex-president had tried to introduce changes to PEMEX, but was not as influential as Vicente Fox.

Due to Fox's outbursts, representatives of parliamentary factions in the Standing Committee signed an agreement that stated:

> *The letter of appointment written by the President on behalf of four Mexican businessmen to serve on the Board of Directors of PEMEX are, obviously, contrary to the letter and spirit of Articles 25, 27 and 28 of the General Constitution of the Republic and violation of Article 7 of the Organic Law of Petróleos Mexicanos and Subsidiary Entities ... Therefore, I believe it is necessary to undertake a review of such appointments by the president himself, in order to make new appointments in strict accordance with the established conventions in the Constitution and the Organic Law of the public sector in question.*

Upon assuming his position as PEMEX "advisor," Slim said it was possible to convert it into the best publicly owned oil company in the world, with the application of operational efficiency.

Later, through a decree published in the Official Journal of the Federation, a withdrawal was formally made of the appointments that had been made by the Board of Directors of Petróleos Mexicanos. The Organic Law of PEMEX established integration of the council of eleven members, six appointed by the president and five representatives of the oil union.

Finally, the business went from advisors to consultants and the Board of Directors of PEMEX was restructured.

On the eve of reforms to the Board of Directors of PEMEX, Slim said he would not withdraw because the company Petróleos

Mexicanos is the country's development lever for its fiscal strength. "It is key that it remain in possession of the State, and must get stronger and stronger," Slim said.

The prestigious journalist Alan Riding of the influential *The New York Times* and author of the classic *Distant Neighbors* wrote:

The reality of a country that runs in a two-speed gear was further aggravated by the gradual inclusion of Mexico into the global economy. Mexico's misfortune was that during the crashes of 1982 and 1994, revenue was concentrated in the hands of a few. But when it came to economic recovery, together with the liberalization and privatization policies, concentration of income continued. This phenomenon was by no means exclusive to Mexico: the US and Britain, the first two countries to take this route, had shown a steady expansion of the gap between rich and poor since the early eighties. The arrival of the "New Economy," built around new media and high technology and inflated by speculation in the stock market, accelerated this process.

Mexico was slow to enter this cycle, but they acknowledged that it was now the only business model available. Two decades ago, developing countries thought they should be given special treatment. Today, countries like Mexico have had no choice but to join the global economy and play by their rules.

Fox needs to be able to count on the support of big business tycoons, many of them familiar faces from the past that have adjusted to economic change, such as the dynasty of Garza Sada of Monterrey, Lorenzo Zambrano of Cementos de México, and Alfonso Romo Garza of Pulsar, but also new rich men whose names have been unknown for the last twenty years: Roberto Hernández, president of Banamex, and especially Slim Helú, billionaire and head of Teléfonos of México and a number of other companies, and the richest man in Latin America. What they and most other business leaders have in common is a long history of supporting the governments of the PRI, but they are all now in agreement that Fox is a good choice for Mexico.

Slim always has attracted the gaze of the press while attending any public event.

Despite his relationship with the government of Vicente Fox, Slim never stopped expressing his point of view. Since the beginning, he was against the proposed tax reform by the president. When he proposed to exempt VAT on food and medicine, Slim said, "as long as you are careful about the selection of what products are taxed."

Slim was against a position that he called *nacioglobalifóbicos* (national-globalizophobic), in which those who thought that foreign is always better and that nationals do not have the ability to confront transnational corporations.

"I differ from those who think that Mexican entrepreneurs cannot manage their own businesses or the many authorities that think it's better to favor foreign over domestic investment," Slim said.

Slim has confronted the left-wing politicians as much as the right. Porfirio Muñoz Ledo, who was one of his main challengers, was seduced by the King Midas of business.

When Muñoz Ledo became a PRD senator, he bluffed that he had in his possession a record that showed the punishable irregularities in the divestiture of Teléfonos de México, and the immeasurable stock market speculation that ultimately ended with Slim becoming the owner of public goods.

With the sale of Telmex, he went from an economic monopoly to a private company. As with the popular saying that money has no homeland, the argument that Telmex was in Mexican hands is very relative. It was a triumph of privatization over Republicans.

Overnight, Muñoz Ledo took a turn in his attacks on Slim. On July 7, 2000, five days after Vicente Fox's presidential victory, the ex-legislator and ex-PRD president attended the wedding of Slim's daughter Soumaya Slim Somit.

Muñoz Ledo was with a group of PRD supporters devoted to praising Slim, among whom were Payán Velver, Samuel del Villar, and other supporters of the left such as Epigmenio Ibarra, and other beneficiaries of the country's richest man. They also coincided at the parties of such intellectuals as Monsiváis, Enrique Krauze, Iván Restrepo, Héctor Aguilar Camín, Ángeles Mastretta, Rolando Cordera, David Ibarra and Guillermo Tovar y de Teresa.

Years ago in the tribunal of the Congress Standing Committee of the Union, the engineer Heberto Castillo, a PRD senator, bitterly challenged Slim. The legendary fighter of the student movement of 1968 had demanded the investigation of the large fortunes forged during the administration of Salinas de Gortari.

Six weeks into the Zedillo government, Heberto Castillo questioned Slim's wealth in the case of Telmex. Weeks later, Castillo published an article in *Proceso* magazine in December 1995 and sustained that President Zedillo's government had no political will to prosecute the ex-president Salinas, as was noted in his appearance before the Chamber of Deputies. Attorney General Antonio Lozano Gracia argued that there was no basis to proceed against Salinas and his top aides, as well as businesses that benefited from the privatization program.

In an article dated January 1998, Ben Heff, a reporter for *Universal News Service and RM* in Washington, announced the existence of encrypted files in the Federal Bureau of Investigation (FBI) tracking the movement of hundreds of millions of dollars deposited by order of Salinas de Gortari in banks in the Caribbean.

While Salinas was suspected of having benefited and of having made a group of his business friends rich, he was not required to clarify the allegations of corruption against him.

Back in the splendor of the campaign of Luis Donaldo Colosio, the PRI called the barons of money to a fundraising dinner for the party. The event brought together the country's richest families and was held in the lounge of Las Constelaciones del Hotel Nikko (the Constellation of Hotel Nikko). A special guest of the candidate, Slim grabbed the spotlight of the press.

The reporters swarmed around Slim's table, where he was sitting among family and friends.

"Engineer, tell us about Teléfonos de Mexico. Cuauhtémoc Cárdenas has warned that if he wins the presidential elections, he will submit the company to a new contract. Cárdenas said that privatization was marred by irregularities. What is your opinion?"

To which Slim responded, "The bidding process was very clear."

A SUCCESSFUL MAN
Paradigms and Standards

Success is associated with paradigms and standards that don't necessarily conform to the expectations that all people possess. Slim is a successful man who will remain a symbol for new generations.

Some may think that a person's wealth is defined by how much one has, how much one earns, the clothes one wears and the way one lives. We now know this is not at all true. That is to say, we now know that this is not an absolute certainty. Slim does not associate success with money. He has a rare sense of social value, not only in his business leadership, but also in his human sensitivity. Of his secret to success Slim said, "I believe that success is not economical. I think that viewing success from a material point of view is not accurate, [...] I think for me, success is the family I was born in, grew up in, my marriage, my children, my grandchildren, my friends."

For Slim, success is not only succeeding in business. For him, the word success means values and principles, which do not always bring good and favorable results in business.

Some personal development experts caution that success has its secrets. For example, successful men have a certain quality of persuasion and security in public speaking. They are organized in their thoughts and this is reflected clearly in the act of speech writing; they are organized and productive, innovative and creative; they have critical thinking skills to analyze and evaluate information; they are good listeners and know how to make decisions and answer questions quickly and efficiently; they have the ability to make accurate estimates and work with a mind for numbers, to read and use this knowledge productively and efficiently; they are relaxed and face problems with wit; they know how to hug a child and how to track and record expenses and revenues that are vital not to survive, but rather to thrive.

The Slim genetics for businesses attracts a spotlight on him. Every day, from many parts of the world, he takes requests for interviews from the most influential publications and even the more frivolous ones. The tabloids search for whatever pretext they can to put him on their covers. The Spanish social commentary and entertainment magazine *Semana* attributed a supposed romance with the Queen of Jordan Noor al-Hussein (whose birth name is Lisa Halaby). The publication made claims that the widow of King Hussein and the Mexican tycoon were in a relationship, but Slim took care of the rumor. "We are just friends," he asserted.

The truth is that Slim is seen as one of the entrepreneurs with the most sex appeal. Dr. William M. Brown and a group of British experts in developmental psychology from the University of Brunel argue that sex appeal is not a matter of chance nor is it based on fashion. The characteristics of sex appeal have to do with a person's genetic potential, the symmetry of his personality. It is known that symmetrical faces are more attractive, but corporal symmetry is a fundamental added value for sex appeal. For men, that symmetry should include a large torso, good shoulders, small chest, strong legs and an acceptable height. In the case of female sex appeal: long legs, chest of considerable size, small shoulders and a proportioned waist to hip ratio.

Entrepreneur magazine was given the task of exploring Slim's personality. Reporter Doris Gómora consulted a group of specialists to try to decode the "enigma" of Slim.

Being an entrepreneur is to live one step ahead of the majority. But when does an entrepreneur become an influence for other entrepreneurs?

A group of experts in the fields of small- and medium-sized enterprises and entrepreneurial talent talked about exemplary entrepreneurial personalities and what characteristics make them successful. Here are their answers.

Leadership and Vision

Francisco Martínez, coordinator of the program Entrepreneurs of the National Autonomous University of Mexico, considers Slim an example of a successful entrepreneur.

"I think the most important thing is recognizing the needs of society and we can discuss any of his companies," Martínez said. "In addition, he is one of the few that brings seed capital to create start-ups or reactivate bankrupt firms."

But according to Martínez, what makes Slim different?

"He is an analytical leader and above all he is always ready for change, so in that way, if anything should come up or affect any of his companies, he is ready to take the necessary measures."

Discretion

Miguel Torruco, a hotelier in Mexico City, said, "Slim is a successful entrepreneur because he is a person who has a unique vision for business, he knows how to buy and sell. Additionally, he is discreet and unostentatious, personal qualities not very common nowadays."

Security

For Erika G. Bello, from the School of Business at the University of the Americas (UDLA), Slim is also the most outstanding Mexican entrepreneur today.

"He has the necessary personality traits to continue succeeding: leadership, charisma, creativity and safety," she said.

Innovative

"Slim is the prototype of a successful entrepreneur," said Imanol Belausteguigoitia, director of the Center for Development of the Family Company, from the Autonomous Technological Institute of Mexico (ITAM).

"Slim has five characteristics that meet the definition of an entrepreneur: proactive, risk-taker, innovative, competitive and adaptable; he is flexible," he said. "He anticipates events or problems. He takes calculated risks, breaking with paradigms. Finally, he is an aggressive competitor; it would seem that for Slim, competition is incentive."

Successful men

Angélica Arreola, Director of the Center for Assessment of Human Resources of the Technology Institute of Superior Studies of Monterrey (ITESM), Mexico City campus, said that for her, the most emblematic of the country's entrepreneurs are Lorenzo Zambrano, Cemex's president, and Carlos Slim, president of Grupo Carso.

Why did she choose them? Zambrano and Slim are two entrepreneurs who have shown that big business can thrive in Mexico.

"Innovative people are breaking paradigms, they have the capacity for innovation and a strategic vision of future business, which is vital to the development and expansion the business," she said.

The magazine *Quién* analyzed the personality that Slim projects. Under the title "The face of the Billionaire," the publication gave the following outline of the image of the engineer:

> *Power, money and knowledge are the traits that stand out in tycoon Slim Helú and this is identified through his drooping eyelids and his small eyes, reflecting that, from childhood, much has been demanded of him.*
>
> *Here are some of the conclusions reached by the psychographic researchers Alma Leticia Márquez and Martha Patricia González when analyzing the facial features of the entrepreneur.*
>
> *Rectangular face, straight hair and prominent features: these traits are characteristic of analytical people with a taste for mathematics and who are result-oriented. The prominent features reflect that he spends much energy on long-term situations.*
>
> *Small and widely spaced eyes indicate analytical skills and reflect an open mind. He is a good strategist who likes to multi-task, taking on many projects at once.*
>
> *A drooping upper eyelid reflects expectations that are self-demanding and demanding of others.*
>
> *Bags under the eyes: these signs on the face express exhaustion and excessive stress.*
>
> *Discrete lips indicate an aggression in achieving objectives.*
>
> *A broad nose indicates that he has great ability to concentrate. His nostrils are barely visible, which means he*

knows money management.

Attached earlobes: they are stuck, this means he listens, has great ability to put ideas into practice, he likes to make things work well.

A prominent chin indicates that he often exercises a strong influence on others and is an ambitious person. It speaks of leadership, of his constant victories, and that he often reaches his goals.

His handwriting has also attracted the interest of the media. Usually, the engineer handwrites his speeches and lectures. He is obsessive about even the smallest spelling errors, reviewing them again and again. Though it is rare to see corrections, this does not mean he doesn't make last-minute changes. Furthermore, the texts he reads to the public are on paper with a letterhead of his name.

Under the title of Slim, with the power of his signature, *Expansion* editors also asked: What personality traits does the employer emit when he signs his signature?

The president of the Psychografology Society of Mexico Victor Piá Arreguín said the analysis of the writing of the employer concluded that his lines show signs of a nervous temperament and a hardiness, which speaks primarily of his drive, dynamism and result-orientation.

In an article by reporter Gisela Vázquez, a handwriting expert, she rises to the task of analyzing Slim's handwriting. Here are some of the highlights that were discovered through his handwriting:

The angularity of some parts of his writing indicates that he may act directly and assertively, saying things as they are or as he feels.

"We can see that his personal life is more relaxed than his professional life, where he can be more rash and domineering." His strokes are very similar to those of the artist Pablo Picasso. These strokes occur in people who are creative, resourceful and able to read the current situation.

Inclined and slanted writing reflects dynamism, energy, and self-improvement. This person denotes ability to interact with others and express their views to others.

He signs his full name. What you see is what you get. He doesn't take on a different attitude when it comes to his desires and interests.

He writes his letter "S" with angularity on the bottom. This reflects the gift of command, assertiveness, and organization in every one of their activities. The ascending letter "S" reflects a person who has many ideas, is creative, inventive and self-improving.

His spaced writing can be seen in those taking time to think, giving space for his ideas and projects.

A signature that ends with a period, such as Slim's, is seen in those who tend to impose their point of view.

A down-sloped writing style may be due to any situation that causes nostalgia or a decrease in energy management. Here it is important to consider whether a situation here and now, or there and then.

Accents on the "I" that are high are also seen in people who like to dream, innovate, anticipate events, and especially in people who have the intellectual ability of strategic planning.

Letters "C" and "S" are elevated which is seen uniquely in people who want to stand out from the crowd.

Plato is best known for his philosophical work. However, his influence on mathematics is quite considerable. He thought it was impossible to study philosophy without the knowledge of mathematics. Perhaps this is the reason why his famous and significant phrase is placed at the entrance of academies: "Let no one ignorant of geometry enter." This and other propositions like "numbers rule the world" show us that he was directly influenced by the Pythagorean theory.

"Numbers speak to me, they dance," Slim said when asked about his fondness for accounts. His addiction to mathematics led him to opt for studying engineering and economics.

Fans of numerology argue that this "is a science or a set of laws verifiable and repeatable, which aims to study the entire human being." As its name indicates, numbers and numerical calculations are used for the analysis of name and birth date, from the point of view of their psychological behavior and the most significant events of his life. The result is in a way similar to astrology's ability to divine past events, present and individual futures, as well as certain inclinations that one will inevitably meet throughout his life.

Thoth, or Hermes Trismegistus, is considered the father of numerology. The Greeks called him the "God of Wisdom."

Numerologists ponder the teachings of Pythagoras, the numerical Kabbalah and Christian symbolism of the Middle Ages, and even exalt the Arabs and Celts who studied the power of numbers and considered it as "reflection of the divine."

The following is Slim's Numerology chart, which explains his strengths and the predominant traits of his character.

Numerological Chart for SLIM HELÚ, born January 28, 1940.

Central Elements of his Personality

Name:	Carlos	5	Adventurous
Surname:	Slim	8	Executive
Surname:	Helú	1	Leader
Date of Birth:		28	Unique & ambitious
Birth Path:		7	Expert
Destiny:		14/5	Rebel
Achievement:		3	Communicator
Heart's Desire:		6	Master
Personality:		8	Executive
Habits:		14/5	Rebel / Prone to addiction

Temperament

Physical Response:	2	Calm, Sensitive, Work-oriented
Mental Response:	4	Practical, Planner, Realist
		Committed, Demonstrative,
Emotional Response:	6	Worried
Intuitive Response:	2	Rebel / Prone to addiction

Specialty and Numbers

Distribution of Numbers	1 2 3 4 5 6 7 8 9
In his Name:	3 0 5 1 1 1 0 1 2

Karmic Read

2 Camaraderie, patience, tact

7 Pessimist, confident, knowledge

Periods of Transition

	Age	Pinnacle	Challenge
First:	Birth to 29	2	0
Second:	30 to 38	6	4
Third:	39 to 47	8	4
Fourth:	48 to Death	6	4

EXPANSION
Latin America, Challenges

Slim's challenge in the coming years will be to create the physical and human capital in Latin America, to the extent of his business potential, to contribute and combat the remnants of poverty and unemployment that afflict the region. The tycoon said that the gap between rich and poor doesn't matter. There is a Chinese proverb that said: "Bad governments care about the rich, good governments care about the poor."

The journalist Diego Foneca wrote in *Rostros*, "Who can question the desire of a man who has created more wealth than dozens of Latin American presidents? With a personal fortune of more than the sum of the GDP of Costa Rica, Uruguay and Ecuador combined, and with his decision to work to improve the regional economic development, the engineer has been preparing over the last decade to become part of textbooks."

Slim knows of the circumstances lived by many Latin American countries with economies that are immature and in urgent need of a strong social investment. In this regard, Slim reflects:

> *I think Latin America as every country has its own conditions. A country with a billion people is different from a country with a million. A country with so many people has a very large domestic economy and so that is the main issue to handle. But, I think every country has its own situation and its own pace (rhythm) of development, but what is clear is that everyone will learn or should learn from China or*

Korea. From them, one can emulate an advanced education, which ranges from traditional literacy to the intel-literacy (computer literacy). Not just teaching the ABCs, but rather convergence, connectivity and modern education with average and superior school level focusing greater efforts in education of science, technology and engineering.

Keeping with the quality of Cardinal Richelieu, the prime minister of France in the first half of the eighteenth century, said it was necessary to support the mechanical arts. He spoke of mechanical education. I think it is important to teach all these aspects, without putting aside humanism (humanities), education, creation of jobs, economic activity, investment, or reinvestment.

Slim's concern for the future has led to new commitments.

I like knowing history; I love the history of my country. But I am also interested in the universe, the origin and development of man. If you look at the development of man over five or six million years to date, the different ages and how everything started, it took only ten thousand years to discover agriculture and civilization. In this new civilization, the good thing is that the welfare of the people is what brings success in this society. In the agricultural civilization, man exploited man and earth. That's why there were slaves and social immobility. And as you were born, you lived your life in the same place and in the same social atmosphere. And power was monolithic as was political power, economic power, military power and religious power were linked. The emperor came from God, Pharaoh came from the Divine and the same happened in Mexico as it did in Egypt and Japan or anywhere else. Power was not flexible. With the new civilization, up until the industrial age, up until industrial civilization, everything completely changed. The paradigms of democracy, freedom, pluralism, human rights, environment, globalization, competition are very different. Previously, we exploited the raw materials, land and people. Slavery was not an accident; it was part of a paradigm of civilization. But in the new civilization, poverty is not a business as it once was. It is necessary to have people who are involved with the new economy, with time to relax and find areas of entertainment and other areas. I think that is where the future of civilization resides.

I think governments should have a clear vision of this new civilization to drive change. In the past, poverty was an ethical and moral problem and one of social justice, but now it is an economic necessity. A country like the US, which is called a consumer society, is actually a society of work and welfare. It is a welfare society. It is possible that a "Third World War," as you could call it, could break out against poverty around the globe. It is clear to me that this "war" will come and lift the poor out of their condition, but to achieve this we require education, health and employment. And so, if there are more people employed and receiving better incomes, we will have bigger markets. Therefore, it is very important for governments to achieve this, as there will be much bottlenecking in the future. Energy is one of those aspects; one in which we will see much bottlenecking because the poor people of the world, like in China, India and Latin America, to name a few examples, will be incorporated into markets and sooner than is expected.

Latin America is the name given to the twenty-something countries and nine dependencies of America that speak Spanish, Portuguese and French (all Romance languages derived from Latin) but there are a dozen English-speaking and Dutch-speaking islands, which were erroneously included despite being non-Latin countries. However, one should remember that the term Latin America was first used in 1856 by the Chilean philosopher Francisco Bilbao and Colombian writer José María Torres Caicedo in his poem *Las dos Américas*[35]. The term was even supported by the Napoleon III during the French invasion of Mexico as a way to include France among the countries of America, and especially to exclude Anglo-Saxons.

Slim, who is seen as a modern conqueror whose presence now extends throughout almost the entire continent, is passionate about history and Latin American cultures.

He is aware of the enormous amount of work that needs to be put into the development of most of these countries, many of which face problems of social and political stability. Despite all this talk, Slim speaks with conviction of the challenges for the future knowing that one races against the clock; in the morning with US companies, in the afternoon with European companies, and with Asian companies at night:

My priority is to create the physical and human capital in our countries of Latin America. That's my challenge. That's what I'm most involved and interested in at this time: health, nutrition, health education, labor and physical infrastructure. That means new projects such as airports, ports, roads, power plants, energy, telecommunications, and homes. That is what I'm trying to do within the next few years.

Since appointing his heirs to manage his companies, Slim has been concentrating on this challenge. He has been actively helping, supporting and participating through foundations and companies that have been creating employment by means of huge investments.

I believe that poverty cannot be addressed through the donation of alms. You can't fight poverty through charity and social programs. Poverty is faced only with good education and good jobs. Employment is the only way to fight poverty; in the past, the problem of poverty was an ethical and moral problem, a social justice issue. Today in this new civilization, fighting poverty is an economic necessity. If we do not fight against poverty, we are not going to develop. In the past there were slaves. There were struggles for land and soil and people worked for nothing. Now you do not need physical work, you need knowledge. You need to use your work skills and abilities. That is why we need education: for human capital. Of this I am convinced and that is what I am working for and that's what I'm interested in.

Slim has proposed a Latin American alliance of the rich against poverty. Along with the majority of the most powerful businessmen in the region, he has taken the first steps to form a company to finance development in Latin America that would involve investors, private banks, stock markets, and perhaps the development of banks and global financial institutions.

From their perception, the Washington Consensus did not yield the expected results. For two decades, the region had a growth rate of zero percent and there were many zigzag periods. "Several of its postulates are very good," said Slim, "but others are pro-cyclical and unsustainable."

During the golden years of "Reaganomics," and of course, the "Chicago Boys," when the majority of the debt crises erupted, the Washington Consensus emerged. The term was coined by British economist John Williamson who picked up on the principles of the economic plan in a book published by the Institute of International Economics in Washington. In compiling the findings of fifty economists from Europe, the United States and Latin America who analyzed the experiences of policy adjustment, the Washington Consensus implemented reform structure in many countries, mainly the so-called Third World, which have always been indebted to other countries.

The Washington Consensus was integrated into programs implemented by the World Bank, International Monetary Fund, the Inter-American Development Bank and major economic and financial agencies of the US government.

The Ten Commandments of the program consisted of the following: fiscal discipline, inflation, public spending, tax reform, interest rates, exchange rates, trade policy, foreign direct investment, privatization and deregulation.

Strictly speaking, the Washington Consensus was a true recipe of neo-liberalism and it began to sprout the seeds of globalization.

Some analysts came to categorize the measures of this consensus as Draconian, in reference to the character of ancient Athens, Draco, who was the first to write laws in the seventh century B.C.

Far from the Washington Consensus, Slim believes one option to get rid of lags in Latin America makes for a more social investment in the region.

In late 2005, Slim started his new business project by Fostering Development and Employment in Latin America (IDEAL), with an initial investment of about US$800 million to promote the acquisition, management, construction, exploitation and development of road works, energy, water and everything related to the infrastructure for developing countries in the region.

The strategy consisted of associating with local investors in each of the Latin American countries with great needs for material and infrastructure development, which constituted a potential for important business.

This daunting task has made Slim bring together recognized experts with business experience from his milieu, including former Treasury Secretary David Ibarra Muñoz; Fernando Solana Morales, former director of Banamex and former Secretary of Education and Foreign Affairs; and Daniel Díaz, former Secretary of Communications and Transport.

Slim also acknowledges Ignacio Ponce de León who was director of analysis in the area of debt research in emerging markets for investment bank JP Morgan Chase in New York between 1995 and 2005 as a true genius.

Slim has been committed to Latin America and even acknowledges that after the stock market boom, many assets were left orphaned. Shareholders decided to abandon them, so the Mexican entrepreneur who had the commitment and vision, as well as having the capital and the ability, reaped the rewards. "Only Slim," said Ponce de León, "can see value in companies where no one else sees them ... Yet, before 2000," he added, "no one expected that Slim would be a big player in telecommunications in Latin America. We thought we were going to be technology developers, not managers of services."

The first steps in the region were through his companies América Móvil and Telmex. From 2005, Slim's companies in Latin America began to expand and consolidate financing itself from international markets.

While Telmex is among the ten best positioned Latin American companies with a market value estimated at around US$15 billion, América Móvil is triple the value of Telmex. It is a monster that not only operates in most countries in Latin America, but has also expanded to the United States through marketing. In terms of subscribers, this company ranks among the top five major mobile phones in the world.

Apart from telecommunications, Slim has been given the task of acquiring, creating and managing companies engaged in the infrastructure of Latin America through IDEAL. This will surpass

US$100 billion by 2015, mainly for the construction of infrastructure such as hydropower, energy, highways and bridges.

In order to promote their projects, he created Carso Infrastructure and Construction (CICSA). CICSA was created in only two years and is the size of ICA (Ingenieros Civiles Asociados), which took half a century to reach its size. Other CICSA companies are Swecomex and PC Constructions, specializing in construction of oilrigs and many other projects related to the energy sector.

Undoubtedly, there is much to do in most countries of the region. Rebecca Grynspan, director for Latin America and the Caribbean for the United Nations Development Program (UNDP), speaking about poverty and inequality said, "We are trapped because we don't grow to reduce poverty. Currently, there are two hundred million poor people, but there would only be one hundred million if they had held rates of inequality in the sixties."

Another United Nations agency, U.N. for Food and Agriculture, FAO has noted the Latin American reality: fifty-three million people, equivalent to ten percent of the population, have insufficient access to food while chronic malnutrition affects ten million children.

The Economic Commission for Latin America and the Caribbean (ECLAC) has also warned that failure to act soon to promote more investment will inevitably lead ten million more Latin Americans to fall into destitution, while a similar decay will happen to the condition of the poor.

Grynspan proposes that to reverse this situation, it is necessary to invest more in education. How can we build a common project of society if we do not know each other? According to Grynspan:

For starters, we should encourage the education of skilled workers, better training for teachers, see education as an indivisible chain that begins in preschool, going to basic and secondary education and ends with technical university. As for social protection, only 50 percent of workers in Latin America have some coverage of social protection. It takes more integrated social systems, based on the principles of universality, efficiency and solidarity, systems that combine solidarity and non-contributory systems. It is important to add that 25 percent of young people in these countries neither study nor work, and many come from broken families.

Regarding the relationship between state and society, Grynspan continues:

The characteristics of families have changed. Many of these changes require more flexible labor markets, but that does not involve social vulnerability, which is why, within economic government, social policies have pre-market and post-market policies. However, we have no equity in the market, which would be met with corrective regulations.

From the new private and state investments in most Latin American countries, this region has shown a slight growth rate of around five percent and even external debt has declined, unemployment has decreased and there are a higher number of salaried jobs. While poverty is also a little lower—forty percent of the population lives below the poverty line—it is clear that we have just reached the end of the first decade of this century at the same level of the eighties, which means that it took Latin America more than twenty-five years to recover from the crisis of that decade.

Given the interest shown by investors in Latin America in recent years, Grynspan believes that the main challenge is a long-term growth. One important aspect, she insists, is how to enhance the trade liberalization that is taking place at different rates for countries and the rapid increase in welfare. A study in sixteen countries in this region showed that the impact of trade liberalization on poverty levels has been very small.

According to this Grynspan, they need to diversify markets and products, strengthen supply chains and generate added value with an emphasis on SMEs (small- and medium-sized enterprises), which must be prepared to be pulled.

Faced with the reality of Latin America, one can analyze the situation of other nations, which have higher and better social stability and strong economic, cultural and educational process.

Based on indicators of Human Development, it is important for us to reflect on what has long been called "the wealth of nations."

The first surprise is Norway, a country with the highest human development, has a GDP equivalent to less than thirty percent of Mexico's GDP, or three times smaller than that of Mexico. The GDP is also seventy times less than the US and five times smaller than Brazil. These facts break the myth that only rich countries can achieve great economies and wealth. Among the top ten countries in human development is Iceland, with a GDP of just 1.5 percent of that of Mexico and an insignificant fragment of the US GDP.

Comparisons can provoke distortions and usually incur absurdities and fallacies, although it should clarify some data. For example, a study by *Time* magazine indicates that in Latin America, the economic upswing in the twentieth century was clearer despite many ups and downs. This analysis was based on the value of calculating income in purchasing power parity. Early last century, the average income in Latin America was approximately fifteen percent of the American equivalent and in the early twenty-first century, it represented twenty percent. The backlog is still brutal and convergence is still minimal.

Of course, it's surprising and shocking that in the twenty-first century, a large part of the world's population lives in poverty. That is, many people do not have access to basic goods to ensure their survival (food, clothing and housing). And although there are different criteria, always relative to defining poverty, the driving figures are devastating.

For governments and for investors, it is a great challenge to reverse the current situation in Latin America. Slim's companies are present, so far, in seventeen countries in the region. In the last decade, his companies have invested US$60 billion dollars worldwide. According to World Bank figures, of all global business groups, Slim's companies made the most investments on the planet in the last ten years.

Like him, many businessmen have placed more emphasis on Latin America. In 2003, the first summit took place in Ixtapa, one of the principle ports in Pacific Mexico, of the richest men in Latin America to analyze the economic and social situation of countries in the region.

The conclave brought together thirty-two of the most powerful businessmen in the area. The president of Spain, Felipe González, spoke to them. He is considered one of the greatest statesmen of the twentieth century whose reflections are accompanied by a calm analysis of the various conjectures of the time.

The magnates had the opportunity to hear the reflective views of a statesman distanced from political power. "No emerging country, and Spain is no exception, became a central country without making trade liberalization with social equity and income distribution," González said to the assembly.

One year later, held in Santo Domingo, Dominican Republic, a second summit assembled and the futurist Alvin Toffler was invited to speak to businessmen and their heirs.

The third summit, convened by Slim and Venezuela's Gustavo Cisneros, took place in Buenos Aires, Argentina. The hosts were Paolo Rocca, Federico Braun and Alfredo Román. The Pérez Companc and Fortabat families were notably missing.

A fourth would come in 2009, with a meeting in Cartagena, Colombia, which the media called the Summit of Billionaires. The hosts on this occasion were magnate Julio Mario Santo Domingo and the banker Luis Carlos Sarmiento. "The purpose of the meeting," Sarmiento explained, "is that now with globalization, the problems of our countries are similar. So we will try to find and discuss solutions to common problems, now compounded by the economic downturn."

Included in the billionaire's club, as the powerful businessmen in Latin America are called, was the Venezuelan businessman Gustavo Cisneros, the main shareholder of the largest Hispanic television network in the US (Univisión) and owner of various telecommunications companies. He is associated with Venevisión International, Venevisión Productions y Movida in the US, and Cervecería Regional in Venezuela, all grouped under the tutelage of the Organización Cisneros (Cisneros Group) emporium. He also owns the Venezuelan baseball team Los Leones de Caracas. The Venezuelan magnate's companies operate in more than fifty countries in Latin America, Asia and Europe. In the US alone, 35,000 people work for the conglomerate. According to *Forbes*, Cisneros ranks number two on the list of Latin American billionaires.

Also a part of this select group were Brazilian businessman Marcelo Odebrecht, owner of the Odebrecht organization, which has modernized petrochemical construction; the billionaire Joseph Safra and his brother Moisés, who have sown banks as though they were planting wheat throughout the continent; and Argentine Carlos Miguens Bemberg, a descendant of the wealthy family of German immigrants. Bemberg was also president of the International MBP and is currently the president of MB Holdings and Agropecuaria Cantomi. Additionally, he holds a very active mining industry in Argentina, being the director of Patagonia Gold S. A. since its inception. He is the former director of Minera El Desquite. To the list of Latin American billionaires, we can also add the German-born Argentine businessman Alberto Roemmers, founder and owner of Laboratorios Roemmers, a leader in prescriptions and units sold in the pharmaceutical market in Latin America; Federico Braun, manager of the group of imports and exports from Patagonia; Paolo Rocca, president of Techint Group and CEO of Tenaris, a world leader in the production of seamless steel tubes, with presence incountries around the world, and chairman of board of directors of Ternium, a manufacturer of various flat steel products.

In Ecuador, we have Álvaro Noboa, the richest man of his country, who has been a candidate for the presidency of the Republic four times (1998, 2002, 2006, 2009), and in the 2007 elections, succeeded in obtaining the post of National Assembly Member. As a businessman, Álvaro Noboa controls Grupo de Empresas Noboa and Noboa Corporation, with over 110 companies in Ecuador and around the world including offices in the United States, Antwerp, Rome, Japan, Argentina and New Zealand. In Colombia, there is Julio Mario Santo Domingo, the largest brewery employer in the region, the banker Luis Carlos Sarmiento Angulo and industrialist Carlos Julio Ardila. This list also includes Chilean businessman Andrónico Lucsik, the largest retailer of bottled or dehydrated food and drink in his country.

Mexicans who have attended these meetings include Lorenzo Zambrano, owner of Latin America's largest cement company, which has industries around the world, mainly in China; María Asunción Aramburuzavala, Mexican beer heiress whose company exports to all continents; Emilio Azcárraga Jean, heir to the consortium of the largest telecommunication facilities in Latin America and the most important Spanish-speaking television network; and Ricardo Salinas Pliego, the millionaire furniture trader and banker and owner of the Mexican television network that is seen around the country.

The recession of 2008 that engulfed the United States swept the whole world, especially Latin America where the red flags lit up on investors' switchboards. On one hand, this crisis occurred in the context of the presidential succession to the White House. George

W. Bush's successor Barack Obama inherited the world's most powerful country in a state of bankruptcy. Wall Street and The City—as London's financial district is known—warned from the beginning that the United States had many years earlier shown symptoms of a much greater economic depression than that of 1929. Obama was forced to implement a plan of emergency economic recovery in the amount of US$500 billion to the industrial sector. One-third of their resources, it was announced, would be earmarked for infrastructure projects to create jobs. The plan would include construction and rehabilitation projects for roads, bridges, transit systems, railways, schools, plants for water treatment and infrastructure networks, broadband telecommunications, among other projects.

The banking system, equal to the most powerful companies of the most emblematic multinational companies of US origin, had the worst rates in their financial returns as well as the largest frauds (Ponzi schemes). The downturn can be traced to several missteps including poorly-handled accounts on the New York Stock Exchange, over-enthusiastic lending practices by banks, and fund managers choosing risky investments with supposedly high returns that in the end, were never recognized. In this gloomy picture, millions of citizens faced the highest record of bankruptcies, loss of investments and savings, and defaulting mortgage payments.

In the context of Mexico, everyone wanted to listen to Slim, who many consider a financial guru. The tycoon was summoned to discuss the global crisis.

Slim criticized the government's mismanagement of the US economy. In his view, Washington acted a little late and made some mistakes: "Hopefully, they are little mistakes, and hopefully they won't make big mistakes." According to Slim, the government began buying assets, which to him was a mistake. Sooner or later, the amount would become unmanageable because there would be trillions of dollars that would have to be bought.

"Underneath all this, in my opinion, there is poor regulation and even worse supervision. I'm speaking on a global level," he said.

For Slim, this crisis will allow real structural solutions, not just for Mexico, but also for the United States. "We were worried about bird flu, but instead we got the US financial pandemic," he said.

It was then that Slim referred to the fact that with this crisis, it wouldn't be long before we would see the rise of numerous geniuses, but also financial Rambos who are not interested in winning the war, nor having power, but who are just interested in taking part in the war.

Regrettably, we are living a very special situation that unfortunately will not last a year, it will last longer. I am not speaking of the stock market, I mean the real economy, and we must take measures to prevent impacts it will have on the real economy. It must be borne in mind by all debtors that what happened with Fobaproa[36] cannot happen again; where the debtors ended up losing their homes because they sold the mortgage at 11 or 12 cents to groups that wanted to recover, instead of giving it over to the debtor ... In our case, it is important that the GDP grows by two, one or negative one percent. In fact, I do not think the GDP growth is really significant in these conditions and will surely be a very bad thing. What we need to take care of is the wage sums and total employment.

As the recession began to wreak havoc all over the world and in Mexico, the debate was slowly heating up. Slim, who had been a special guests of the Senate during the "Forum of Mexico Facing the Crisis: What to do in order to grow?" called the global crisis the worst in recent history, even worse than 1929. The scenario for Slim was even more disturbing. "I don't mean to be catastrophic," said the tycoon, "but it's a delicate situation and we must be prepared so that later, we don't cry."

The GDP will collapse. Unemployment levels will be higher than we have ever seen before. "We will see the bankruptcy of large companies, businesses will close and buildings will be empty," he predicted.

Slim argued that the weakening of the economy mostly affected the middle class, which was shrinking because their income was evaporating. As fiscal initiatives thrive in Congress, the government tries to compensate for these resources by raising energy, gas or electricity prices.

"In this sense, they shouldn't use state monopolies for revenue purposes, as these should be companies that are managed independently," he said.

In the political context, Slim's recommendations to the senators were taken as confrontational to President Felipe Calderón. Days earlier, the president in his working trips around the country had launched a barrage of criticism and insults in which he predicted a bleak future for the country.

Knowing that his relationship with President Calderón had always been cordial, Slim did not flinch. However, some of his competitors took the opportunity to undertake a media campaign against the president using journalists, academics and politicians who identified with one of these groups.

The following is the full text of the controversial address of Slim to lawmakers from February 9, 2009:

Thank you, good afternoon. I am very pleased and honored to be with you in this important forum.

There was no record, I believe, since 1931, at the time of the Great Depression, when there was a great cooperation between the revolutionary block of the Congress and the Commerce and Industry Chambers. That was a very important coalition or alliance that allowed, along with the public policies adopted back then, a growth of 6.2 percent from 1932 to 1982.

Such sustained growth during so many years has been spectacular. That was the famous "Mexican Miracle" and the country achieved a huge transformation, thanks to those efforts and those public policies in which State policies were written and remained for many years.

It is a shame that since 1982, after the big crisis of the external debt, we have grown zero percent per capita. It is not mediocre; it is zero. That is worse than mediocre, mostly if we consider the population that has been expelled. That is a zero percent, including Mexicans that had to leave the country for not finding job opportunities here.

That '82 big crisis of external debt had various reasons. One was, maybe, significant public expense. Another was, no doubt, the availability of petrodollars, financing and credit, which allowed an excessively large debt. But the main cause was external. It was the twenty-one percent interest rate.

You know that an economy, a company or a normal person whose financial cost is raised four times must be in trouble.

And from that external debt, came the plan and model of the Washington Consensus, which had various purposes, one of them to collect. This model has many virtues, but we have suffered its weaknesses for many years and of course, the developing countries do not notice or pay attention to them.

We have seen that on these abuses that have been imposed on the International Monetary Fund, technocrats, academics, dogmatic and ideologues never showed up or brought this to our attention.

The nearest thing was Greenspan's irrational exuberance of the markets on December 1996, when the rate was 6,500 and went up to 13,000.

Well, that is a really clear situation; we need to have a long-term vision towards the future, but we have to know what has happened in the past.

There are no simple solutions for sustained development. The country passed from being an agricultural society to an urban and industrial society and now we have to move on to be a tertiary society: of services, technology, knowledge, and to keep in mind what this society and its new paradigms require in order to go in that direction.

I was very glad at the opening of this Forum—not the Forum itself—but the words by the President of the Congress, Deputy Cesar Duarte, who said, "We need to go over a structural revision of the model and redesign of the financial system." That is what we need.

The President of the Senate talked about proposals and commitments and talked about structural changes to improve productivity and competition, which in fact are the two essential arguments in this whole situation we are living.

This crisis which started in the nineties (which Greenspan tried to stop with his irrational exuberance), by 2000, 2001 was a shock for the destruction of that time's richness and there came a series of excessive, aggressive policies, monetarily and fiscally permissive, which made that crisis, which was getting better in 2000, 2001, 2002, blow out of proportion and lead us to what we are living today.

The centerpiece of the big crisis of the financial institutions, because of the excessiveness in their liberal policies, neo-liberal policies as well as a total lack of sense of caution, is mostly the government of the United States. Obviously, the consequences came with the lack of regulation and supervision of the international financial institutions, creating new instruments and products in which their main feature is what we call "leverage," or the possibility to turn one peso into twenty, thirty or fifty.

For example, in order to buy commodities, we used to grant five percent guarantees. To buy products, we did not grant guarantees, and then the risks would multiply by hundreds, and this is what we are suffering now.

It was the speculation with oil, speculation with food— which fortunately collapsed - commodities in general, because we did not have to give anything that created a series of players, gamblers, newcomers, boys who came believing that everything was going upwards forever, and they would bet and bet, and, well, this is what we are paying for.

But, the serious matter is that even though the centerpiece is in the United States, the bigger consequences are appearing outside, in Japan for example. While in the United States the GDP dropped 3.8 percent, in Japan it dropped eight percent, in Germany eight or nine percent alone in the last quarter.

We are now in the moment, I would say. We have already been through the twenty-nine[percentage drop in GDP], we are living the thirty, we need to avoid the thirty-one, thirty-two and thirty-three. We need to avoid the financial market, which has not been stabilized or is not stabilizing and of course, it contaminates real economy through credit. It collapses the economic world as it did back then and as it looks it is doing, in many ways, at this moment.

Unemployment increase is excessive; we are talking about two digits. Spain is already in two digits as well, high digits; Japan, Germany, the whole [world's employment] is decreasing very much.

Our countries have the strength. Our countries, I am talking about Latin America, have the best strength in terms of exchange in these last years. We have oil; other countries have sorghum, or wheat, etc., and we also have minerals.

[Our countries] have an economic strength and we have to take care of it and apply it very carefully in order to avoid these physical collapses.

There is no doubt that the Mexican Gross Domestic Product is going to drop; it is going to fall down, it will be negative. It has already [fallen] since the last quarter of 2008. We do not know how long it is going to last, but the effect is going to be very strong.

This is where I say: the GDP is going to be negative, substantially negative, because of the fall of oil and exports, among other things, and the consequences, also internal. But we have to watch over employment.

We do not have to worry if it is negative two, negative one or zero. We have to pay attention to which is the salary mass, which is the employment rate, and we need to establish, like the national agreement led by the President of the Republic Felipe Calderón Hinojosa, to seek actions to protect the employment and the family income. That is the critically important thing to do at this moment.

I am glad that in this agreement, it has taken up what all these models and ideologies, dogmatisms and doctrines have been living in for so many years, since '83, but mostly, when the Washington Consensus started applying more firmly in our countries, has maintained us in a zero growth.

I think that the main goodness we are ending up with, just as it happened in that meeting with the revolutionary block of the Congress, is that we are turning over to the internal economy as we are realizing that thinking outwards is not everything.

We used to think that foreign investment was wonderful— it seemed like a donation. Foreign investment is not a donation. Foreign investment comes because we are offering good profits.

Modern companies are like old armies. Armies used to conquer territories and collect taxes. [Now,] companies conquer markets and collect dividends, royalties, and transfers from one or another source.

I mean, we need to turn over to the internal economy. We obviously need foreign investment and to adopt technology and such, but we have to turn over to the internal economy [and] take good care of our internal economy. Encourage small and medium sized enterprises, decrease business mortality, encourage [business growth] in Mexico... There are strong enterprises that compete internationally, but there are no strong countries without strong enterprises.

If the countries do not have strong enterprises, they are turning into neo-colonies. In a certain way, they need to have the strength, not internally, but outwards, to be able to project themselves.

Therefore, we see countries that have encouraged strong enterprises in their trans-nationalization, even with fiscal incentives, like Spain, which gives a seventy-five to ninety percent deduction to the investment, or Brazil, which gives support with the development bank, etc.

We need, as the United States has done since 1823 with the Monroe Doctrine, to help the Independence control our economies and markets until now.

I think it is very important to pay attention to the internal economy. It is great that we return to development banking. We used to neglect it, but development banking is essential for our country's growth.

We also have to get back to building infrastructure to improve our human capital since we have a huge budget.

And there is [the matter of] quality. It is low quality and we need to modernize it, improve quality and pass to a digital culture, not only alphabetize, but digitally alphabetize the population.

We need to be competitive in this civilization of knowledge, of information, etc. We need competition and I agree with competition, it is very important. It is as if we are athletes. If we do not compete with anyone, we will never progress.

We need to use international references in competition. What was the record time for this? How high does he jump? How well does the baseball player play? How well does the football player play? Who is the best coach?

Clearly, we have to be open to [the fact that] competition and globalization is not an alternative, it is a necessity. This new civilization is a paradigm, even though at this moment it is retracting because of the economic collapse; the lack of employment, the lack of consumption, the fall of the American economy and of the developed economies as well.

269

Obviously, the exporting countries will see their imports reduced, the prices of primary products will be lowered, actually they already were, etc., etc. Then, there is going to be an important fall of the international trade.

But besides that, international trade is going to fall and employment is going to fall as well. There is going to be a high unemployment rate. Unemployment indexes are going to go higher than we have ever known, [as high as in the 19030s].

The companies are going bankrupt, many of them small, medium and large. Businesses are going to close and there are going to be closed storefronts everywhere, the buildings empty. So this is going to be a very delicate situation.

I do not want to be catastrophic, but we need to be prepared to foreshadow and not just look at the consequences afterwards and cry.

I think that, as we did back in 1931, we have to review our decisions, see which model we need to generate, how it is supposed to work, how we are going to get out of this crisis, because we have to get out of it much stronger. How do we do that? Well, by creating human and physical capital. If we have a good physical capital, human capital is going to be very important.

Employment is encouraged through the small- and medium-sized enterprises, we all know that, but we also have to pay attention to our agricultural sector, which may be a little abandoned, and of course, infrastructure. [We need] an even faster, more effective and more job-generating infrastructure and the construction itself of the infrastructure, which is essential, is infrastructure maintenance. For that we do not have to wait for the plan, the project, the engineering or the right of way, or such. This is done overnight.

There are 30,000 schools in bad condition. We need to repair them, modernize them. We need to repair windows, bathrooms, ceilings, which are really deplorable, and painting. [We need] to do the same thing with hospitals, health centers, government offices, archeological zones, taking care of the environment biodiversity, etc.

I believe there is such ability in Mexico to give intensive employment with very little money, and of course, we have to look for the combination of public and private capital to drive those projects that justify it.

I think we have to try to get out of this, as I was saying, much stronger; it particularly catches my attention that the dogmas are still on after twenty-six years of failures.

They still find new formulas, new blames to justify that it is not so, even though those who have been more important have recognized it.

I think we should [recognize it]. Besides, in the situation of these last years, we have reduced the middle-class and we have affected it very much.

A good part of what the President of the Competition Commission indicated, of which thirty or forty percent was income, because they have no income, people do not have an income.

One-third of the students at the UNAM live on a monthly family income of four minimum-wage salaries, which today is equivalent four hundred US dollars. Is that an income? We need to improve the people's employment and income.

There is often a debate between wealth and income. I think the fact that richness is private, collective or public has to be handled efficiently to generate more richness. Its product, which is income, has to have a better distribution.

And we see how, without question, one of the ways to improve income distribution is with education, employment and sources of employment. Education not only has the advantage of creating human capital, but it is a better offer, and one who has a good education has better job alternatives.

There are still some issues to go through, but basically to insist [on higher] employment in Mexico. I think we have to search, no doubt, for strong and competitive national capitals, stand face to face with transnationals, create more public richness and when a fiscal initiative fails in the congress, do not to use the monopolies of the state to collect or to substitute tax collection. [We should ensure] that energy is not summed up, as it has been done, for tax collection; that gasoline is not used for tax collection, those things should be separate. Those companies should be handled with autonomy and out of the budget to avoid the fact that when an income is not authorized, a point is not added to the net, or such, the prices are rising and the tax is not collected.

Last, I want to tell you here, [just as they say in the United States, to "buy American," and] Minister Sebastián, from the Spanish industry said, "There is something our citizens can do for their country, which is to bet on Spain, on our products, our industry and our services, bet on ourselves." There is starting to be economic nationalism in consumption. Hopefully we are not [saying], "Sell Mexico."

I am leaving information for the legislature about competition as referred by the president of the Commission.

It is indicated here that the main reasons and more problematic factors in Mexico are government bureaucracy, inefficiency, corruption, inadequate infrastructure, restrictive regulations, tax regulations, financing access, tax rates, crime and robbery, and inadequate education of the workforce.

I am leaving you this: for the third time, we are in sixtieth place. It is not God's law either, because the United States is in the first place. We already know they are not the most competitive in the world, since they are spreading their products everywhere.

So then I am leaving you this information and I thank you very much for your attention, time and invitation.

THE AMERICAN DREAM
The Don of Ubiquity

Not even Slim's fiercest critics can deny that the investor and wealth-maker generates jobs and well-being. Even in the early nineties, many Americans were asking, who is this Mexican who wants to buy everything?

Since he was very young, Slim was noticed for his insightful personality, which allowed him to have a greater understanding of himself. His business acumen showed that he had a great capacity for insight, which allowed him to gain maturity in assuming responsibilities. This led him to act more freely and consistently as a leader in his businesses.

Far from the argument that Slim is the richest man in Mexico, the perception Americans have is that he's impressive for building his empire in Mexico. He is seen as a winner because his way of generating wealth is not beyond anyone's reach.

From an early age, he learned the codes that govern American society. Much of his knowledge of how businesses operate in the United States he learned from his multiple readings in the New York Stock Exchange Library, where he examined hundreds of books and records on financial issues. This only added to his habitual readings about American literature and history, as well as his contact with the elites of power and money of that nation.

By the weight of his business in the United States, Slim projected himself as a person with enormous influence and has gained an important voice as one of the most influential people of his country and of the world.

Fortune magazine has compared Slim's profile with that of another great American magnate, John. D. Rockefeller. The television network CNN and *Time* magazine reviewed him as among the twenty-five executives of the most influential entrepreneurs in the world, next to the Brazilian Ghosn, CEO of Nissan; the American Bill Gates of Microsoft; Steve Case, president of America Online, and Jerry Levin executive director of AOL; Robert Rubin, CEO of Citigroup; Michael Dell, CEO of Dell Computer; Stanley O'Neal, chairman of Merrill Lynch; Andre Action Jackson, president of VITB Corporation; Rupert Murdoch, president of News Corp; Jeffrey Immelt, CEO of conglomerate General Electric; Oprah Winfrey, the queen of daytime talk shows; Andrea Jung, CEO of Avon beauty products; and Britain's Sir John Brown, chairman of British Petroleum.

The New York Post also considers him among the twenty-five most influential Latinos in New York in areas such as arts, fashion, health, politics, media and philanthropy. In this list, Slim is highlighted alongside: Virgilio Garza, Head of Latin American art auction house Christie's; Julián Zugazagoitia, director of the Museo del Barrio; the Brazilian fashion designer based in New York, Francisco Costa, creative director of Calvin Klein; the Colombian Nina García, fashion editor of *Marie Claire* magazine; Rossana Rosado, CEO of *El Diari/La Prensa*; Rosario Dawson, co-founder of Voto Latino; Puerto Rican Luis Ubiñas, president of the Ford Foundation; the Dominican Yaz Hernández; René Alegría, of publishing house HarperCollins group; the Dominican writer Junot Día, Pulitzer Prize winner; Lin Miranda, writer of *In the Heights*; the Cuban actor Raúl Esparza; Cesar Perales, head of the Foundation for

Legal Defense and Education of Puerto Ricans; Anthony Romero, CEO of American Civil Liberties Union in the United States; and Supreme Court Judge Sonia Sotomayor.

Slim's presence in the United States is becoming more important. He is part of the board of directors of the RAND Corporation (Research and Development), an organization of nonprofit research offering advice and solutions around the world on issues like trade policy.

He is a strong advocate of the Clinton Foundation, led by former President Bill Clinton, which targets a fund of US$100 million to fight poverty in Latin America.

Similarly, Slim is an important contributor to the World Wide Fund for Nature, which has provided funds of US$100 million to preserve the biodiversity of Mexico in seventeen areas grouped into six natural regions. The World Wide Fund for Nature is the largest and most respected independent conservation organization in the world. Its mission is to stop the degradation of the planet's natural environment and build a future in which humans live harmoniously with nature.

The WWF has about five million members and a worldwide network of twenty-seven national organizations, five associates and twenty-two program offices, working in over one hundred countries. The international headquarters is located in Switzerland and the Latin American headquarters is located in the United States.

To Americans, it may have seemed odd that the secretary general of the Organization of the United Nations, Ban Ki Moon, invited Slim to a meeting of notables for advice on climate change.

It was no surprise that by mid 2009, Slim received the President's Medal from the George Washington University for the philanthropic work he does on the various foundations he chairs.

This award was instituted in 1988, and since then this medal has been given to personalities like Mikhail Gorbachev, Walter Cronkite, the Israeli prime minister and Nobel laureate Shimon Peres, among others.

Other awards that Slim has received are the Golden Plate Award, awarded by the American Academy of Achievement; the World Education and Development Fund; Entrepreneur of the Year (Latin Trade 2003); the Alliance Award 2004, awarded by Free Trade Alliance; the Hadrian Award (2004), awarded by the World Monuments Fund, and he was recognized as the Entrepreneur of the Decade (Latin Trade 2004).

Slim's prize list is impressive. His multiple awards range from Mexico to Latin America, the United States to Europe. In China and Japan, he has an unusual interest in non-governmental organizations because in public schools, he is taken as an example of success and perseverance.

The international media has focused its spotlight on the makings of the Mexican billionaire. At the beginning of 2007, when multibillionaire Bill Gates visited Slim's office for an exchange of views on the Internet market in Mexico and the United States, the meeting caused a stir, mainly in the local media. The Microsoft founder visited Mexico City to receive the silver award of the Mexican Order of the Aztec Eagle, which is the highest honor the Mexican government can give a foreign figure for his prominent service in the country. Gates had donated thousands of computers to public libraries and offered assistance to the Mexican government for the care of multiple diseases such as AIDS, malaria, tuberculosis and other conditions common in developing countries.

At that meeting, Gates and Slim discussed the market for Internet advertising. They discussed the need to work together to increase the penetration of services they could provide through their companies. Microsoft and Telmex created an alliance to offer Internet services and advertising in Mexico through the website prodigy. msn. It should be noted that Slim rescued Internet service provider Prodigy in 1997 from bankruptcy, adding a Spanish interface and increasing the number of customers from less than 200,000 to over 3.5 million subscribers.

Slim's presence in the United States is getting stronger, which shows that he is an investor by nature. For example, in late 2008 he acquired eight percent of the Bronco Drilling Company at six dollars per share, which amounted to approximately US$32 million.[37] This company is dedicated to the production of oilrigs and has contracts to drill three wells in Mexico.

Among the many Slim family investments in the United States, those carried out in early 2009 include the purchase of twenty-nine million shares of Citigroup by the brokerage firm Inbursa worth US$150 million, and the acquisition through Inmobiliaria Carso of 300,000 new shares of the luxury retail chain stores, Saks Fifth Avenue, as described earlier.

Slim's group owns shares in Global Crossing, Office Max, Circuit City and Borders. As if that's not enough, Carso Global Telecom's repository of most of the control shares of Telmex operate telecommunications services in the United States, just as América

Móvil provides wireless services in US territory. It should be said that the Carso Global Telecom serves low-income consumers, especially Hispanics in the United States, who have little to no access to credit.

In a world where there is never enough time, it seems that Slim has the gift of ubiquity. He is omnipresent. On any given day, someone may find him leaving a business meeting on Wall Street or find him at a concert in the John F. Kennedy center for the Performing Arts in Washington, or lecturing in any American university.

From a young age, Slim has been involved in the problems and the evolution of American society. In the sixties, he traveled through major US cities. Those were the times in which they debated the ideas of the best-known thinkers of the conservative American world like Sidney Hook, who came from the extreme left, or Norman Podhoretz, one of the intellectual gurus of the Jewish world. In those years, the old leftist Irving Kristl founded the magazine *The Public Interest*, aimed at renewing North American politics.

To the south, Latin America was in a state of social, political and economic turbulence. Inspired by the Cuban Revolution, intellectuals wanted to get rid of what was perceived as decades of foreign control through the stranglehold of the traditional oligarchy. The war in Vietnam was being fought and American students were protesting against it. The disorderly streets brought an onslaught of racial riots in that country. Then Fidel Castro and Che Guevara earned more and more popularity under the banner of socialism as a more viable system. In Latin America, the so-called theology of liberation was underway. "The duty of the Church is to achieve freedom," condemned the Archbishop of Recife, Brazil, Helder Cámara.

In the United States, it was the golden age of soul and the influence of the Rolling Stones, the Manfred Mann's Earth Band and the Beatles was well underway. Music was a kind of catalyst and movements like *free love* emerged. One important legacy of the social movements was the changing role of women in American society. In congress, there were only four black congressmen and the number of black students was also low. Also prevalent was sexual repression, literary censorship and family authority. Amid confusion and frustration, the United States was plunged into a vicious circle where poverty seemed to have no end. The effervescence of social movements was slowly breaking down much of the social, political, cultural and economic activism.

That was the world that Slim found as a youth in his first trips to America.

As in many parts of the world, Slim is now one of the most heard and respected voices in the United States and has been criticized by some of the most influential Americans who have speculated about the role of the Mexican investment tycoon.

The purchase of shares of the most influential US daily, *The New York Times*, put him in the limelight. Fame, power, success and authority all came together in this operation which represented in an outlay of US$250 million; a pittance of his fortune, but a stock of high social and political impact.

The voices grew louder when he made his purchase of the *NYT* stock public.

"Many foreign magnates are buying cheap stocks. The United States must get used to it," noted the recognized analyst Armand Peschard-Sverdrup of the Center for Strategic and International

Studies in Washington. "We'll have all foreign interests as owners of US companies. It is one of the events that hastened the recession. By participating in *The New York Times*, Slim is basically being projected as a person with enormous influence in this country, no matter how his investment goes."

George Grayson, academic researcher at the College of William and Mary in Virginia, and one of Slim's fiercest critics, did not believe that the Mexican tycoon would interfere in editorial politics just because he purchased shares in *The New York Times*. "For those who read *The New York Times* every day, you will probably pop champagne bottles, because unless they gain capital, these newspapers are going to reduce their services."

In line with Grayson, professor of sociology at Columbia University, Todd Gitlin, pointed out: "investing without seeking to influence will enhance Slim's reputation ... I think it would be foolish on his part to interfere with the newspaper. He would benefit from a global reputation by being above a simple interference."

For Alex Jones, a professor at the University of Harvard and author of *The Trust*, considered the definitive biography of the Sulzberger and writer for *The New York Times,* Slim "is the closest to the ideal investor, because Slim is a man who has already made his fortune and is an entrepreneur as was Adolph Ochs (the patriarch of *The New York Times*)."

Tom Rosenstiel, from the Project for Excellence in Journalism and former media critic at the *Los Angeles Times*, said the acquisition of shares by Slim "is that of a strong ally by giving them the cash they need to strengthen, not weaken, the position of management of *The New York Times*."

Shannon K. O'Neil, Latin America expert at the Council on Foreign Relations of New York, said "What is clear is that the newspaper needs money and Slim has it and could help rescue the newspaper with financing, giving them the time to make the necessary changes to keep the company profitable."

In this sense, the chief executive of *The New York Times*, Janet Robinson, stated that the capital injected into the company by Slim would be used immediately to refinance debt and give the company greater financial flexibility.

Long before 2007, *The Times* had reported some gains, but they were facing financial problems with a reduction in advertising, which provoked cost cuts while increasing competition from *Wall Street Journal*, which had been acquired by media mogul Rupert Murdoch.

The sale of audiovisual media division contributed to sixty-six cents per share to earnings of the company. *The New York Times* also reported a loss of twenty-nine cents per share from other asset sales, such as a printer, and a loss of five cents per share due to accelerated depreciation expenses.

"While our second quarter results reflected the weakness of a graphical advertising market [...] we continue to move aggressively into the development of new products, cost cuts and a rebalancing of our portfolio," said chief executive officer Robinson.

The truth is that the editorial firm had been hit by a drop in advertising revenue due to the migration of readers to the Internet, as well as the decline of the US housing market and other economic factors.

The crisis had knocked on the doors of the most influential newspaper in the world and the third largest circulation daily in the United States, with a million copies sold per day. In financial terms, 2008 was hard for the *The New York Times*. The company had a commitment of thousands of millions of dollars in debt and a credit of US$400 million that matured in May, but in stocks it only counted for US$46 million in cash.

They desperately needed a transfusion of money for a newspaper that, for the first time in history, had to cut and reduce staff. They were freezing wages and selling ads on the front page. To try to solve their financial problems, the owners of *The Times* sought to sell nineteen floors of the fifty-two-story building in Manhattan, where its headquarters are located, to an investment and management firm. The company would occupy the other floors and would use proceeds from the sale to pay part of their debts. Among other assets they put on sale was the Boston Red Sox Baseball team and the *Boston Globe*. In the midst of crisis, *New York Times* executives announced the closing of its distribution of its subsidiary *City* and *Suburban*, which meant lying off 550 workers, 5.4 percent of staff, and prepare a plan to reduce the number of sections and increase the price per copy.

The situation for *The New York Times* became untenable because of the seventy percent drop in its share price, from a maximum of US$21.14 reached in April 2008.

Slim came to the rescue of *The New York Times* by endorsing agreements of US$250 million with two of his companies. Through Banco Inbursa, he purchased US$125 million in stock and the same amount through Inmobiliaria Carso.

The agreement was to purchase 9.1 million Class A shares for a period of six years with guarantees that are convertible into common shares. The shares carried an interest rate of fourteen percent of which eleven percent are payable in cash and three percent in additional bonuses. In principle, Slim will get 6.4 percent of the shares.[38]

Based on the terms of the agreement, Slim would not be represented on the board of The New York Times or have special voting rights. But when exercising the warrants, he would have seventeen percent of the common shares of the company, becoming the largest shareholder, where the principal owners are the Ochs-Sulzberger family with nineteen percent of company shares and special voting rights.

In late February 2009, according to documents submitted by The New York Times Company to the Security and Exchange Commission of the US Stock Market, Slim's companies increased their shares from 6.4 percent to seven percent of the capital through multiple stock purchases that brought in US$3.7 million by Inmobiliaria Carso.[39]

Before Slim's injection of funds became public, investment firm Harbinger Capital and Firebrand Partners bought major shares in The New York Times. Slim's investments and those of these two companies together represent more than thirty percent of the capital, thus exceeding Sulzberger's nineteen percent. Another one of Times shareholders is the fund T. Rowe Price Group, with eleven percent, which is the second largest shareholder.

Some analysts believe that this infusion of resources does not guarantee a restructuring of the newspaper because the shareholder structure and control exercised by the Sulzberger family, which through ownership of ninety percent of the shares of Class B, maintain their so-called right to vote.

Slim, in an interview with *The New Yorker,* reported that his investment in *The New York Times* was not motivated by interest in the contents of the medium, but rather the channels of communication that transmit said content, including television, Internet and mobile phones.

On celebrating the first anniversary of his investments, Slim set out to exercise the right to purchase his own investments in the *New York Times*, a company that was forced to suspend payment of dividends to shareholders by not surpassing the crisis that enveloped the majority of print media in the United States.

With all his problems, the executive chairman of *The New York Times* company, Arthur Sulzberger, praised Slim as "truly loyal to *The Times*," in an article published on the website of the newspaper about "The 100 Most Influential of the NYT in 2009."

"While it would have been a good idea to get to know me and my colleagues, it was obvious from the moment we met that Slim was truly loyal to *The Times* […] Slim is a very astute businessman who understands the big brands […] and shows a deep understanding of the role that news, information and education has in our interconnected world society," Sulzberger said.

Power Without Borders

In the world, as of right now, there are only 1.210 people with fortunes that amount to over 1 billion dollars. Perched at the top, sits Carlos Slim Helu, a Mexican businessman who gets US$30 million daily earnings. Thusly he is not only the richest, but one of the six most influential men on the planet.

No millionaire has been so methodical as Carlos Slim. His fame and power have transcended borders, which is why he has earned the nicknames "The Greatest Tycoon" and "King Midas" in America. But his influence doesn't stop at this continent. In Japan, Slim is seen as a example to follow, and they refer to him as "Taikun" - An extremely rich and powerful man.

Some have even called him "Mr. Sell" for his influence in the stock market. In the jargon of the stock exchange a popular phrase says "Sell in May and go away", suggesting to sell in May and stay out of the market until October.

1992 was the first time that Carlos Slim appeared in the elite group of *Forbes'* World's Richest Men list. At the time, 51 years old, Carlos seemed to be a newcomer, however *Fortune Magazine* as well as *The Wall Street Journal*, were taking good care and keeping an appreciative eye on Carlos Slim.

Founded in 1917, Forbes is an American magazine with a circulation of several million copies worldwide. *Forbes*'s List of The Richest in the World began publication in 1987, and soon attracted the spotlight of tabloid media hoping to discover the eccentricities of the truly rich. But beyond the infamous list, *Forbes* magazine is one of the most trusted information resources for the world's business leaders. Slim has appeared consistently in this publication since 1991.

As we began the new millennium, in 2001, Carlos Slim stood at 25th place on the Richest People in the World List. In 2006 Carlos ascended to the podium and joined the club of the three richest in the world alongside Bill Gates and Warren Buffett, with a fortune of US$30 billion. If his fortune were a symphony, and in many ways it is, it was reaching the crescendo, foreshadowing a series of financial moves and decisions that would help it grow exponentially.

He was crowned by Forbes as the richest person in the world in 2011, when his fortune reached, according to the Wall Street Journal, US$69 billion.

América Móvil, considered the largest and in many cases only mobile phone company in Latin America, has a base clientele of 260 million customers. Consolidated in Latin America with a fiber optic network of 290,000 kilometers, making it the largest telecommunications infrastructure in the world.

His power and influence reaches everywhere and in places you might not expect. According to the Securities and Exchange Commission, of U.S. government, Carlos Slim has 8.2 percent of controlling shares in AT&T, as well as owning 10 percent share for both the high end store Saks Fifth Avenue as well as the prestigious periodical *The New York Times*.

As if this weren't enough, Slim also attained 58.7 million shares (totaling a controlling action of 2 percent) of BlackRock, one of the titans of international finance.

BlackRock is perhaps the main institution for high-risk investment fund management of around the world. To give you an idea of BlackRock's assets (which include banks, investment funds and corporations) BlackRocks combined assets represent the equivalent of 100 percent of gross domestic product of China or 11 times more than the GDP of Mexico.

But what significance did this investment have for Slim? Why would he take such a personal stake in a company like BlackRock? Omar Escamilla Rodrigo Haro, specialist in regional integration between Mexico and the United States and professor at the UNAM, theorizes that Slim's strategy was two fold, both financial and strategic.

Among the largest shareholders of BlackRock, are Bank of America, Goldman Sachs, Bank of New York Mellon, Morgan Stanley and Citi group.

What is surprising is that it is these banks that, according to Simon Johnson, economist at the International Monetary Fund, are responsible for the economic meltdown of 2007-2008. Some of these entities are still under investigation by the U.S. federal government.

According to Omar Escamilla Rodrigo Haro, one of the most disturbing issues when looking at BlackRock is the network of economic and political interests that are found internally. With a staff that includes former ministers of finance, such as Roger Altman; Former head of the World Bank, Abdlatif Yousef Al-Hamad, who was also Minister of Finance and Planning of Kuwait, former CEOs of banks, like Deryck Maughan of Citigroup, and vice president of companies such as Dennis Dammerman from General Electric.

These are just some of the names that make up the network of influence and power within BlackRock which aims to ensure the development of investments and interests for it's customers around the world.

But there are important elements that can help us understand Slim's acquisition of the 2 percent of BlackRock, and these are the assets (common and preferred shares) that the firm has in four of the ten largest mining companies in Latin America, which contributed, in 2009, more than three quarters of the US$63.6 billion generated by all ten companies. Let's take a quick look at what these mining assets are exactly:

The following data was taken from the Securities and Exchange Commission of the U.S. government, according to reports in 2010:

Iron and Nickel.

Minera Vale, a Brazilian joint venture, and the world's largest exporter of Iron and second largest of nickel. BlackRock has over 45 billion shares of Vale, with assets valued over US$1.4 million.

Copper.

The Chilean resort's Mina La Escondida, the world's leading producer of copper, is controlled by BHP Billiton. BlackRock has 1,526,898 BHP shares with a value of over US$106 million. It also has controlling shares in Southern Peru Cooper, a copper mining company controlled by Grupo Mexico, BlackRock controls 19,643,996 shares worth US$690 million.

Gold.

Yanacocha Gold Mine is the largest gold mine in the world, located in Peru and controlled by Newmont Mining Corporation. BlackRock has 40,511,663 shares valued at US$1.8 million.

There are two relevant aspects to consider in order to clearly understand Slim's large investment in BlackRock. The first has to do with the 41 percent increase of Slim's company, Grupo Carso's gains over the previous year, driven by - in large part - his mining and real estate businesses. The second relates to the investment of MX$4.5 billion Grupo Carso had made earlier that year towards gold mines in San Francisco and La Concheña, another mine in Ocampo, Chihuahua.

And this isn't the only time these two giants have done business together. When AMX (América Móvil) went under it's restructuring, part of the $25 billion spent on the acquisition of Carso Global Telecoms (who control Telmex and Telmex International) came from the sale of 19,877,633 shares of AMX to BlackRock.

What the above shows is the connection and shared interests between the world's most powerful financial and investment group and one of the world's greatest monopolists. A relationship in which Mexico's role becomes that of a transitional economy that allows for the restoration and the profitability of large investment blocks, because while natural resources are extracted, tax levy's will be allowed to support infrastructure construction and outside investments.

Carlos Slim's expansion didn't stop at the Americas. With the goal of truly becoming a man of international influence he expanded across the seas. A great example of his international business roles with his work in Spain.

In 2011, Slim acquired through his company, Carso, more than a million shares of Criteria which went on to become Caixabank. following the agreement of the general meeting of shareholders. La Caixa, controls 81 percent stake in CaixaBank.

Caixabank is the financial arm of La Caixa, which had been using Slim as an advisor since May of 2010.

The Mexican billionaire became the advisor and shareholder with the second most shares. In 2008 Caixa was considered as the sole partner in the expansion of Mexican company Inbursa. The company invested €1,500 billion (about US$2 billion dollars) to buy 20 percent stake in Inbursa. La Caixa has presented ambitious growth plans.

When local Mexican business all going to Caixa, the chairman of Banco Santander, one of the competitors Caixabank, immediately recognized the vision and ability that Carlos Slim has for business. And going so far as to tell reporters "The exciting thing is to see him find something new. When he invests, then you know he see's a great business model that won't fail."

In 2007, when Carlos Slim was already a worldwide celebrity with about US$50 billion dollars.

That led to The Wall Street Journal's David Luhnow, entrusted with a more comprehensive report, to finally find out just who Slim was and how to explain his wealth rapid and seemingly unstoppable wealth.

David Luhnow wrote in The Wall Street Journal:
How did this Mexican, son of Lebanese immigrants, reach these heights? He did it by assembling monopolies, something similar to what John D. Rockefeller did with the oil refining industry. In the postindustrial world, Slim has built a stronghold around the phone in Mexico and Latin America.

Teléfonos de Mexico (Telmex), Telcel controls 92% of all fixed lines and 73% of mobile phones, respectively. Like Rockefeller at the time, Slim has accumulated so much power that is considered something of a myth in his country, a force as large as the country itself.

It would be impossible to stop Luhnow from making the contrast of how could the world's riches man live in one of the world's poorest countries.

To quote a study by the UN: "In the last two years, Slim has won nearly US$25 million dollars a day while 20% of the population lives on $2 or less a day."

In response to this and because of his strong belief in community and family, Slim has undertaken and become serious about his philanthropic work. A colorful advertising campaign of its foundations was intended to emphasize the trait of Slim, who was not quoted by name: "Within the Telmex Foundation we have changed the history of hundreds of thousands of children, adults and seniors, with programs that seek out to help solve the core structural problems of Mexico: education, health, nutrition and justice, among the most important."

He is also a strong advocate of the Clinton Foundation headed by Former US President Bill Clinton, which allocated a fund of $100 million to fight poverty in Latin America.

Not even the fiercest critics of Carlos Slim can question his magic touch as an investor, a real maker of wealth that creates jobs and welfare in any business he chooses to involve himself with and his ability to give back to the community he lives in.

Fortune magazine has compared the Slim profile with that of one of the great American magnates, John D. Rockefeller. CNN and Time magazine executives are among the twenty most influential companies in the world, next to the Brazilian Carlos Ghosn, CEO of Nissan, and Americans Bill Gates of Microsoft. And like Rochefeller his influence and reach for the philanthropic, go global.

Slim is an important collaborator to the World Wildlife Fund, which provides funding to preserve biodiversity of Mexico in seventeen natural areas grouped into six regions. And takes a lot of interest in the preservation of the world's natural resources. It was no surprise that General Secretary of the United Nations, Ban Ki Moon, invited Carlos Slim to a meeting seeking out his advice on climate changes and fluctuations.

Slim received the "President's Medal" from George Washington University, for his philanthropic work, joining fellow award winners Mikhail Gorbachev, Walter Cronkite, the Israeli prime minister and Nobel laureate Shimon Peres. His awards are many and his recognitions are deserved, for his tireless efforts and financial support for education and preservation.

Among the awards Slim has won, are the Golden Píate Award from the American Academy of Achievement for his work in education; Entrepreneur of the Year (Latin Trade 2003), the Alliance Award, awarded by Free Trade Alliance, the Hadrian Award, awarded by World Monuments Fund and recognized as the

Entrepreneur of the Decade by the Latin Trade in 2004. The merits of Carlos Slim and his international reach are impressive. His awards and acknowledgments range from his home country to Europe and the United States. In fact, in some schools around Japan, Carlos Slim is used as a model example for business and success.

The international media focused a spotlight on all that makes the Mexican tycoon tic, when the multi-billionaire Bill Gates visited Slim to exchange views on the Internet market in Mexico and in the United States. The meeting caused a stir, especially in the U.S. media. The Microsoft founder was visiting Mexico City to receive the Silver Mexican Order of the Aztec Eagle Award, the highest honor the Mexican government gives to a foreigner for outstanding service to the country. Gates had donated thousands of computers to public libraries and offered assistance to the Mexican government for the care of diseases like AIDS, malaria, tuberculosis and other conditions common in developing countries.

In 1997 Slim rescued the fledgling internet company Prodigy from bankruptcy. Adding a Spanish interface and increasing its number of customers from less than 200,000 to more than three and a half million subscribers.

During the meeting with Slim, Gates addressed the theme of the advertising market on the Internet. They discussed the need to increase the penetration of the services that could provide through their companies. Microsoft and Telmex have an alliance to provide Internet services and advertising in Mexico through the joint forces of Prodigy and MSN.

Slim's presence in the United States is getting stronger, for example, in late 2008 he acquired 8 percent of The Bronco Drilling Company for an amount close to US$15 million. This company is engaged in the production of oilrigs and has contracts to drill three oil wells in Mexico. The Slim group owns shares in Global Crossing Limited, Office Max, and, as if that weren't enough, Carso Global Telecom (Telmex), now controls several outlets for telecommunications in the United States, like América Móvil, which provides wireless services in U.S. territory. It should be added that Carso Global Telecom serves low-income consumers, primarily U.S. Hispanics, who have little or no access to credit.

As in many parts of the world, Carlos Slim is now one of the voices heard and respected in the United States. Of course it has not been without criticism from some of the most influential U.S. media outlets, who have debated the intention of the Mexican billionaire's big investments.

Buying a stake in the most influential American newspaper, the *New York Times*, put him in the center of the media hurricane. Fame, power, success, authority, everything came together in this operation that although it only represented a cost of US$250 million, it was, however, an invaluable investment in making a high social and political impact.

"Many foreigners are buying cheap magnates. America must get used to it ... We have all these foreign interests as owners of American companies. It is one of the phenomena that accelerated the recession ... By participating in the *New York Times*, Carlos Slim basically is being projected as a person with great influence in this country, regardless of what he does with his investment," noted the recognized analyst Armand Peschard-Sverdrup from the Center for Strategic and International Studies, Washington, DC.

"What is clear is that the newspaper needs money and Slim has it, it could help rescue the press - lending daily financing, and giving them time to make the changes necessary for the company to remain profitable," was the opinion Shannon K. O'Neil, an expert on Latin American at the Council of Foreign Relations in New York City. With that spirit in mind, Janet Robinson, Chief Executive of the *New York Times*, stated that the capital invested by the Slim's company, immediately be used to refinance debt and give the newspaper greater financial flexibility.

Long before 2007, the struggling paper was dealing with financial problems. The loss of advertising dollars, triggering cut costs while increasing competition from *The Wall Street Journal*, bought by media mogul Rupert Murdoch, did not help the *New York Times* gain back its momentum. But by the end of the second half of 2007, the company reported that its quarterly net profit growth was US$118 million.

The sale of the media division contributed to a 66 cent earning per share of the company. The *New York Times* also reported a loss of 29 cents per share on sales of other assets and a loss of 5 cents per share due to accelerated depreciation expense.

"While our second quarter results reflected the weakness displayed in the advertising market, we are moving aggressively towards the development of new products, cost cuts and a rebalancing of our portfolio," said Janet Robinson of the *New York Times*.

The truth is that the publishing firm had been hit by a fall in advertising revenues due to the migration of readers to the Internet, as well as the decline of the U.S. housing market and other economic factors.

In financial terms, 2008 was very hard year for the *Times*. The crisis had knocked on the doors of the world's most influential newspaper. The company had a commitment of over US$1.1 billion of debt and a credit of US$400 million maturing in May but had only boxed US$46 million in cash. The *Times* was on its last legs. It was in desperate need of an angel. An angel investor that would give it the cash flow it needed and save a New York institution. A newspaper that, for the first time in its history, had to cut down wording in articles, freeze salaries and sell ads on the front page. Trying to solve their financial problems, the *Times'* owners sough desperately to sell 19 of the 52 floors of the historic New York Times building in Manhattan. Proceeds from the sale would be used to pay part of their debts. Other assets offered for sales were the baseball team Boston Red Sox and the *Boston Globe*. The situation at the *New York Times* became unsustainable, due to the 70 percent fall in its share price in April 2008.

Enter Carlos Slim. To the rescue. Carlos entered into agreements with the struggling paper and through two of Carlos's companies, Banco Inbursa and Inmobiliaria Carso, he invested US$250 million into the *New York Times*.

The deal was the purchase of 9.1 million shares for a period of six years with guarantees that they are convertible into common shares. The notes carry an interest rate of 14 percent, of which 11 percent is payable in cash and 3 percent in additional bonds. In principle Slim gets 6.4 percent of the shares.

Based on the terms of the agreement, Slim will not be represented on the board of the *New York Times*, nor will he have special voting rights. But when exercising warrants, he would have 17 percent of the common shares of the company, making him the majority shareholder, although the company will remain in control of the owners, the Ochs-Sulzberger family, who have 19 percent of the company shares and special rights vote.

In late February 2009, according to documentation submitted by The New York Times Company to The Exchange Commission and U.S. Securities, Carlos Slim's companies increased their share from 6.4 to 7 percent of the capital, through multiple actions that rounded off to an added expense of US$3.7 million for Inmobiliaria Carso.

Slim, in an interview with the *New Yorker,* reported that his investment in the *New York Times* was not motivated by interest in the contents of the medium, but in the communication channels that transmit such content, such as television, internet and mobile phones.

Nevertheless, the chairman of The New York Times Company, Arthur Sulzberger, praised Slim as "loyal to the Times," in an article published on the website of the newspaper that was part "The 100 Most Influential People of 2009"

"While it would have been a good idea my colleagues and myself to have spent more time with him, it was obvious from the moment we met, that Slim was truly loyal to the Times ... Slim is a very astute businessman who understands big business and shows a deep understanding of the role that news, information and education play in our global society."

Another example of Carlos Slim's relationship with news media came with the purchase of 1 percent of the shares of London's *The Independent,* a newspaper published by Independent News and Media (INM). The investment was for an estimated amount of €18 million and led to much speculation.

For years the main shareholders of *The Independent* have been deadlocked in conflict. Sir Anthony O'Reilly and his partner Denis O'Brien have prolonged a fierce dispute over control of the newspaper. The O'Reilly family controls 28 percent of the INM, which controls not only *The Independent* and *The Telegraph* but also a slew of other newspapers in Ireland, Australia and South Africa. While O'Brien owns 20 percent of INM's shares. The English media speculated about the reasons Carlos Slim had to acquire the shares in *The Independent.* It was assumed that there would be a negotiation with Denis O'Brien, owner of Di-gicel, considered the leading mobile operator in the Caribbean, and Slim's competitor in that region.

But amid the conflicts between partners at INM, shares of the company who published *The Independent* depreciated by 85 percent. The shares previously worth €4 fell nearly to less than US$2. Dollars in the London Stock Exchange between May 2008 and June 2009.

Therefore, the Mexican businessman admitted that investment in that newspaper "Was a wrong decision." It's obvious that Slim is unwilling to play the part of Citizen Kane, as most other big media moguls tend to do. Ted Turner, the controversial Rupert Murdoch, Anthony O'Reilly and Denis O'Brien, who may crave to be as powerful the great William Randolph Hearst was in his time.

Unlike Hearst's Napoleonic desire for power, it is the challenge of the years to come for Carlos Slim to create real capitol, both physical and human, in Latin America. To contribute, to the extent of the possibilities allowed to him through his many enterprises, to fight the ravages that poverty and unemployment have left upon the region, to engage and shorten the distance between the poor and the rich of each country and between countries. Perhaps we could find wisdom in an old Chinese proverb that states, "The unwise governments worry about the rich, the wise worry about the poor." In other words, what good is being at the top of the ship if the wood at the bottom will give, and the boat will sink.

From journalist Diego Fonseca's book *Rastros*:

"Who can question the desire of a man who has generated more wealth than dozens of Latin-American presidents? With a personal fortune greater than the sum of the GDP of Costa Rica, Uruguay and Ecuador; and the desire to work to improve conditions for regional economic development, this man has been preparing himself over the last decade to become part of the history books."

Slim understands the situation facing so many Latin American countries with emerging and struggling economies, desperate for a strong social investment. On this particular he has been quoted to say:

"I think every country in Latin America has its own specific conditions and solutions. A country with a billion people is different from a country with a million. A place with a billion people has a very vast interior economy, which would be the principal focus for me. But like I said, each country has it's own unique situation and it's own path for development. But one thing is for certain, they could all learn from China or the South Korea, but specifically learn that they have a very advanced system of education, that goes from learning their traditional alphabet to the intelalphabet (the language of computers). They're not teaching the A to B to C to D - but instead are teaching the convergence, connectivity and interactivity of modern education. Focusing great efforts towards the education of science, technology and engineering. As the Prime Minister of France, Cardinal Richelieu, said in the first half of the sixteenth century, he said it was necessary to support the mechanical arts. He spoke of mechanical education. I think now it is very important to teach all these aspects, without putting aside the humanity of it all and to create jobs and economic activity, investment and reinvestment."

Slim's concern for the future has led to new commitments. He is aware of the enormously daunting task that is the aiding in the development of a grand majority of these underdeveloped countries. Many of which are faced with problems of social and political unrest.

Undeterred, Slim speaks with conviction about the challenges that await his immediate future, aware that he will be in battle twenty-four hours a day: In the morning with U.S. companies, in the afternoon with the Europeans and in the evening with the Asian companies.

"My priority is to create the physical and human capital and social change in our countries within Latin America. That's my challenge." Says Slim. "This is what I'm more involved with and interested in at this time: health, nutrition, education, health, labor and physical infrastructure. That means new jobs such as airports,

ports, roads, highways, power plants, energy, telecommunications, etc.."

Since leaving his heirs to manage the businesses inside and outside of Mexico, Slim has focused himself on facing this challenge. Through foundations and companies that have invested the required millions, into his dream for a unified and advanced Latin America.

"I believe that poverty can not be tackled through handouts. You cannot fight this scourge through tax-deductible donations or social programs. Poverty is faced only with a good education and job opportunities. Employment is the only way to fight poverty. In the past, the issue of poverty was an ethical, moral one, about social justice. Today, in this new civilization, fighting this problem has become a necessity of development. If we don't stand up to poverty no country will be able to develop. And the best way to do that is through education."

Slim has proposed an alliance of the wealthy to help defeat poverty. A union of the most powerful businessmen in the world taking the first steps to establish a company for financing Latin American development that would involve investors, private banks, stock markets, perhaps development banks and global financial institutions. For Carlos Slim, one of the options for removing Latin America from its backwardness is making more social investment in the regions themselves. Based on this thought, Slim began his new business project in late 2005, with an initial investment of around 8 billion dollars to boost acquisition, management, and the construction of roads, power plants, and everything related to infrastructure development in the countries of the Latin American region. The strategy was to partner with local investors in each of the countries that have a large need for infrastructure development in addition to being be default a significant business ally.

His first steps towards investing back into the regions initially went through his two main companies, América Móvil and Telmex, but in 2005, Slim's companies in Latin America began to diversify and consolidate. It became clear that he has generated so much wealth that the challenge to explore new territories became almost obligatory.

América Móvil, the pioneering company of Slim's enterprise, was even named the highest performing technology company in the world by Businessweek in 2007. Beating out companies like Apple, Google, Dell and Microsoft.

Although Telmex is among the ten top ranked Latin American companies with a market value estimated at around US$40 billion, América Móvil triples Telmex in value. It is a monster that not only operates in most Latin American countries, but also has expanded into the United States and Spain. This company is one of the five largest mobile phone operator in the world with the most number of customers.

But Slim's investments and companies began to reach far beyond telecommunications. He knew that to help rebuild a country they needed access to their raw materials, innovative technologies and new energy. Slim created Carso Construction (CICSA), a company formed in just two years, yet is as big an organization as the ICA (Ingenieros De Civiles Asociados), a company that took half a century in building it's ranks and fleshing out its many dimensions. It bears repeating that CICSA did this in only two years.

Other companies that make up part of the Slim group are Swecomex Carso and PC Constructions, two companies specializing in oilrigs and the construction of all types of projects related to new energy. There is also Inbursa Financial Group which amongst it's many subdivisions we find the The Development Project, a private scientific and technological research fund for studies on infrastructure projects.

There is obviously a lot of work to be done. Many of the poorer countries in Latin America have a big whole to dig themselves out of before any re-building can actually happen. The United Nations Organization for Food and Agriculture (FAO), has gives us this recent poll on the reality in Latin American: 53 million people, basically 10 percent of the population, live with insufficient access to food, and 10 million children suffer from chronic malnutrition.

The Economic Commission for Latin America and the Caribbean (ECLAC) has also warned that if nothing is done soon to promote more investment into these countries, it will inevitably lead to a substantial increase in extreme poverty.
Rebeca Grynspan, ECLAC director, proposes that to reverse this situation we need to invest a lot more into education:

"How can we come together and build a common project when we lack the knowledge to do it. We have to begin with re-educating the lesser skilled of our workers, give our educators better tools and have them better equipped. We must see education as an invisible chain that begins in pre-school, flows through primary and secondary school, and ends in university."

According Rebeca Grynspan only around 50 percent of workers in Latin America have social benefits. It will take a more integrated social consciousness and participation, a system based on the principles of universality, efficiency and solidarity. One should also take into consideration the added challenge that 25 percent of the youth in the countries of this region are unemployed and many come from broken homes.

It seems that for this economist, Latin America needs to diversify its markets and its products, strengthen productive chains, and generate added value with emphasis on SMEs, small and medium enterprises must be prepared to be "dotted" to higher levels of efficiency and productivity.

Faced with the reality of Latin America, we can analyze and compare to the situation of other nations that have a higher social stability and stronger educational programs.

The first surprise is that Norway, the country with the highest human development, has a GDP equivalent to less than 30 percent of Mexico's GDP, is seventy times less than the United States and five times smaller than that of Brazil. Similar data helps to disprove the myth that only developed countries can achieve great economies and wealth, as we see that among the top ten countries excelling in human development is Iceland, with just a GDP which represents 1.5 percent of Mexico's and a figure almost nonexistent compared to U.S. GDP.

Of course comparisons can lead to twisting the truth and usually incurs fallacies, but it's worth our time to look over some data, for example, a study in *Time* magazine on Latin America indicates that economic improvement in the twentieth century was even clearer despite the many ups and downs it suffered.

Of course it's surprising and shocking that we live in the twenty-first century and much of the world's population is living in poverty, without access to basic goods to ensure their survival (food, medicine, clothing and housing). And although there are different criteria for the definition of poverty, the figures as they stand today, regardless of your definition are truly devastating.

For governments and for investors it is a real challenge to reverse the current situation in Latin America. Carlos Slim's companies are present throughout the region and in the last decade his companies have invested a total of US$80 billion worldwide. It is the business group that has singlehandedly made the most investments in social growth for Latin American countries in the last ten years.

A Self-Made Man

Benjamin Franklin used to say that man ought to be frugal. One of his supposed favorite quotes was:

"The way to wealth is as plain as the way to market. It depends chiefly on two words, industry and frugality: that is, waste neither time nor money, but make the best use of both. Without industry and frugality nothing will do, and with them everything."

Franklin's philosophy has many similarities with the thought of Carlos Slim Helú.

Regardless of his wealth, many wonder: "What does this man posses that he can seduce both friends and strangers?" The immediate response could be " his money". Which is a silly answer since it is the same thing as his wealth. I guess a better way to say it would be the secret to attaining it. Everyone who dreams of success would kill to be let into Slim's private study, and told the secret of his success and what he did to make it to the top of the mountain. Whenever he's pressed to divulge this information Slim responds that there is no hidden secret. It's just to work, save and invest.

Slim is perhaps the prime example of the self-made-man. He's not just the lucky main player in the classic story of being "in the right place at the right time." Carlos Slim's story differs from that of many millionaires, however he does share one trait with many of his multi-millionaire clubhouse friends, and that's his tenacity and his mental sharpness. His tenacity and dedication but, above all, his passion for business.

Interest of this man flows everywhere. In this café you can overhear a conversation about his wealth or his recent investments.

In a museum people marvel at the art he has donated, millions of people around the world look up to him or emulate his success and his ethics. And although industrious countries like China and Japan teach classes on Slim's business method, in his home country of Mexico, there is still some stigma surrounding the inescapable fact that the richest man in the world has become so while in a country where some of the most painful social contradictions reign supreme.

Carlos Slim has never seen his business as a job. As a child, his father, Julian Slim, introduced him to the business world and taught him that he must "Enjoy what you do and believe that success has nothing to do with the short term, with the today or the tomorrow, but with the vision."

It seems that Carlos isn't really concerned or interested in the magazines that rank this man over the other, and that track the fortunes of people around the world, however he is not unaware of his responsibility as one of the most important businessmen in the world. In this respect it's important to note that Carlos Slim's many companies generate hundreds of thousands of jobs in more than twenty countries. He is one of the largest investors in the world.

When Slim is asked about how it feels to be the world's richest man, Slim replied that "It's a matter that is not relevant, this isn't a competition, I'm not playing football." Ultimately, he adds, "When you die you can't take it with you." However he has stated time and again "wealth must be managed with efficiency, honesty, and simplicity."

Carlos Slim, for the most part, keeps a healthy distance from most of the rich and powerful. For four decades he has occupied the same residence and has said that the only way he'd leave that house is feet first. Now, he lives alone, widowed nearly three decades ago, with his children growing up, getting married and starting a nest of their own.

Carlos has stated that in his opinion a man has up until his 60's to be able to give 100 percent to both work and the enjoyment of life. Regardless of this, he retired from the boards of his companies before reaching his sixtieth birthday because of health reasons. He is still very much active and maintains an honorary seat on board as patriarch and founder of this vast Slim Empire. What has also attracted a lot of attention is the fact that despite the company's vast earnings, Carlos has given himself the monthly salary of merely US$25,000, a lower salary than that of some of his corporate executives at Telmex.

He travels around the world doing business, attending and lecturing at conferences and schools, but even still he carves out a large chunk of his time for family life. Carlos spends time with his six children, twenty grandchildren, wife and a few select friends such as renowned authors Gabriel Garcia Marquez and Carlos Fuentes. When they have been asked about what makes Slim so unique Gabriel Garcia Marquez said he seeks out Slim because "There is a shine to him, a luminance to him."

Some cultural promoters, like the writer Fernando Benítez, have maintained a close relationship with Slim. In an article written in 1996 and published in *La Jornada,* entitled "The Self Made Man" Benitez said that his relationship with the tycoon went back just before the 1985 earthquake.

Benitez recalls:

"I met Slim over twelve years ago, and since then I have been his friend. After a few months of knowing each other, Carlos, as tactfully as one could, donated a large sum of money to myself, Guillermo Tovar and José Iturriaga. Carlos knew we were masters of our field in history research, which has always been a poorly rewarded task. He came in and helped us be able to continue our work.

Carlos, then a younger but remarkable entrepreneur and art enthusiast, came with me on an unforgettable trip to the ruins of Palenque, Yucatan, Yaxchilan. We spent beautiful moments together.

Carlos bought the old golf club in Cuernavaca, which was about to be turned into an empty lot, and happened to be the only green space in the city, in order to preserve it. I admired the care he took in the trees, especially the bald cypress that was about to disappear from the region. Carlos dug a small pond to save the tree. He told me: 'If they do the same in the Chapultepec, all these amazing trees would not die.'

At lunch we ate at tables beautifully adorned by his wife Sumy. The nights would be full of talks and spirited debate in the parlor. Reading *Forbes* Magazine and marveling how did I become friends with a man so rich as Carlos Slim!"

Fidel Castro himself, ended seduced by Carlos Slim. During certain meetings where talks turned to the virtues of socialism versus capitalism, Castro and Slim came together to enjoy their love of cigars. The mogul used to smoke two to three Cohibas a day.

However, he stopped in 2007, for health reasons. In August of 2012 in the Cuban newspaper *Granma,* Castro spoke glowingly of Slim, saying that not only is his wealth impressive and massive but he is a highly intelligent man, with an instinct and knowledge of finance and the stock market that is unrivaled. He is also a very generous man, Fidel spoke of when Carlos came to visit him in Cuba and brought for the Dictator a new state of the art Television set that Fidel claims he kept until only recently.

Like Fidel Castro, many other celebrities have spoken of the virtues of Carlos Slim, such as Bill Clinton. Clinton praised the altruism of Slim and hundreds of thousands of jobs that he generated with his many companies. Together they have traveled the world, giving lectures on sustainable development.

Carlos Slim enjoys the perks of being accepted in the corridors of power and money in the United States, not an easy feat for a Latin American without absorbing the patterns of hedonism, aggression and defiance sometimes associated with the North American culture.

Felix Solomon, one of the most respected journalists on Wall Street, addressed the rise of Carlos Slim as the richest man on the planet:

"You could earn a billion dollars a year over a lifetime of work and you will not be as rich as Carlos Slim. To get that kind of wealth, it's not enough to make money. You need to build and own a company, and most people would say you need a monopoly. But while Microsoft's monopoly has been global, Slim's is locally confined to Mexico. And a very important part of his wealth comes from his properties in other countries and other industries, where he has no monopoly."

But just as there are voices of authority that recognize his merits, there are also those who criticizes him, like Denise Dresser, a renowned academic with a strong presence in the national media. Who referred to Slim's conduct and monopolizing as "truly unnamable."

With a PhD in political science from the University of Princeton, a specialist in contemporary Mexican politics and the US-Mexico relations, Denise Dresser talks about Carlos Slim in these terms:

"Why doesn't anyone question the talent or the business sense of Carlos Slim?

All he's done is buy a monopoly that has become an empire, decision after decision, investment after investment, acquisition after acquisition. What he has done is, essentially, know when to buy and what to buy.

He has performed with intelligence and shrewdness, has acted with great instincts and a great sense of timing. He understood how to operate the codependent relationship between government and the business class and because of this the media and has exploded in his favor. Hence the success, hence the recognition, hence the pedestal on which the country has placed him. The Mexican Midas: everything he touches turns into a million more."

It is undeniable that just like the figures and data turn and evolve around the Slim business empire, the legitimacy of his wealth will always be a source of debate especially in Mexico. For many it is intolerable that in a country where four out of ten people living in poverty there is a small group of eleven multi billionaires with a fortune of US$130 billion, exceeding the international reserve currency, and is equivalent to 12.4 percent of the value of all goods and services produced by the national economy. But while other wealthy Mexicans are questioned for their economic power, experts and officials from several delegations of governments seek out Slim for his advice on financial issues.

Slim is seen as a guru, so his presence is essential in both multilateral forums and with corporate events worldwide. That's the difference between Carlos and others who have occupied the title of the richest in the world.

Recently Slim has been caught in the eye of the hurricane, so to speak, when he announced he was pulling the advertising for his many companies away from local Mexican television outlets (Televisa and TV Azteca) since these companies were standing in Slim's way for his goal of a triple play. Which means being able to offer not only phones, but Cable TV and Internet as well. He was showered with negative reviews, smear campaigns, to which we add multimillion dollar lawsuits from competitors. The truth is that the Slim Business Group is fifteen times larger than what Televisa and TV Azteca represent together. In court, Slim's group has put up an unprecedented battle and is very likely to win this war.

Current technology allows Slim the ability to offer voice, video and Internet services through in a single connection. With this in mind, the companies specializing in integrated services that are associated with the Slim Business Group have been positioning themselves as principle providers of content and internet in 16 of the 18 countries in which Slim operates. All the while his core business, telephones, continues to thrive with more than 230 million customers spanning the U.S. to Argentina, which accounts for his company América Móvil's, revenue of US$45 billion during 2010.

Controversial and daring, Carlos Slim tries to keep a distance from the media. Very rarely does he give interviews. Daily office applications from journalists worldwide remain ignored. Hundreds of invitations to have him speak at this international forum or receive this award or that honor pour into the office, but Slim is usually more interested in the stock markets and his businesses.

The most private and therefore coveted sanctuary for the tycoon is his well-lit and sober office. Decorated with no lack of Auguste Rodin sculptures, a large desk surrounded by six comfortable arm chairs, and a large sculpture of "The Last Days of Napoleon" by Swiss artist Vincenzo Vela sits in the room, prompting Slim to point out that the statue is there "to never forget to always keep your feet on the ground." The energy in this room is palpable, you can feel that so many amazing and life altering business decisions have been made in this room.

A classic Slim story goes that some tourists strolling through Shanghai were astonished to find Carlos Slim standing in a huge line for a major international exhibit. He could have easily gotten a private tour, or bought the museum for himself, but he chose to stand in line like everyone else. That same scene could have happened in New York, Paris, Madrid and Sao Paulo. This billionaire likes to walk everywhere, even in Mexico. When someone spots him, the crowds usually gather around him as if he were a rock star, some will ask for an autograph, others are content to shake his hand or take a picture, but many more just want to get some of that golden Slim business advice.

While many entrepreneurs have confessed to being devotees of Sun Tzu's *"The Art of War"*, whose maxims have become a kind of sacred scripture for business strategies, Slim think the important thing is to have companies that are leaders in their field. Innovators and trendsetters.

Far from self aggrandizing himself with all the success and the praise thrown his way, he remains believing that it is the customer and the consumer that should be above everything, and to satisfy the customer it's necessary to have the best people always look out for the best. This way of operating, which has not changed for Slim's companies significantly in recent decades, has enabled his exponential success despite the various political changes and financial tides that have come and gone in that time.

Where There is Money There is Dynasty

The fortunes, eccentricities and scandals of the world's richest people have captivated the interest of people all over the world, resulting in the desire to delve in deeper in the lives of these titans of industry. Carlos Slim does not escape this fate.

With the media constantly looking for headlines, it's hard to remain outside of the public eye. Being a father of six and grandfather of twenty, his time belongs to his family, his business and his philanthropic activities. However, those in his inner circle know his understanding and concern of bearing the responsibility that comes with being the "richest man in the world" and the media attention that comes with it.

Another millionaire who attracted the international spotlight was the Greek ship-owner Aristotle Onassis, who used to say that "a rich man is usually nothing more than a poor man with money." He was a mythical figure who created his own legend. In time he became a celebrity both for his vast fortune, his eccentric lifestyle and his love scandals. Born in 1906 in the small Turkish village of Izmir, Onassis took over the family business and became a mogul by the time he was 40.

To contrast, the Rockefeller family never enjoyed the prestige and admiration that most millionaires and billionaires enjoy. Since the beginning of their dynasty they were criticized for having very little scruples for business.

The family's public perception and discrediting was such that the University of Columbia rejected a million dollar donation to avoid being associated with the Rockefeller Foundation. John

Rockefeller II was accused of doing business with the Nazis, selling them formulas patented in the United States.

In an attempt to restore their tarnished image, the Rockefeller clan took refuge in philanthropy. Always, however with self-promotion on their mind. Erecting what would later become landmarks in order to gain more positive celebrity, erecting buildings such as the famous Rockefeller Center, and Radio City Music Hall, in the heart of New York City.

Within all families exist the tongue in cheek tradition of sharing family anecdotes that showcase the stinginess of the patriarch. It was told, for example, that on one occasion at the luxurious Waldorf Astoria Hotel a waiter complained about the small tip that was left by John Davison Rockefeller. The gutsy waiter addressed this by commenting to John that his grandson, Nelson, was much more generous in this regard. The patriarch replied: "Yes, but my grandson has a millionaire grandfather. I don't."

John Pierpont Morgan or JP Morgan, as he was known, was famous for his greed and his sinister personality, reflected in his threatening eyes and disfiguring nose. Despite his ugly appearance, JP Morgan (1837 - 1913) has been widely recognized as one of the most important bankers in history and one of the fundamental personalities in the United States during the nineteenth century. His father, Junius Spencer Morgan, though born in the United States, developed his professional career in the United Kingdom, where he sought to facilitate access to European funds for private companies and the U.S. government.

Although the Morgan family had sufficient economic resources, Junius refused to coddle JP, despite the fact that his parents realized early on that he was a sickly child. This didn't stop Junius from making sure his son was prepared and would often prepare and encourage him to take trips on his own. Long before he entered his adolescence his parents sent him to live on the island of Madeira for one year in order to strengthen his lungs with the island's pure air.

The sickly Morgan studied at the English College in Boston and some of the most exclusive schools in Switzerland, where he learned French. Later he enrolled at the prestigious University of Gottingen in Germany, where he excelled in all matters relating to the exact sciences, specifically mathematics. When he reached fifteen, his parents made him travel Europe by himself. It was during this trip where his admiration for the arts began, which would shortly thereafter turn into his passion.

JP Morgan believed that languages are fundamentally important for business and, in that respect, it was important to be a well-educated person. This drove him to travel throughout Europe visiting museums, libraries and attending concerts. When he was twenty he graduated college and returned to live in New York, where he began his career in finance, working for Duncan, Sherman & Co., the U.S. representative of George Peabody & Co., which his father owned. This job would provide a good foundation for his eventual management of his father's company through his own company, JP Morgan & Co., from which he began to build one of the largest financial and industrial empires impressive.

In 1890, upon the death of his father, JP Morgan was placed in charge of all family businesses, with banks in England and France. Three years later his business partner Anthony Drexel also dies, thereby leaving him as sole administrator of the vast financial empire.

In 1871 JP Morgan founded, the firm Drexel, Morgan & Co., the largest and most successful investment firm on Wall Street, which became the main source of financing of the U.S. government. He also invested heavily in railroads. In 1900 he had five miles of railroad. His wealth was such that in 1912 he controlled 70 percent of the funding sources of the country and their companies were estimated at US$25 billion. He was the subject of an investigation, accused of monopolizing many of the sectors in which he did business, but claimed that his empire was the simply the fruit of the new economy. In 1913 the legendary JP Morgan died, he bequeathed his amazing art collection to the New York Metropolitan Museum of Art.

Jean Paul Getty, one of the richest men in the world, was famous for his stinginess. Getty, a Minnesota native, was born into and became immensely rich investing in oil. He was one of the first to make a personal fortune that exceeded US$1 million. He founded the Getty Oil after buying and then merging a number of small companies. His heirs sold it shortly after he died. In his time he established more than 200 companies and accumulated a wealth of more than US$3 billion. He was a tireless collector of art, both as a hobby and as an investment. He enjoyed living in large mansions and castles, but would have pay phones installed in them to make sure the staff or the guests wouldn't use his phone.

His fame for greed transcended fame during an incident involving the kidnapping of his grandson J. Paul Getty III while the young man was studying in Italy. The kidnapping occurred on July 10, 1973, in Rome, and the criminals demanded a ransom of US$17 million dollars. At first the tycoon believed this was a self-kidnapping and that his own grandson was behind it to get money, however, Italian police confirmed that it was an actual kidnapping.

The millionaire then refused to pay the kidnappers, claiming he had fourteen grandchildren, and if he paid the ransom that would set a precedent and in the future he could be a victim of even more extortion. Given the lack of cooperation from the Getty family, the kidnappers sent a local Italian newspaper a lock of the boy's hair and the boy's right ear. A note along with them threatened to send the second ear within ten days if their demands were not met. Getty reluctantly agreed to negotiate. He refused to pay the US$17 million that his grandson's captors demanded and negotiated a payment of "only" US$2 million.

He then ordered his administrators that this amount be turned over to his son as a loan, so that after he could get paid back with "comfortable" payments with low interest of 4 percent.

According to *Forbes* there are only 1,200 multibillionaires worldwide. One is the American mogul Donald Trump, who has never been in the top ten, but is a media figure of some significance. He is famous for his scandalous love affairs. He has openly spoken up against gay marriage, and during another one of his public blunders he announced his candidacy for President of the United States in 2012. Perhaps such rash moves have lead to his rising unpopularity, some people have decided to protest Trump by openly boycotting not only his television shows and hotels, but also the products that sponsor anything related to Trump.

Of course, there is another type of millionaire, whose talent and generosity is actually committed to social causes and the betterment of their communities and countries.

Warren Buffett, Bill Gates and Carlos Slim are the trio of the richest in the world. The former two have launched a program called "The Giving Pledge" ensuring that the richest people in the U.S. and around the world pledge to donate at least 50 percent of their fortune before dying or through their will towards charities and social betterment. The call was successful. Gates, co-founder of Microsoft, was the one who set the example by promising away half his fortune to charity and Buffett followed soon after, pledging to give away 99 percent of his fortune, amounting to about US$50 billion.

Joining the pledge with Gates and Buffett was Facebook founder Mark Zuckerberg and sixteen of the richest people in the United States, to which hundreds of millionaires in other parts of the world have been added, including Star Wars creator George Lucas, located at position 61 of the richest men in the world according to *Forbes*, Ted Turner, founder of CNN, and billionaire founder of Oracle, Larry Ellison.

While Carlos Slim Helú did not join the project, because from his perspective social issues "are not fixed by giving away money." He doesn't see himself as a Santa Claus, however he *has* chosen to spend a quarter of his fortune on social projects, through his foundations and other international organizations like the one headed by former U.S. President Bill Clinton.

The story of the world's richest men is surrounded by myth and suspicion. By envy and often times by greed and ruthlessness. But it is also engrossed in philanthropy and strategy, and few scholars have delved into a serious analysis of these characters.

Daniel Alef, a versatile man (writer, lawyer, entrepreneur and professor) has been given the task of following the lives of hundreds of men and women who have excelled in their fields and made their fortunes in America. Within this task he has shadowed and written about the Rockefellers, the Morgans and the newly rich such as Mark Zuckerberg and Steve Jobs, among many others. In doing this Daniel has been able to establish a common denominator within the vast variety of these fascinating characters. Many of them left school and opted for the title of Millionaire. Many came from rural families and left their studies in search of the American dream. According to Daniel's assumptions, a college education is not a prerequisite for success in business, although many of the tycoons and millionaires stress the importance of their educational base and what they learned and how they learned to apply it. Others consider it a circumstantial benchmark like Steve Jobs, who attended Reed, or Bill Gates at Harvard.

Daniel Alef says that those who had access to the universities were able to maximize the value of networking within these prestigious houses of study. This is the case of Brin and Page, the famous founders of Google, who were supported by an investor to develop their project. One of their professors at Stanford was the key, which, together with another investor, each provided US$100,000 long before Google even existed on paper.

But this does not mean that just because they have passed through a prestigious university that they will have secured business success. In fact 80 percent of Americans have amassed their wealth through the accumulation of one dollar at a time, designing and following through on a plan to grow that money before becoming a millionaire. With great self-discipline and skill, and without losing focus of their objectives. A simple but arduous path. The important thing is to take the first step, as the first million is always the hardest.

LEGACY
Heirs of An Empire

It is clear by now that Carlos Slim will go down in history as one of our culture's largest influences in the world of business. Both the Chinese and Japanese regard him with admiration, he has won over the most powerful groups in the United States and in all of Europe he is considered a respected celebrity. There are only a handful of men in history who have attained and cultivated such power and control while simultaneously attracting fans and critics, love and hate, admiration and envy. There is no doubt that as his empire continues its rise, he will be famous for being the richest man on the planet, but it seems clear that to those who know him, who deal with him, he will be remembered for his honesty and his consistency.

"How will history remember Carlos Slim?" I asked the tycoon one afternoon, while chatting and enjoying some coffee in his office. Undeterred, Slim replied, "I am not interested in them building a monument, or putting up a plaque or giving me a prize for what I do." He didn't explain any further and the matter wasn't pressed. Obviously he tries not to think about how he will be remembered, Carlos lives in the present, and is focused on the now. He continued to say:

"Personally, what I worry about and think about the future is how it will be for my family. My children, my grandchildren. I want them to be united, to love each other and help each other and their communities. To know that I have taught them how to do this. This is really my main concern. Other than that, I don't care if I will be remembered, or if the perception of me will be this or that. The people I care about and love will remember me fondly, and that's all that matters."

"Well then, what would you consider your legacy to be?" I asked.

"My main legacy are my children," he replied. "Many people think that they need to make their countries better for their children, but I believe in making my children better for the good of my country." He continues to say,

"Many people have asked me or wondered if I will leave money to my children. I believe that if you leave them a company you leave them work, purpose, responsibility and commitment. Yet if you leave them money, whatever that amount may be, 100 million, or 50 or 20, you would give it to them to encourage them to be lazy, to not have to work. No? Having something to do in order to earn that money is different. When you are the head of a company that you have to administrate, even if you are not there every day and you delegate, it's a job. It's a responsibility, an effort you must make for the company and for yourself, and for the country to begin to make money. That's a very different lifestyle then just going digging into endless bank account, and laying around scratching your stomach all year, and eventually your whole life."

Slim has taught his children that "We must keep active and do things in life. And we should be careful and responsible and efficient in managing wealth."

For Carlos Slim family values have been the core of his life and something essential he has transmitted to his many children.

"My dad gave us an education based on well-defined values. He was a kind person of strong character and who lived by a very ethical code. He always made having a strong and united family a priority in his life. Infusing in all of us a sense of happiness and harmony and a profound love and connection, and thus a deep concern for, our country."

Carlos has a close relationship to both his parents. He remembers them as "open-minded people with great human values. That's what I've passed on to my children, and that's why I say that they will be my legacy."

Being a millionaire in a country of enormous social contradictions is seen by some as less of a burden and more of a sin. Mexico's past has been no stranger to injustices. The fact that Carlos Slim is the richest man in the world and is from Mexico aroused unusual interest, especially since for many years the World's Richest Men had primarily been American moguls.

On one occasion, the editors of Mexico's leading financial magazine asked me the question: "How do you think the world will remember Carlos Slim in a hundred years?"

I replied that Carlos Slim, along with Bill Gates and Warren Buffett, were the trio of the most richest men on the planet, however it is only Slim whose connections, charm and political and global pull that make him not only the richest, but one of the six most powerful men in the world, according to *Forbes* magazine. So if you were a reporter, one hundred years from now, and you were researching Carlos Slim in the year 2012, you would find a Mexican mogul who fit the profile of a modern day conquistador whose empire spanned across over 20 countries, including the United States.

This future reporter would then try to seek out the origins of this man's exceptional rise to power, the secret behind his wealth, but would be remiss to find only the fact that Carlos Slim's big secret was simply to negotiate shrewdly and inflexibly, down to the last cent. A mogul that unlike many before him, reinvests his capitol back into the country that helped him make that money instead of taking his wealth out of the country that needs it so. Never wavering from this promise, through revolutions, economical crisis, and turmoil, the Slim family has never left Mexico or stopped investing in her progress.

In one of my meetings with this legendary founder of Grupo Carso, he told me he wanted for Telmex, which for a while was the crown jewel of his empire, before that honor went to América Móvil, to remain in the hands of his family, for at least two generations.

The eldest of his heirs, son Carlos Slim Domit, along with his brothers, stated that they will make sure that the company remains in the family and remain a Mexican company, not only for posterity but as a strategic support system for the country. This mentality and business acumen is what Carlos Slim has passed on to his descendants.

A Carlos Slim will also be remembered as a man who invested millions so that new technology would be available to everyone, and his work through his many foundations on the advancement of medicine and medical care.

A question that comes up often among us journalists is what will happen to the Slim empire once he retires or is no longer with us? Seemingly, Slim has left nothing to chance and just like he demonstrated when he stepped down from the board of his various companies, he had already ensured that his children and his family were more than well equipped for the task at hand, and with the secure knowledge that they will continue to grow the business in exponential ways, repeating the pattern taught to him by his own father, Julian Slim Haddad, who has spent much time forming Carlos into the man he is today, and inspiring in his son an entrepreneurial spirit. The same was extended to Carlos's siblings, but it was young Carlos that took the most fervent interest in his father's business and was the one who would always accompany Julian on his excursions.

His father educated him on the virtues of savings and investment, taking him on weekend business trips where Carlos would learn a lot from his father's learned colleagues. "They were all very wise, you could learn a lot as a young man by listening." recalls Slim.

The tycoon has followed this example with his own children. For example, when Carlos Jr, Marco Antonio and Patrick (Slim's sons) were teenagers, Carlos Sr would gather them all in the home library and give them lessons in economics, taking out handwritten notes and teaching his children about the follies and successes of his own companies, and comparing Mexican economics to those in the US and overseas.

Even in the early eighties, Slim used to bring his firstborn to the Stock Exchange. Carlos Slim Jr remembers his father's teachings:

"My father always included us in his business ventures. From a very young age he talked with us about the problems within various enterprises and the solutions you could find by tackling the problem uniquely."

Thanks to these life lessons and a lifetime of insight from the world's most successful business man, Slims children have made fundamental decisions in the advancement of the Slim empire. Some close to the company recall an instance of Slim's son Carlos Jr, figured out the link between a drop in profit margins in one of his 200 stores and the electric bill of that location. It's that obsession for detail that has been passed down from father to son, and it's what will keep the enterprise going strong.

"I have to stress," recalls Slim, "that I always had my family's support. Which is not at all limited to the material and the monetary, but more so in the moral example and the time dedicated to me and my development. When I was twelve, with the hopes of one day helping with the organization and management of the family's finances, my father set up a savings account for me in order to see how I would invest it. At the end of every week we would go through the activity together. And so it went for several years. Thus, in January 1955, just three years after I had been given this saving account, I had $5523.32 pesos in the bank, and by August 1957 it had increased to $31,969.26 pesos and continued to grow. Mainly through investments in shares of the National Bank of Mexico, and other smaller investments, by early 1966 my personal capital in that savings account had increased to $5 million."

It's clear that Slim has prepared his progeny well and that they are more than equipped to carry the torch and ensure the legacy. Carlos Jr, Marco Antonio and Patrick all have common traits. They are all charming, sociable and there is no rivalry or competition between them. They seem to share victories and triumphs together.

Of his children's work conduct Carlos Slim says,

"If my kids had wanted to be boxers or athletes they would be forced to compete against each other. Real life is not like that. You are only truly happy when you're not competing with anyone."

"I think we all have different vocations in life," says Slim, "there are some who are born bullfighters, other have the drive to be doctors, another person winds up a journalist, for me, I always liked investments."

Slim's children have stated that their father never pressured them to work in the family business, and always encouraged them to find their own passion.

"We always had the freedom to study or not to study, to work or not to work. To feel free to try different things." Carlos Jr remembers. "Besides, the way our parents raised us was to do something with your life for the pleasure or the responsibility of it, not for the ambition or the power. My dad says it's always worse to do something you don't love, you'll be hurting yourself and your business. If you don't feel you're doing something that makes you a better person, or makes you feel better then change course, do something else."

Carlos Jr. began working for his father at a very young age and, like the other two heirs, studied business administration at the Universidad Anáhuac. And all three are aware of the large responsibility and expectations that have fallen on their shoulders.

Marco Antonio has a passion for mathematics and is considered the financial guru of the family. Patrick, the youngest, works with his brother-in-law, Daniel Hajj, and oversees everything related to telecommunications within the Slim empire. Since Patrick took over América Móvil, the company's worth in telecommunications has tripled and he is considered one of the main new sources of the family's expanding wealth.

To explain why there is no nepotism behind his choices Slim uses a simple baseball metaphor:

"These positions in my companies, my children don't have them simply because they are my children. If you're playing baseball and you're pitching, what do you do when your son comes up to bat? ... You strike him out! Obviously. And if you're the one at bat, and your father's pitching, you still try to get that hit. Otherwise it's bad baseball. You have a responsibility to the team and the people to give it all you've got regardless of who's at bat. I think it's a bad decision to give a child a great job simply because he is your child, and I don't like it when someone places too much pressure or over expects from them because they are your child. You must find the job that goes with their strength, their talents, their personality, pleasure and drive. Otherwise no one wins."

Thus, the larger of the heirs, Carlos Slim Domit toured during training every corner of the empire of his father, was soaked and raised in the area of operations Inbursa financial, immersed himself in the business of Hotels, paper mills, Sanborns chain, department stores and Telmex.

Mr. Slim's decision to entrust the success of their companies to his children seemed like a lot to handle for a young trio of brothers. The decision was first met with some criticism, but the fact is that the heirs have continued to grow the business substantially. The three brothers have given ample proof of their leadership, and are handling the responsibility of shepherding the empire into the new phase of it's dynasty.

The decision to carry out the generational change in power occurred because Carlos Slim Helú faced a severe health problem in December of 1992. The tycoon was rushed to a hospital in Houston, because of an aortic aneurysm, where a team of specialists proceeded to extract the blood that had invaded his heart. Slim recovered a few hours after the surgery. In October of 1997, he underwent surgery again to address a problem that lingered from the previous surgery. This time his recovery took three and a half months, prompting a series of rumors speculating the "death" of Carlos Slim. The experience of being on the verge of death made him reconsider his own style of doing business. Upon his return he gathered his staff and board members and announced he was stepping down and entrusting the companies to his sons.

So, Carlos Slim Domit Jr came to be the general director of Grupo Carso and The Sanborns Group. Patrick Slim Domit became general director of Condumex-Nacobre and all manufacturing and industrial subsidiaries resulting from these companies, and Marco Antonio Slim Domit became the head of Grupo Financiero Inbursa and its subsidiaries. Taking command of Telmex was Jaime Chico Pardo and Slim's son-in-law, Arturo Elias Ayub. Another of Slim's sons-in-law, Daniel Hajj, was appointed CEO of Telcel. He then went on to América Móvil, where he works closely with Patrick Slim Domit.

The main piece of advice that Slim has given his successors is "Always stay away from politicians."

"I think," says Carlos Slim, "a business man must stick to his business and his community, and stay away from political interests, projects, and agendas. I'm not a member of any political party nor do I ever care to become one." Slim jokes that his children are "vaccinated" against the temptations of political power.

To further explore Carlos's disdain for politics and nepotism the Slim empire has had many people that are not in the Slim family rise to the highest ranks of the company and have been entrusted with many parts of the empire. Likewise, many family members have been let go after honestly assessing that they were not adding value. However, this is rare since the Slim clan is made up of fervent and intelligent hard workers. Even his son-in-law, Daniel Hajj, is one of the executives with the greatest authority at the company he works at, and has one of the best work ethics. Hajj is the first to arrive and one of the last to leave.

On the shoulders of Carlos Slim Helú's children rests a huge responsibility: to continue the expansion and maintain his vast empire. Carlos, Marco Antonio, and Patrick are the heirs of the planet's largest fortune. All three have helped to consolidate their businesses. They are billionaires, famous, and have a name that surely will open doors in all areas all over the globe. All three hold distinct talents and different keys to the expansion of their businesses. And it is up to them to write the story of what happens next to one of the world's most important dynasties.

APPENDIX A

The White Paper
Privatization to the Highest Bidder

High above the sale of banks and other companies held by the State, privatization of Teléfonos de México during the administration of former President Salinas de Gortari was the most coveted jewel for businessmen.

On December 1, 1988, when Salinas de Gortari took office, there were a total of 618 public sector businesses, 399 of which went to the private sector before his administration concluded. The state participated in fifty branches of economic activity and presidential decision was reduced to just twenty-one. So the "White Paper," in which the operation of privatization is registered, affirmed that ninety-three percent of the property is in domestic investors. It is recognized that in Telmex the most foreign investment is concentrated, even though it is established that absolute control of the telephone company was in the hands of Mexicans.

For the two leaders of the privatization process, the former Finance Minister Pedro Aspe and former Secretary of the Comptroller, María Elena Vázquez Nava, the sale of companies such as Telmex, among others, was achieved because:

> *The State had been overwhelmed by activities and entities that were blocking the possibility of development from social energy, and foreseeing the fulfillment of their basic commitments being diminished precisely in the outline that had been given as reason for the active participation*

in the enforcement of social justice. It was the case for advising risks of heavy apparatus that, including its volume, had lost the ability to meet the basic levels of technological change and meet basic levels of financial efficiency. It was not intended only to improve administrative levels, but the responsible use of the scarce resources of the people of Mexico, which cannot be distracted in the unproductive sustenance of dispensable areas—not to be strategic or of priority—that ultimately turn against social interest causing more gaps than satisfiers.

Under this perception of inefficiency and a supposed burden to the government, it was decided to privatize Teléfonos de México, which turned out to be the most profitable company for its new owner. In just the first year, it reported earnings of US$2 billion. Telmex was a profitable company even before it was privatized. Its sale represented, for the Salinas administration, forty percent of the total income of the 399 privatized companies. The telephone company was sold to the highest bidder.

The following is a summary of the White Paper report on the privatization of Teléfonos de México, which brings together a total of twenty subsidiaries.

Entity:

Teléfonos de México, S.A. of C.V.[1] and Subsidiaries (Telephones of Mexico)

Alquiladoras de Casas, S.A. of C.V. (Housing Rentals)

Anuncios en Directorios, S.A. of C.V. (Advertising on Boards)

Canalizaciones Mexicanas, S.A. of C.V. (Mexican Pipes)

Compañía de Teléfonos y Bienes Raíces, S.A. of C.V. (Telephone Company and Real Estate)

Construcciones Telefónicas Mexicanas, S.A. of C.V. (Mexican Telecommunications Construction)

Construcciones y Canalizaciones, S.A. of C.V. (Construction and Pipes)

Editorial Argos, S.A. of C.V.

Fuerza y Clima, S.A. of C.V. (Force and Climate)

Fincas Coahuila, S.A. of C.V. (Farms Coahuila)

Imprenta Nuevo Mundo, S.A. of C.V. (New World Press)

Impulsora Mexicana de Telecomunicaciones, S.A. of C.V. (Driving Mexican Telecommunications)

Industrial Afiliada, S.A. of C.V. (Affiliated Industrial)

Inmobilaria Aztlán, S.A. of C.V. (Real Estate Aztlán)

Operadora Mercantil, S.A. of C.V. (Commercial Operator)

Radio Móvil Dipsa, S.A. of C.V. (Dipsa Mobile Radio)

Renta de Equip, S.A. of C.V. (Equipment Rental)

Sercotel, S.A. of C.V.

Servicios y Supervisión, S.A. of C.V. (Services and Supervision)

Teleconstructora, S.A. of C.V.

Teléfonos del Noreste, S.A. of C.V. (Northeast Telephone)

Legal status: majority state-owned enterprises

Sector: Transport and communications

Purpose: to use local and long distance telephone services, and associated activities carried out by subsidiaries.

Formalizing the Proposed Divestment:

The SCT, with trade No. 5-1986 of March 30, 1989, proposed the sale of the Federal Government shareholding of the capital stock in Teléfonos de México, S.A. of C.V. (Telmex). On August 15, 1989, the Economic Cabinet approved it through the Agreement No. XXXVIII. On September 21 of the same year, the President of the Republic announced the federal government's decision to divest its shareholding in the company to achieve a more competitive telecommunications sector and maintaining effective stewardship of the state. They also issued guidelines for those that had to be adjusted for its sale.

Based on the Agreement No. XXXVIII of the Economic Cabinet of August 15, 1989, the Inter-Ministerial Commission on Expenditure and Financing, through the minutes of October 23, 1989, ruled favorably on disposal of representative shares for Telmex held by the federal government and state entities and, through the Agreement No. 90-III-E-7 of February 12, 1990, ruled that the divestiture of Teléfonos de México, S.A. of C.V. involved its eighteen branches plus two in a merger.

Dated October 15, 1990, by the office No. 1.0.00784, the SSP ordered to re-sector the Secretaria de Hacienda de Crédito Público (SHCP)[2]. On October 27, the holder of the Ministry of Finance was appointed Chairman of the Board of Directors. On January 30, 1990, by office No. 1.0.00071, the SSP communicated to the Shareholder of the SCT and authorized to disincorporate the entity. On that same date, the SPP asked the Secretary of the Treasury in letter No.1.0.00072 for the designation of the National Society of Credit through which the sale of state participation in the social capital of the company was affected. On March 26, 1990, the Ministry of Finance, through the office No. JRS/0124/90, designated Banco Internacional, SNC, as responsible for the propagation, assessment, evaluation and sale of Federal Government shareholding in the capital of the company and its subsidiaries.

The Extraordinary General Meeting of Shareholders of Teléfonos de México, S.A. of C.V. of June 15, 1990, agreed among other things:

- *To modify the system of actions that comprise the series "AA," which should represent fifty-one percent of common shares with voting rights that may only be subscribed or acquired by Mexican investors;*

- *To increase social capital and declare a dividend in shares of Series "L" to be distributed at a rate of 1.5 of "L" shares for each common share of Series "AA" and "A" which the social capital is divided, while capitalization of profits earned in previous years;*

- *To increase the number of members to serve on the Board of Directors to nineteen members;*

- *To change the rules of society so that they reflect the new structure of social capital and the new composition of the Board of Directors; and,*

- *To authorize the Board of Directors to serve on a*

> *plan of employee participation in the social capital of the entity.*

After the capital increase and under the new ownership structure, 20.4 percent of the social capital would have majority and control the vote in the Board of Directors, subscription only for Mexicans, 19.6 percent in Class A shares with complete vote without property restrictions and sixty percent in Class L shares, with limited voting.

Appointment of External Auditor (Art. 12 of the Regulations of the Federal Law of Public-Sector Entities in effect as of January 27, 1990).

On June 18, 1990, in letter No. DA-90-003, the Secretaría de la Controlaría General de la Federación[3] (SECOGEF) designated Roberto Casas Alatriste to conduct the audit for the sale of the Financial States of June 30, 1990, which were considered by the financial agent for the development of Technical and Financial Evaluation of the entity.

Sales Prospectus: The prospectus for the sale was determined by the agent bank in August 1990, and delivered to groups of qualified investors, between August 13 and September 21, 1990.

Public Bidding: In June 1990, Banco Internacional, SNC, and its financial advisor, Goldman Sachs & Co., completed the Technical and Financial Evaluation of the entity.

The National Securities Commission granted on August 10, 1990 the authorization No.5860 for the sale of Class AA shares without the corresponding dividend coupon to the Class L shares with limited voting rights.

On August 13, 1990, in *Excelsior, La Prensa, La Nacional, El Economista, Novedades, El Día, El Universal, La Jornada,*

Unomásuno, El Sol de México, El Heraldo de Mexico, Ovaciones, Segundo Edición, El Norte, El Porvenir, El Diario de Monterrey, Ocho Columnas and *Occidental de Guadalajara,* the official announcement and the tender of Class AA shares owned by the Federal Government was published, representing 20.4 percent of the capital stock and the option of 5.1 percent of "L" shares series. On August 16, 1990 in *Novedaded, El Día, El Universal, Excelsior, La Jornada, El Heraldo de México* and *El Nacional* published an invitation to investors to express their interest in participating in the process of divesting the institution. Between August 20 and October 31, 1990, the Banco Internacional, SNC, coordinated visits to the company as well as interviews with officials from Telmex and Communications sector.

On November 15, 1990, between Public Notaries numbers, 1, 74, 87, 89 and 181 of the Federal District received proposals to purchase the following:

Group led by Acciones y Valores de México, S.A. of C.V. represented by C. Roberto Hernández Ramírez; together with the Comptroller Mextel, S.A. of C.V.; Accitel de México, S.A. of C.V., Teléfonos de México, S.A. of C.V., and GTE Mexican Telephone Company, which offered to pay the amount of 0.780 US cents per Class AA share with the amount of US$1.687billion by 2,163,040,972 shares plus the option to purchase 5.1 percent of Class L shares.

Group led by Grupo Carso, S.A. of C.V., represented by Slim Helú, Chinese Jaime Pardo, Fernando Pérez Simón, Alejandro Escoto Cana and Sergio F. Medina Noriega, along with Seguros de México, S.A., a group of Mexican investors Southwestern Bell

International Holdings Co. and France Cable et Radio, offered 0.80165 cents per share for a total of 2,163,040,972 Class AA shares without the corresponding coupon of the dividend in Class L shares of Telmex along with the option to purchase shares of Class L, which represents a 5.1 percent stake in Telmex, according to the share option agreement and to increase the value of the bid, offered US$23.6 million in dividends.

Group led by Gentor, S.A. of C.V. represented by Humberto Acosta Campillo and Salvador Benítez Lozano, who offered to buy only 10.4 percent of the social capital; 1,103,151,000 shares out of the 2,163,040,972 Class AA shares in auction, at the price of 0.634546 cents per share amounting to US$700 million plus the option to purchase 5.1 percent of Class L shares.

Formalization of Sales: On December 6, 1990 and the Inter-Ministerial Commission on Expenditure and Financing issued the agreement. XXIII-90-E-2 on Telmex whereby the CEO of this company should conclude negotiations with the union to clarify its shareholding before the announcement of the sale.

In the session held on December 6, 1990, the Inter-Ministerial Commission on Expenditure and Financing, through the Agreement No. XXIII-90-E-1, agreed to sell Telmex to Grupo Carso, S.A. of C.V., Seguros de México S.A. and a group of Mexican investors and Southwestern Bell International Holdings Co. and France Cable et Radio, for having presented the best conditions for acquiring all the Class AA shares.

On December 9, 1990 the SHCP issued resolution No. RVP-179-A, which approved the sale of Class AA shares property of the Federal Government for MX$1.76 billion in favor of the offer made by Grupo Carso, S.A. of C.V., Seguros de México, S.A., and a group of Mexican investors and companies Southwestern Bell International Holdings Co. and France Cable et Radio, of. On that same date, SHCP issued the trade No. JRS/0457-A/L90 through which Banco Internacional, SNC, was authorized to effect the sale of the shareholding of the Federal Government, motive of the tender for the company Teléfonos de México, S.A. of C.V.

That same date and based on Article 32 of the Federal Public-Sector Entities, the Sindicato de Telefonistas de la République Mexicana (Union of Telephone Workers of Mexico) and Nacional Financiera, SNC, signed a trust agreement by which workers through a loan granted by the Nacional Financiera, SNC, acquired 4.4 percent of the share capital of the company shares 186,615,300 Class A for a loan of US$325 million, equivalent to MX$9.55 billion. The actions would be a guarantee of loan repayment as authorized by the SHCP in tender no. JRS/0457-B/90and Resolution of Sale no. RVP-179-B, both on December 9, 1990.

Completion of the Process: December 13, 1990 the Purchase and Sale Agreement was signed with Grupo Carso, S.A. of C.V. by Bernardo Quintana I. and Rómulo O'Farrill N. and thirty Mexican investors, Southwestern Bell International Holdings Co. and France Cable et Radio, winners of the tender. On December 20, 1990, in the presence of the holders of the SHCP, SCT, SECOGEF, SPP and the Secretary General of the Union of Telephone Workers of Mexico and representatives of the winning group signed a trust agreement on all the actions Class AA, motive for buy-sale with validity of ten years to ensure compliance with the obligations assumed by the buyers.

First stage: The shares acquired by the national investors, equivalent to 10.4 percent of the social capital of the entity while the two foreign investors each bought five percent, bringing the total shares purchased amounted to 20.4 percent of the social capital of the entity.

The transaction amounted to US$1.76 billion corresponding to 1,734 million of the shares and US$23.6 million in dividends. The total equivalent was MX$5,171,216.0.

The tender was broken down into partial payment in cash and the alternative of six months pay accrued in interest at market rate. Foreign investors paid cash after the agreed period so to suit their interests.

With the above operation, Telmex stopped being a majority state-owned entity.

Between September and October 1991, Southwestern Bell International Holdings Co. gained 5.0 percent, France Cable et Radio 0.033 percent, and two Mexican investors 0.067 percent of the Class L shares for a total of US$476.6 million dollars, equivalent to MX$1,454,078.70.

Second stage: The international placement of the secondary public offering of 16.45 percent of the Class L shares of Telmex was prepared by SHCP, Banco Internacional-ISEFI and Goldman, Sachs & Co., consisted in basically as follows:

- *Increasing the liquidity of the stock through public offering;*
- *Hiring Goldman, Sachs & Co. as global coordinator and co-leader in international syndications;*
- *Select underwriters for the meeting; and*

- *Define bank and brokerage firms for placement in the world.*
- *In Mexico, recording the Class L shares on the Mexican Stock Exchange and abroad to make a program sponsored by Telmex. American Depositary Receipts (ADR), representing a twenty pack of Class L series called American Depositary Shares (ADS).*

In April 1991, the Securities and Exchanges Commission (SEC) of the United States was filed with the registration of the initial public offering (IPO) of Class L. On the same date, the price of the Class' A shares was US$2.69 each. On April 19, 1991 the Banco Internacional, SNC, informed the Inter-ministerial Commission on Expenditure and Financing that Class L shares were listed on US$3.12 per share.

Between April 26 and May 20, presentations were made in Spanish, English and Japanese to investors in twenty-five cities in Mexico, Japan, Europe, the US and Canada. The placement of the Class L shares on the market was made with reference to the fundamental values of Telmex, their future prospects and their contribution in the days prior to the placement.

On May 13, 1991, rules for the international public offer were published in the Diario Oficial de la Federación. On May 14, 1991 simultaneously in Mexico, the United States, Canada, Europe and Japan an international public offering of Class L shares property of the Federal Government was made. It placed 15.7 percent of the social capital of the company, result from the sale of 1.665 million Class L shares, of which 1.377 million were placed in the markets of more than twenty countries and 288 million shares in the domestic market, of these, 150 million shares acquired by Telmex for the pension fund for administrative employees. On May 20, 1991, it received a net commission of US$2,166.7 million. On June 6, 1991, 80 million Class L shares were acquired by the international underwriters, exercising a part of the oversubscription option "Green Shoe" made available by the Federal Government, the amount of this latest sale was of US$104.1 million. The total amount of the placement of 1.745 million Class L shares amounted to US$2.27 billion, equivalent to MX$6,818,006. 00.

With these operations, the entity ceased to be of minority state participation by keeping the Federal Government only 9.52 percent of the capital.

Third Stage: Based on the success of the company, the financial performance of the stocks and the desire to reaffirm Mexico's presence in international capital markets, in early 1992 the Federal Government decided to make a second offer of Class L shares of Telmex through Banco Internacional-ISEFI and Goldman, Sachs & Co.

The strategy was meant to pulverize the offer to prevent competition for the same market and achieve greater liquidity. On April 27 and May 8, they made presentations to investors in Mexico, Japan, Europe, the US and Canada, since they were essential to promote the sale of the shares of Telmex. They distributed over 60,000 preliminaries for Telmex in Spanish, English and French in over twenty countries.

In determining the offering price of the stock, they carried out an analysis of the prospects of the company's telecommunications market on an international level and conditions in different capital markets.

On May 11, 1992, they held a second public offering nationally and internationally of Class L shares. The volume guide placed 500 million shares, corresponding to 4.7 percent of the social capital. On May 18, 1992, they received an amount of US$1.360.4 million, equivalent to MX$4,212,735.30.

On December 17, 1992 in letter no. JRS/232/92 Unidad Desincorporación of the SHCP solicited the Ministry of Planning and Budget of the same ministry for the cancellation of the key program-budget allocated to Telmex and its subsidiaries from the Register of Public Administration.

Fourth Stage: From October 29 to December 14, 1993, a public offering of "L" shares was achieved on the open market, for a total of 329 million shares corresponding to 3.1 percent of the social capital. The above transaction amounted to US$902.8 million, equivalent to MX$2,912,933.60.

By December 31, 1993, the Federal Government owned 20,420,175 shares of Class A shares and 160,431,473 Series L stock, representing 1.7 percent of the social capital of Teléfonos de México, S.A. of C.V.

Opinion of Public Commissioners: Public Commissioners appointed by the SECOGEF issued their opinion with respect to the way they conducted the process of divestiture on December 20, 1992.

APPENDIX B

Auction
A Bargain

For Slim's business group, the acquisition of Teléfonos de México was an open operation and was outside any political interest. In order to break the stigma of having been favored by former President Salinas, Slim said he would be willing to open the company books.

By paying US$441.8 million and buying 5.17 percent, the Grupo Carso won the operating contract for Teléfonos de México. A group of investors made a superior payment for each Class AA share. They covered the transfer amount before the deadline. He also argued that there was no property damage whatsoever against the nation.

Officially, the privatization of Telmex was announced on September 21, 1989 and three bidders submitted bids on November 15, 1990, announcing the winner on December 7 of that same year.

On the eve of the process, the federal government reported that in the case that the Mexican and foreign groups established separate positions, this would guarantee US$25,000,000 for each bidder.

In the case of the Banco Internacional, SNC, additional information is required in order to make a comparison on the positions. Such information had been agreed to be applied directly to each of the groups and should hand it in within seventy-two hours from when the Bank requested it. This period could only be extended at the Banco Internacional, at the justified request of the applicant, within seventy-two hours indicated. Once the bids are matched, they are handed over to the Ministry of Finance and Public Credit.

It was also agreed that the terms of Article 32 of the Federal Law of Public-Sector Entities organized workers of the company were entitled to preference shares in the auction.

So the following was established:

The Winning Group of the auction for 20.4 percent of the social capital represented by the Class AA series, which in turn represents at least fifty-one percent of common stock, payable on the date of signing Buy-Sale contracts respectively, for the sum of US$250,000,000 (two hundred fifty million dollars). A selection made by the Winning Group, will segregate the previous payment of US$125,000,000 (one hundred twenty-five million dollars) for each of the Mexican and foreign groups.

To make such payments, the groups could apply, as part of the same, for amounts they had deposited as collateral as provided in Section 6. The balance is paid in cash or in part with shares of Class L Series, property of the Winning Group, at a pre-agreed upon price not to exceed 180 calendar days bearing interest at market rates guaranteed the payment of the balance of shares of Class AA Series of Telmex (in any case) that remain affected by the trust referred to in paragraph two of these rules. This procedure is detailed in Scheme of Divestiture.

And when you have met the conditions of this notification and bases specified here, the Ministry of Finance and Public Credit, through the Banco Internacional, SNC, will announce the outcome of this auction, and will be returned once assurances have been given by the participants with accrued interest.

Failure to make payments in the time signaled in the guarantee and the initial payment will be lost for the Federal Government in a matter of contractual penalty.

In a press release dated December 10, 1990, the following dimensions on the divestiture of Teléfonos de México were made.

On September 21, 1989, the President Salinas de Gortari announced the Federal Government's decision to divest its stake in Telmex to make the telecommunications industry more competitive and efficient while retaining the leadership of the State. The stated objectives were to:

- *radically improve the service;*
- *steadily expand the current system;*
- *strengthen research and technological development;*
- *guarantee the rights of workers and give them shares in the company; and,*
- *ensure majority control of Mexicans.*

Since the announcement of the divestiture of Teléfonos de México, they worked to ensure the achievement of each and every one of these objectives.

The first stage of the process concluded on Thursday, December 6 1990—it was commissioned to acquire the shares of the company's control. On December 7, once the operations of stock markets had closed, the Winning Group was notified of the decision.

The process was as follows: first, recognizing the need to expand telecommunications services in Mexico, they made a number of necessary modifications for Telmex to fulfill the commitments of its expansion program.

On the other hand, they changed the Telmex concession title to ensure the achievement of the objectives of improving service, expanding the system and strengthening research and technological development.

The Concession Title also states that control of the company will remain in Mexican hands. This title facilitates the development of telecommunications, with a modern and flexible conception of regulation within a competitive framework. The modification of the current title, signed by the Ministry of Communications and Transport and Teléfonos de México last August 10 was published in the Official Journal of the Federation on Monday, December 10.

A modification to the structure of Teléfonos de México was proposed to ensure control by the Mexican company with such a high market value while ensuring the rights of minority shareholders. This change was particularly complex given that the shares of this company were listed on both the domestic and on the New York Stock Exchange. The proposed changes to the shareholding structure of Telmex were approved and made public in Asamblea Extraordinaria de Accionistas (Assembly for Extraordinary Shareholders) on June 15, 1990.

Moreover, to comply with the offer of the President of the

Republic, a scheme for workers to acquire a part of the social capital of Telmex was established. The corresponding contract was signed by the Secretary General of the Telephone Workers Union and the Chairman of the Board of Teléfonos de México, signed by witness of honor, Secretary of Labor and Social Welfare and Secretary of Communications and Transport.

The timetable for the divestiture was published on August 13 in the major newspapers and was strictly carried out and the process was completely transparent.

The companies that qualified to participate in the auction (five domestic and eleven foreign) and the list of which was released to the public the December 21, 1990, had access to the same information to make their assessments and prepare their positions. The Banco Internacional, SNC, received more than three hundred questions from various participants. These questions were answered directly by the bank and in some cases, were turned over to the Ministry of Communications and Transport, the Ministry of Finance and Public Credit and Teléfonos de México. All questions and all answers were provided to each and every one of the participants. The groups also made visits to Telmex where they were given presentations of all areas that made up the organization by providing information with the relevant documentation for the evaluation of the company. All groups were always accompanied by officials from the Banco Internacional.

As it was made known to public opinion and according to the schedule established on November 15, the bids for the auction were presented for 20.4 percent of the shares of Teléfonos de México, owned by Federal Government officials and representatives of the Secretary of the General Comptroller of the Federation and the Ministry of Finance and Public Credit. They specified the amounts offered and the operating conditions of buy-sale, as well as proposals for programs of modernization, technological advancement, expansion and training of personnel for Telmex.

Immediately, they began to assess and approve bids in terms of both financial and technical aspects. The results of the evaluation were presented to the Inter-ministerial Commission on Expenditure and Financing, Thursday, December 6, and the winning group was appointed. The bidders were notified of the decision the next day, after stock markets closed. In turn, it was decided that, being a listed company active in both the Mexican and New York Stock Exchange, it was essential to announce to the public the outcome of the auction before the markets opened on Monday, December 10.

It should be noted that three bids were successful and each guaranteed the Mexican majority control of the company. They all fully met the requirements stated in the scheme and the rules for the auction of Teléfonos de México, and all groups were properly qualified to participate in the auction. Likewise, all bidders decided to commit to the growth of the company and therefore in their bids for the 20.4 percent of Telmex's social capital included the option of 5.1 percent of the Class L shares offered by the Federal Government. It was concluded that the technical aspects "do not contain significant differences that clearly allow warn advantages of one over another." Consequently, the amount offered was, finally, the decisive variable for the decision.

The main features of the three positions were the following:

First Position:

Presented by Grupo Carso, France Cable & Radio and Southwestern Bell.

Offer MX$5,138.7 billion (US $1,734 million), plus cash dividends corresponding to 20.4 percent of capital up to a total amount, present value of MX$69.938 million (US$23.6 million). Thus the total payment offered is MX$5208.6 billion (US$1757.6 million).

The equivalent price per share of that position, including the option, is MX$6.022 (US$2.03).

Second Position:

Submitted by Acciones y Valores de México, S.A. de C.V., Stock Market, GTE and Telefónica Spain.

It offers MX$5,000 billion (US$1687.2 million).

The equivalent price per share of that position, including the option, is MX$5.779 (US$1.95).

Third Position:

Submitted by Grupo Gentor.

For only the Mexican component, it provides MX$2.074 billion (US$700 million).

The equivalent price per share of this position including options is MX$4.701 (US$1.59).

The Inter-Ministerial Commission of Expenditure and Financing decided that the first position, led by Grupo Carso, was the winner, noting that the payment exceeded the MX$208.6 billion offered in the second bid of (US$70.4 million), ie. 4.2 percent more.

It is important to indicate that the payment of US$1,757.6 million was offered by the Winning Group in auctioned shares, exceeded US$609.8 million to the total capital market of the company in December 1988 (which was US$1,147.8 million).

Grupo Carso, headed by "the engineer" Slim, is bringing together divergent industrial and commercial companies. He has more than US$1,500 million in annual sales, 30,000 employees and a great business capacity.

France Cable & Radio is a subsidiary of France Telecom, with sales of more than US$20 billion a year, with 155,000 employees and to date has installed and operates 28 million telephone lines in their country (compared with 5.5 million lines that Telmex operates in Mexico). The company has shown great ability to expand and modernize the telecommunications network in the country, which has grown at an average annual rate of eleven percent in the last twenty years with a level of the most advanced digitalization in the world. This company is regarded worldwide as one of the most technologically advanced.

The company Southwestern Bell has sales of more than US$8.900 billion a year, has twelve million lines installed and has 66,700 employees. This company became an independent corporation in 1984 to disband the national telecommunications system of Bell in the United States. It is one of the leading companies in local telephone, cellular and paging in the United States.

The above information indicates that the new administration of Teléfonos de México will certainly have the ability to achieve the ambitious growth and quality that has been imposed in the

Concession Agreement. It will be achieved and will lead Mexico to its rightful place in telecommunications and is indispensable for achieving the national goals of economic growth and development.

The divestiture of Teléfonos de México was carried out with transparency and impartiality and has provided the public with an opportunity to understand the different events of this process. This great task was achieved through the teamwork of many public servants from various departments, officials and the Union of Teléfonos de México, and Banco Internacional. This is one of most important privatizations worldwide for its value and complexity, which has been managed with efficiency and professionalism.

The Federal Executive wants to make the fullest recognition to all groups that participated in this auction who performed with great seriousness and, a labor of many months involving a significant investment of resources.

In the coming days, the shares corresponding to 20.4 percent of the social capital of the company will be received, which, according to the new shareholder structure, has the majority needed for management control of Telmex and to appoint the new general director. This concludes the first stage of the divestiture, to proceed later to the placement of the Class L shares owned by the Federal Government in the domestic and foreign securities markets. Like the previous phases, the opportunity will be announced to the public in detail, the steps that will follow are for said loans.

About the Author

José Martínez Mendoza is considered a pioneer of investigative journalism in Mexico. He has received numerous awards for his work. He is a rigorous and acute witness to the reality of the country. He has written a biography of several personalities from the political life of Mexico.

His books include: *Las enseñanzas del professor: Indagación de Hank González* (The Teachings of Professor: Investigation of Hank González) and *La maestra: Vida y hechos de Elba Esther Gordillo* (The Master: Life and Acts of Elba Esther Gordillo), both published by Océano. His research on the reality of Latin America is quoted by the press in several countries.

Footnotes

[1] As of March 2011, Slim's corporate holdings have been estimated at US$74 billion.

[2] Also Ottoman Porte or High Porte

[3] *Diccionario enciclopedico de mexicanos de origenes libanes y otros pueblos del levante (Encyclopedic Dictionary of Mexicans with Lebanese Origin and other Peoples of Eastern Orgin)*

[4] A person from the Mexican state of Chihuahua

[5] National Peasant Confederation

[6] National Unification Revolutionary Party

[7] Order of Cedar

[8] Mexican Stock Exchange

[9] *Delgado* is the Spanish word for thin; a synonym for Slim

[10] The Expanding Man

[11] Association for the Improvement of Mexico, A.C.

[12] Institute of Technology

[13] As of August 2011, Slim became the largest shareholder of the luxury retailer Saks Inc. with a 16 percent stake in the company.

[14] María Félix (April 8, 1914 – April 8, 2002) was a Mexican film actress and one of the icons of the golden era of Mexican cinema.

[15] Basque separatist group known as the ETA

[16] Fideicomiso para la Cobertura de Riesgos Cambiarios – Trust for Hedge Funds

[17] A Mayan people who live in the jungles of the Mexican state of Chiapas, near the southern border of Guatemala.

[18] Ahuehuete is derived from the Nahautl name for tree. It means: "upright drum in water" or "old man of the water."

[19] Fund for Assistance, Promotion and Development

[20] University Corporation for Internet Development

[21] Technological Institute for Telephones of Mexico (notice the play on words "Telephones of Mexico" can also be interpreted as the name of Slim's company Telmex).

[22] Telmex Foundation

[23] Carso Foundation

[24] Fostering Development and Employment in Latin America

[25] Smuggled items or contraband

[26] Center for the study of Mexican History Carso

[27] The company names are officially in Spanish. Though the English equivalent is provided here, it is not to be mistaken for the official English names of the companies listed.

[28] The company names are officially in Spanish. Though the English equivalent is provided here, they are not to be mistaken for the official English names of the companies listed.

[29] Free Enterprise S.A. of C.V. (Variable Capital Company)

[30] In 1993, President Salinas de Gortari altered the value of the Mexican peso as a result of hyperinflation. At the time, one "new peso" was equal to one thousand of the old ones. By 1996, all original pesos had been removed from circulation and the new peso became the standard peso and is still in circulation at present.

[31] Though Slim was not under investigation for insider trading, he was fined US$85.5 million by a US court in 2001. Grupo Sanborns, Grupo Carso and CompUSA were fined a combined US$36 million.

[32] Translated: "My Times"

[33] Popular proverb of the oral Spanish tradition. Refers to the miserly character of the person in question.

[34] A "dollar-remover"; a person who parks money (usually large sums) in foreign banks as a hedge against deflation and various political dangers.

[35] The Two Americas

[36] *Fondo Bancario de Protección al Ahorro* or Banking Fund for the Protection of Savings. A contingency fund created in Mexico in the 1990s to prevent the collapse of the banking system. The fund was later revealed to be plagued by corruption.

[37] In 2011, shortly after Bronco Drilling was purchased by Chesapeake Energy, Slim sold his 4.2 million shares for $11 a share, which equaled about a forty percent profit.

[38] On August 15, 2011, the newspaper announced that had repaid its

US$250 million debt to Slim (approximately US$279 million with interest) more than three years ahead of schedule.
[39] In August of 2011, Slim's stock in NYT rose to just over 7 percent, or 10.6 million shares.